PRAIRIE POWER

PRAIRIE POWER

Voices of 1960s Midwestern Student Protest

Robbie Lieberman

University of Missouri Press
Columbia and London

Library of Congress Cataloging-in-Publication Data
Lieberman, Robbie, 1954–
    Prairie power : voices of 1960s Midwestern student protest / Robbie
Lieberman.
      p. cm.
    Includes bibliographical references.
    ISBN 0-8262-1522-X (alk. paper)
  1. Student movements—Middle West—History—20th century.
  2. Student protesters—Middle West—Anecdotes. I. Title.
  LB3610.L54 2004
  378.1'98'10977—dc22
                                                        2003028077

♾This paper meets the requirements of the
American National Standard for Permanence of Paper
for Printed Library Materials, Z39.48, 1984.

Designer: Jennifer Cropp
Typesetter: Crane Composition, Inc.
Printer and binder: The Maple-Vail Book Manufacturing Group
Typefaces: Palatino, Vendome

The section on Southern Illinois University in the chapter "Three Prairie
Power Campuses" includes material from an essay by the author and David
Cochran titled "It Seemed a Very Local Affair," as it appears in *The New Left
Revisited,* edited by John McMillian and Paul Buhle. Reprinted by permission
of Temple University Press. © 2003 by Temple University. All Rights
Reserved. The same section also includes material from another article
cowritten by the author and David Cochran, " 'We Closed Down the Damn
School': The Party Culture and Student Protest at Southern Illinois
University during the Vietnam War Era," that appeared in *Peace and Change*
(July 2001). Reprinted by permission of Blackwell Publishing Ltd.

FOR RICH FEDDER

a sojourner
in the prairie

CONTENTS

PREFACE

This book began in 1997 when my colleague David Cochran and I organized a forum called "I'm on the Pavement, Thinkin' about the Government: Vietnam, Carbondale, and the May 1970 Riot," featuring a panel of former local activists from the sixties. We followed this with a reunion of former national leaders of Students for a Democratic Society (SDS) who identified with (and perhaps coined) the term "prairie power." Carl Davidson, Jane Adams, Jeff Shero Nightbyrd, and Robert Pardun (who has since published his autobiography, *Prairie Radical*) spoke to a large audience of SIU students and community members about their experiences and ideas in that era, and we interviewed each of them afterwards. At that point we realized there was a unique story to tell. Prairie power was not just a contingent of SDS; it was a set of values and a style of protest that to some extent distinguished student activism at large midwestern state universities from that at more elite and urban institutions. It was not that the local activists and SDS leaders told the same story—in fact, they didn't, as this book demonstrates—but there were striking similarities in their outlook and concerns despite their lack of contact. It also became clear at that point that SDS itself was not always at the center of New Left student protest.

At that point our project split in two. While I continued to explore the meaning of "prairie power" and how it was illustrated in the activism on several campuses in the lower Midwest, David took on a local study of protest at SIU, a project that is still in the works. We were, of course, not the first ones to note something special about radicalism in the Midwest; the heartland has contributed more than its share of radical activists and ideas, from the populists and grassroots socialists of the late nineteenth and early twentieth century to William Appleman Williams and Bob Dylan, both of whom had a significant impact on the New Left. (Our forum's name came from a

Dylan lyric.) But the point was not to suggest that midwestern radicals were somehow more authentic or more violent, arguments that have been made in the past. Instead, the idea was to examine working-class institutions in rural, conservative areas of the country to see how the student New Left developed and made its mark. Since I began this project several local studies of student protest at midwestern universities have been published, all of which confirm my own conclusions about the prairie power experience. What makes this study different is that the activists tell the story in their own words.

I chose to interview former activists from three campuses: Southern Illinois University, the University of Missouri, and the University of Kansas. Perhaps calling these working-class institutions is stretching the point, but all three admitted students from a wider variety of class backgrounds than did their more elite counterparts in the upper Midwest and on the coasts. All three were part of the boom that affected college campuses nationwide in the sixties. There were enough differences among these three schools to make their local stories interesting in and of themselves, but also enough commonalities that I could reach some conclusions about the nature and impact of prairie power activism.

While some readers will perhaps be disturbed by the fact that the oral histories do not reflect the racial and gender balance of the student population then and now, they are an accurate reflection of the makeup of the student New Left at these institutions. It was in many ways a white, male-dominated movement, as several of the oral histories confirm (sometimes inadvertently). And, as in the national movement, black activists tended to pay a much higher price for their involvement than did their white counterparts. There weren't that many African Americans involved in the New Left student movement on predominantly white prairie power campuses (a study of student protest at historically black colleges remains to be done), and it is surely more than a coincidence that the most well known black activists from the campuses I studied suffered harsh fates: Jimmy Rollins was kicked out of the University of Missouri after being charged with possession of marijuana, and he ended up serving time in prison; Leonard Harrison fled to Africa from Lawrence, Kansas, with his wife after she had criminal charges filed against her; and Dwight Campbell, the popular student body president at

SIU (the first African American to hold that office), died in a mysterious drowning accident in Chicago in the early seventies.

There are several recurring themes in the oral histories that appear here. Many people were moved to activism because of similar influences; most of them saw student rights and the war as pressing issues, problems that they wanted to address nonviolently. None of the people I interviewed expresses a clear ideology, most were affected by the counterculture, and virtually all have maintained the values to which they came in that turbulent era. In each case, there was pressure on the university from the surrounding community to deal harshly with student protesters, and the responses of university administrators made a big difference in the outcome on each campus. At the very least, this book documents the fact that there was significant protest that had a lasting impact on campuses and communities, protest that has received little attention in the literature to date. It will hopefully be of interest to future scholars to compare the experience of prairie power activists to that of other New Left student protesters.

Many people contributed to this book. I would like to thank David Cochran first and foremost for working with me to organize the community forums that sparked this project. In addition to his creativity and his research on SIU, his contributions include conducting several interviews with me (Adams, Davidson, Nightbyrd, Lenzi, Ellinger, and Harris) and interviewing Larry Bennett himself.

The Illinois Humanities Council gave me a grant that made possible the 1997 event in which the national SDS leaders participated: "Prairie Power: Midwestern Student Radicals and 1960s Protest." The Department of History at Southern Illinois University also helped sponsor this event, as well as the panel of former SIU activists. A special research grant from Southern Illinois University at Carbondale in 1997–1998 helped with the initial research, interviews, and transcription. I received a Dean's Appreciation Award in 2001 from Shirley Clay Scott, dean of the College of Liberal Arts at SIU, which helped defray the expenses of research travel to Lawrence, Kansas, and Columbia, Missouri. Many thanks to Edna Jan Jacobs for her patient work in transcribing some of the interviews. Thanks also to Jack and Aline Kultgen, my friends in Columbia, Missouri, who not only housed and fed me during the time I was working there, but who also shared documents from the sixties and stayed up late talking with me about this project. John Schuder, who was the SDS faculty adviser at MU in the sixties, was also very helpful, particularly in connecting me with former activists. Archivists at both MU and KU also merit recognition and thanks for helping me locate material, sometimes unprocessed, that was invaluable in enabling me to understand the events that transpired on their respective campuses. Steve Weinberg, a former colleague from the University of Missouri, suggested I contact Beverly Jarrett, director and editor-in-chief of the press at that institution. Her support and encouragement has meant a lot to me in the final stages of the creative process.

Last but not least I would like to thank all of those who were willing to share their time and memories with me. While the interpretation is mine, in the last analysis the measure of these oral histories has something to do with how thoughtful and forthcoming all these people were: Jane Adams, Larry Bennett, Caroljean Brune, Carl Davidson, Bill Ebert, Rory Ellinger, Pat Harris, Ray Lenzi, Jeff Shero Nightbyrd, Wayne Sailor, Trish Vandiver, Larry Vaughn, and Dan Viets. The oral histories in this book, while clearly pointing up some of the weaknesses of the student New Left and the personal foibles of its participants, still may serve as testimony to a struggle for peace and justice that continues in our own time.

SELECTED CHRONOLOGY OF EVENTS

KU   University of Kansas
MU   University of Missouri
SIU   Southern Illinois University

1960
April   Student Nonviolent Coordinating Committee (SNCC) formed at a conference at Shaw University in Raleigh, North Carolina.

1962
June   Students for a Democratic Society (SDS) produces the Port Huron Statement.

1964
Summer   Students from college campuses, including SIU, volunteer for Freedom Summer in Mississippi.
Fall   Free Speech Movement at Berkeley defends the right of students to carry out political organizing on campus.

1965
February   Student Peace Union at KU begins two months of demonstrations against U.S. military involvement in South Vietnam.
March   Civil Rights Council at KU holds a sit-in at the chancellor's office to protest discrimination on campus, especially in fraternities and sororities. LBJ's orders for sustained bombing of North Vietnam (Operation Rolling Thunder) and sending U.S. combat troops into South Vietnam begin steady escalation of the war.
April   SDS sponsors largest antiwar demonstration to date (20,000 people in Washington, D.C.).

May   SDS national office moves from New York to Chicago.

1966
June   Moo and Cackle riots at SIU result in the expulsion of twenty-three students.

1967
April   "Gentle Tuesday" takes place on MU campus. Students begin two months of protests against the "brain drain" from MU, as top professors harassed for their antiwar politics leave the university.

Summer   The Summer of Love brings thousands of young people to San Francisco. The mainstream media run stories on the "hippies," while the underground *Oracle*, printing a record 100,000 copies, warns of growing problems in Haight-Ashbury.

1968
April   Student strike at Columbia University. Student activists at KU plan a dialogue with the administration on the issue of university relations with the military.

May   Agriculture Building at SIU bombed.

August   Protests at the Democratic National Convention in Chicago lead to a police riot.

1969   First black professor hired at MU.

February   Four students are arrested on the MU campus for selling an issue of the underground newspaper *Free Press* with supposedly obscene content. In the largest demonstrations on campus to date, students and faculty challenge the university administration. The four students are convicted on obscenity charges, but the conviction is overturned by the U.S. Supreme Court a few years later. SDS is banned from campus.

April   The *Big Muddy Gazette* is banned from the SIU campus for criticizing the Center for Vietnamese Studies and Programs and the university president.

May   First black student body president elected at SIU. Students at KU disrupt the chancellor's review of ROTC.

June   The Old Main building at SIU burns to the ground. SDS
            disintegrates into several factions at its national conven-
            tion.

October   More than 2,500 KU students, faculty, and townspeople
            in Lawrence, Kansas, observe the national moratorium
            against the war.

1970   The administration at KU refuses to allow the Gay
            Liberation Front to become a recognized student organi-
            zation. The MU administration takes the same position a
            year later. The MU case goes to the U.S. Supreme Court
            and the gay students finally win the right to recognition
            in the late seventies.

January   Students at SIU protest against the Vietnamese Studies
            Center. Students at MU begin two months of protests
            against closing hours for women's dorms. The next fall,
            the Missouri chancellor writes to parents about what he
            calls the "inter-visitation crisis" on campus.

February   Six leaders of student government at SIU are suspended
            in a protest over dorm hours. The SDS chapter at MU
            sponsors a teach-in on women's rights.

April   The student union at KU is firebombed and burned.
            President Nixon orders the invasion of Cambodia. In re-
            sponse to this widening of the war in Southeast Asia,
            student protests erupt around the country.

May   When four students are killed by the National Guard at
            Kent State University (and two more at Jackson State
            University a few days later), the protests increase and
            more than three hundred campuses are shut down as a
            result. Thousands of students demonstrate, peacefully
            for the most part, at MU during the largest protests in
            the history of the campus. At SIU, a student strike, vio-
            lent confrontations, the arrival of 1,200 National Guard
            troops, a state of civil emergency, and a dusk-to-dawn
            curfew lead to the closing of the university.

July   Two people are killed by police in Lawrence, Kansas.

1971

April   Half a million people rally against the war in Washington, D.C., in April and May. Press coverage of protest declines, while polls show more and more people, including students, opposing the war.

May   Students at MU organize a moratorium in memory of the Kent State and Jackson State students who were killed. The rally begins with a prayer service and ends with renaming the park on campus "Peace Park."

1972

February The February Sisters take over a building at KU to call attention to women's issues such as lack of child care on campus.

April   A broad peace coalition at KU protests against the war at the Kansas Relays, with the support of the Student Senate. MU students disrupt an ROTC review on Francis Quadrangle.

May   Several days of rioting in Carbondale follow Nixon's announcement of the mining of Haiphong Harbor.

1973

January Paris Peace Accords.

May   Watergate hearings begin.

1974   More than 700 students at MU protest the lack of minority faculty on campus.

August Nixon resigns.

PRAIRIE POWER

INTRODUCTION

Student Protest and the
New Left of the 1960s Revisited

Protest on college campuses was a hallmark of the sixties. Student demands included curricular reform and a greater role in governance, abolition of women's dorm closing hours and in loco parentis more generally, the right to organize and demonstrate on campus, racial equality in areas from housing to admissions and hiring, and an end to university ties to the military. Contrary to media portrayals, student protests were not typically violent affairs, nor did they take place only at elite institutions on the coasts or in the upper Midwest. The student movement in the heartland, while perhaps smaller and more short-lived than its counterpart on the coasts, had a significant impact. Indeed, it was the students at state universities in the lower Midwest that shaped the New Left in the late sixties and early seventies. Student protest at these "prairie power" campuses led to lasting and profound changes at the university, community, and individual level, while leaving its mark on subsequent movements, notably feminism, gay rights, and environmentalism.

Why have midwestern activists received so little attention? One reason is that the media focus was and is on the large and dramatic demonstrations that took place on the coasts—Berkeley and Columbia still dominate our images of student protest. A second, perhaps more important reason is that in telling the story of the rise and fall of the New Left, both popular and scholarly writers often have treated protest at midwestern universities in the late sixties and early seventies simply as part of the movement's decline and disintegration. The diversity, the contributions, and even the contradictions of prairie power activists get lost in this version of the story. The standard narrative of the student New Left is as follows:

1

Inspired by the commitment and courage of the civil rights movement, with which some New Leftists had firsthand experience, and by John F. Kennedy's idealistic rhetoric and appeal to young people to act, white youths set out to change the world. Disturbed by both segregation and the bomb, which seemed to contradict the idealized picture of America they had been brought up to believe in, and unhappy about the thought of adopting their parents' lifestyle, which seemed to promise affluence without meaning, they created their own movement for social change centered around one major organization, Students for a Democratic Society (SDS). Beginning with a philosophy of nonviolence and a belief in the potential for young people to influence the course of events, SDS leaders set out their ideas in the Port Huron Statement, particularly the notion of "participatory democracy"—that all people have the right to participate in basic decisions that shape their lives. Such ideas served as the basis for attempts to build a multi-issue movement: to organize an interracial movement of the poor in northern cities, participate in the southern civil rights movement, and galvanize students to take action on pressing issues on and off campus. The founders of SDS tried to live the ideals of the movement by downplaying leadership, working by consensus, living communally, and sharing everything from ideas to sexual partners. They were, in the words of Todd Gitlin, "a band of brothers standing in a circle of love," a phrase suggestive, among other things, of women's secondary status in the movement.[1] They were also a small group at this point.

President Lyndon Johnson's escalation of the war in Vietnam changed all this. The New Left was losing its illusions about liberalism even before the Gulf of Tonkin: liberal civil rights leaders forced John Lewis to tone down his speech at the 1963 March on Washington so that it wouldn't sound anti-administration, the federal government refused protection to the freedom riders and then to the volunteers during Mississippi Summer, the Democratic Party denied seats to the Mississippi Freedom Democratic Party delegation

1. Todd Gitlin, *The Sixties: Years of Hope, Days of Rage,* 105. The New Left experience had unforeseen consequences for women, who generally did not claim leadership roles and were often defined by the men with whom they had relationships. Sara Evans, among others, has written about how women's experience in the New Left afforded them the opportunity to develop skills and confidence, while simultaneously making them aware of their own oppression (see Evans, *Personal Politics: The Roots of Women's Liberation in the Civil Rights Movement and the New Left*).

at the 1964 Democratic convention, and young New Leftists could not persuade government officials of the madness of MAD (mutual assured destruction). But it was the Vietnam War that brought this disillusionment with liberalism to new heights. At the same time, SDS experienced a sudden and rapid growth spurt in the wake of its April 1965 antiwar demonstration, the largest of its kind until that time. The scale was suddenly different, the issue of leadership more pressing, and the focus narrower as students on hundreds of campuses started SDS chapters in order to have an organizational mechanism with which to confront their own administrations' in loco parentis policies and complicity with the war machine. Enter "prairie power," a group of southern and midwestern activists who emphasized organizing students around local issues, decentralizing SDS leadership, and focusing on the war in Vietnam.

Kirkpatrick Sale was the first to analyze these activists as a "new breed." In his 1973 history of SDS, he described their "ruralistic dress," which "reflected a different tradition, one more aligned to the frontier, more violent, more individualistic." Prairie power people were, according to Sale, uninterested in the history of the Left and more thoroughly anti-American than early SDSers. Gitlin emphasized their cultural rebellion and style: "[M]any were shaggy in appearance, they smoked dope, they had read less, they went for broke." Prairie power activists became, in the standard historical narrative, "long-haired, dope-smoking anarchists," in large part responsible for the downfall of SDS.[2] The move of the SDS national office from New York to Chicago in 1965 and the takeover of the leadership by decentralists marked the beginning of the end. Midwestern radicals, who came into the movement as political naïfs—obsessed with the war in Vietnam, privileging campus organizing over other sorts of activities, and focusing too much energy on cultural, or expressive, forms of protest as opposed to political, or instrumental, goals—led SDS down the path to the sectarian splintering that took place at the organization's convention in 1969.

The above narrative reflects the point of view of the founders of SDS, the so-called "old guard" who wrote some of the first accounts

2. Kirkpatrick Sale, *SDS*, 204–5; Todd Gitlin, *The Whole World Is Watching: Mass Media in the Making and Unmaking of the New Left*, 30–31; Gitlin, *The Sixties*, 192.

of the New Left. They came largely from professional, middle-class, liberal families and attended elite schools on the coasts or in the upper Midwest. Some of them had ties to the Old Left, and as a group they were disproportionately Jewish. They started out believing they had access to power and, like the early civil rights activists, that they could affect the government by demonstrating what was wrong with American society. SDS developed out of the Student League for Industrial Democracy, whose parent organization was strongly anticommunist and focused on the labor movement as the agent of change in American society. Even when the students broke off from their elders over the issue of excluding Communists, they remained ambivalent about liberalism. Some had experience in the southern civil rights movement, in attempting to build an interracial movement of the poor in northern cities, or in challenging U.S. ties with apartheid South Africa. They sought to build a multi-issue movement as described in their manifesto, the Port Huron Statement. Their biggest contribution to left-wing thought was the idea of "participatory democracy," although they sometimes stumbled over whether it was a means to an end or a goal in and of itself. In any case, from their point of view, prairie power was the movement's undoing. The dominance of prairie power from 1965 on meant a turn toward the more expressive side of the movement and toward a more anarchistic way of organizing.

In the old-guard accounts of the sixties, SDS is at the center. In its early years of hope, it is a multi-issue organization that provides a strong sense of community for those involved. It is the escalation of the Vietnam War and the rise of prairie power in 1965 that mark the beginning of the New Left's decline. While this account is not altogether mistaken, it is problematic for several reasons. One can make a strong case that the student movement generally and SDS in particular reached their greatest strength and influence in the late sixties. The demand for attention to the Vietnam War came from the grassroots and was the central reason for SDS's sudden popularity. One can hardly say objectively that the New Left began to decline in 1965 (when SDS grew and changed), nor even that it ended in 1968 (when the violence at the Democratic convention signaled a more confrontational approach on all sides), or 1969 (when SDS split into competing factions). Both the antiwar and student movements grew in numbers and actions during the late sixties and early seventies, and the main work of the women's, gay rights, and environmental movements was still to come.[3] In any case, the New Left of the sixties is not synonymous with SDS.

Just as important in calling the old-guard account into question is the fact that the continuities between prairie power and the old guard are more noteworthy than the differences. The founders of SDS emphasized the importance of face-to-face relations, local organizing, the relationship of means and ends, and a commitment to nonviolence and nonexclusion. These are all ideas with which prairie power activists strongly agreed. Moreover, some observers of the New Left in its early years saw precisely the same weakness that the old guard later attributed to prairie power. For instance, Christopher Lasch writes: "Both the strengths and weaknesses of the New Left derive from the fact that it is largely a student movement based on 'alienation.' *From the beginning,* the New Left defined political issues as personal issues. How does one achieve personal integrity— 'authenticity'—in a mechanized, bureaucratic, dehumanized society?" (emphasis added).[4]

One can find many of the ideas of both the early and later New Left in the Port Huron Statement, written in 1962: "The goal of man and society should be human independence: a concern not with image of popularity but with finding a meaning in life that is personally authentic." "Politics has the function of bringing people out of isolation and into community, thus being a necessary, though not sufficient, means of finding meaning in personal life."[5] The response to the Port Huron Statement indicates that its emphasis on personal life and community struck a chord: "Barbara Haber, a founder of SDS, says the statement was radical because it went beyond political issues such as redistribution of wealth to look 'at the kinds of relationships people had. . . . We were going to live our

3. Some critics of prairie power comment on the shift from community to mass movement that began in 1965; such terminology reveals the old guard mourning the growth and change of the New Left in the late sixties. See Gitlin, *The Whole World Is Watching,* 136, and Wini Breines, *Community and Organization in the New Left, 1962–1968: The Great Refusal,* 67–68.

4. Christopher Lasch, *The Agony of the American Left,* 180. It is noteworthy that many of the criticisms of the old guard against prairie power are strikingly similar to the Old Left's critique of the New Left.

5. "The Port Huron Statement," in Alexander Bloom and Wini Breines, eds., *"Takin' It to the Streets": A Sixties Reader,* 66, 67.

lives differently than our parents. . . . We were going to use our lives as experiments.' " Another early SDS activist, Andrea Cousins, "cried when she read the Port Huron Statement because she was so happy to find a political statement that embraced who she was, a statement 'about how people live and how they talk to each other and how they relate to each other.' "[6] While prairie power activists strongly promoted the notion that relationships and lifestyles mattered and that political activity should be fulfilling, they did not bring such ideas into the movement.

From the point of view of SDS prairie power organizers, the story should be told differently. While some prairie power leaders emphasize cultural differences as much as political ones, they interpret these in a positive way. The entrance of a "new breed" increased the movement's potential impact rather than signaling its decline. Jane Adams describes what she saw as a cultural divide, which she personally straddled: prairie power activists were more working-class, and lacked ties to the Old Left. In her terms, they were more anarchistic, more influenced by the counterculture, and not as intellectual (although plenty smart). They used drugs, and carried a little red book that was not by Chairman Mao but the Industrial Workers of the World. Many of them experimented with communal living. They were non-Jews who attended less elite universities, often state institutions in the South and lower Midwest. Religious and ethnic background, class, geography, experience, ideas about organizing— all these things separated them from the old guard.

Here it is worth noting that the cultural divide was never about religion as such. The disproportionate number of Jews in the early New Left—and for that matter in most left-wing movements in the twentieth-century United States—came from an Eastern European urban political tradition. Their ideas were often rooted in Marxism, especially the belief that one could end racism and anti-Semitism only by replacing capitalism with socialism. (Of course, not all Jews came out of or accepted this tradition.) By contrast, prairie power was associated more with a midwestern populist tradition, one that came from white workers and farmers, was nominally Christian, and was more closely allied with the direct-action approach of the IWW than with a particular intellectual tradition.

6. Rebecca E. Klatch, *A Generation Divided: The New Left, the New Right, and the 1960s*, 32.

Another insider's view comes from Carl Davidson, a New Left theorist and organizer who claims he coined the term *prairie power* and saw in it an enormous opportunity for building the movement. Davidson, like Adams, describes prairie power as centered around students from large state universities, rather than the elite schools that had produced SDS's founders. These students were home-grown radicals, more activist and less ideological than the old guard. Fueled by the civil rights movement, they were fighting battles for themselves on college campuses over issues that ranged from dorm hours to university complicity with the war machine. They were not controlled from a center. They symbolized the spirit of alienated youth, and, for a brief time, their adolescent rebellion was politicized.

These changes at the grass roots were remarked on by some of the first scholars of the student movement. In a 1971 study, Milton Mankoff and Richard Flacks wrote that the student movement had grown by spreading beyond the offspring of the liberal, educated middle class to include increasing proportions of Catholics and Protestants, children of businessmen and white-collar and blue-collar workers, and increasing numbers of young people raised as "Republicans in 'middle America.' " Activists could no longer be defined by membership in an organization or systematic commitment to political action; the role of the "politico" was no longer central as the movement developed a variety of ways in which allegiance to it could be expressed.[7]

While Mankoff and Flacks focused on Wisconsin (and to some extent Santa Barbara), similar findings emerged from a study of Southern Illinois University conducted by Roy Eugene Miller. Miller found that most student radicals at SIU—perhaps the first "prairie" school to be studied in this manner—did not fit the old profile of people from liberal, Jewish, or nonreligious parents with high incomes and education. Instead these were people who did not have much influence in family decisions, whose parents did not have liberal values or high incomes. Miller also found that single, younger, underclassmen were more likely to be radicals and that student radicals were the most alienated. This was congruent with Carl Davidson's comments about alienated youth. While most were in the liberal

7. Milton Mankoff and Richard Flacks, "The Changing Social Base of the American Student Movement," 54, 55.

arts, they were not on the whole outstanding students. Eighty-five percent had less than a B average and 53 percent were in the lower half of their high-school graduating class.[8]

The implications of these changes in the student movement were spelled out by Mankoff and Flacks: "[T]he long-term viability of the movement depends, in part, on the capacity of those within it to synthesize the spontaneous, anti-political 'gut' radicalism of the new recruits with the more systematically politicized and intellectual radicalism of the veterans." Looking back on this period, one old-guard writer, Todd Gitlin, in his more generous and self-effacing analysis, sees the failure to integrate these new recruits into the organizational networks of the movement as decisive. But, less generously, Gitlin helped set a tone of condemnation and stereotyping of "prairie power" that has rarely been challenged.[9]

Prairie power has not fared well in the literature. Scholarly works on the sixties tend to overlook the diversity and commitment of midwestern radicals, and portray them either as "long-haired, dope-smoking anarchists" from working-class backgrounds or as spoiled rich kids who, lacking experience with the civil rights movement, caused the movement's turn toward violence and self-destruction.[10] Either way, midwestern radicals take the blame for the downfall of SDS and, at least by implication, the sixties student movement more generally.

This is not to say that the account of the New Left from the prairie power point of view is more accurate than that of the old guard. Both offer us significant but incomplete histories of the New Left precisely because they are insiders' accounts. With some historical distance, it is easier to see how one gave way to the other and to acknowledge the important similarities between these two tendencies. The development of the civil rights movement offers a useful parallel. The successes and shortcomings of that movement—the

8. Roy Eugene Miller, "Student Ideology at Southern Illinois University: An Empirical Test of Theory."

9. Mankoff and Flacks, "Changing Social Base," 62; Gitlin, *Whole World*, 129–39.

10. The standard portrait of Weathermen, for instance, is that of privileged midwesterners with violent fantasies, while Kirkpatrick Sale's original characterization of "prairie power" activists emphasized their frontier individualism with its implication of violence. See Sale, *SDS*, 204–7; Kenneth J. Heineman, *Campus Wars: The Peace Movement at American State Universities in the Vietnam Era*; Ron Jacobs, *The Way the Wind Blew: A History of the Weather Underground*.

destruction of the Jim Crow system on the one hand and the failure to address more intractable issues, such as poverty, on the other (to say nothing of the violence with which nonviolent activists had to contend)—helped lead to demands for black power. Likewise, some of the accomplishments of the early New Left, such as its successful challenge to universities to allow greater student participation in decisions, as well as its growing frustration about the Vietnam War and its more general loss of faith in government to solve problems, led to a growing emphasis on direct action. At the same time, the counterculture contributed to ideas about liberation. These shifts were not the result of a linear process—for instance, while the Free Speech Movement won an important victory at Berkeley in 1964, similar issues were still being fought out on many campuses in the late sixties—but it was a process nonetheless. Understanding the links between the early and late sixties helps us break down the distinction that many scholars have drawn between the early sixties, portrayed as "good"—moral, thoughtful, and nonviolent—and the later part of the decade, presented as "bad"—hedonistic, impulsive, and violent. Examining the development of these movements also helps us understand what "prairie power" and "black power" had in common: both emphasized direct action, liberation based on group identity, and organizing one's own community around local issues as an end in itself but also as a means toward a larger struggle for power.

In a provocative piece in *Lingua Franca* in 1996, Rick Perlstein asked, "Who Owns the Sixties?" The article pitted the activist-scholars who wrote the first accounts of the New Left against a younger generation who could see beyond the memories to a more complete history. (Perlstein was using "generation" in the usual way, not the way it applied in the sixties, when a couple of years rather than a couple of decades meant a new generation.) Perlstein saw an important shift going on in the historiography, yet, despite the differences between the two groups of scholars, they tend to agree on the basic issues raised here; both seem to suggest that the counterculture came along and derailed the New Left in the late sixties, and neither group pays much attention to midwestern activists.[11]

11. Rick Perlstein, "Who Owns the Sixties?" Even scholars who challenge the standard narrative of the sixties fail to give prairie power its due. David Farber,

Perhaps the problem is that all grand narratives of the sixties are premature; we need many more local and regional studies before we are ready to make compelling generalizations about the movements of the sixties. It is in recent works focused on the student movement in particular localities that the stereotypes of prairie power activists have begun to break down. The strength of these accounts is in the connecting of local stories to national trends and to events that happened before and after the sixties. Doug Rossinow explains the origins of sixties radicalism at the University of Texas by focusing on the alienation experienced by young people in the post–World War II years, which led to a search for authenticity.[12] Beth Bailey clarifies the link between local and national events in explaining her focus on Lawrence, Kansas, in *Sex in the Heartland:* "[B]oth those who fought for change and those who opposed it acted in local arenas but drew on identities, understandings, and institutions that were defined nationally. Change was introduced in a set of locally negotiated actions by Kansans . . . who were full participants in the national postwar culture."[13] This point is borne out in several of the oral histories included here. For instance, local SIU activist Larry Vaughn suggests that *Life* magazine and the Beatles had a big impact on his view of the world: "I can remember listening to *Sgt. Pepper's Lonely Hearts Club Band* one day . . . and I called up a friend of mine . . . and said, 'This isn't an album, this is a life.' "

Local and regional histories paint a very different picture of sixties protest movements than do the grand narratives. Kenneth J. Heineman's study of the student antiwar movement at four large state universities illuminates the way in which local differences affected the makeup, tactics and strategy, and success and failure of the movement on various campuses. Mary Ann Wynkoop's disser-

touted for challenging the "possessive memory" of New Left scholars, pays little attention to midwestern activists; see Farber, ed., *The Sixties: From Memory to History.*

12. See the introduction and part 1 of Doug Rossinow, *The Politics of Authenticity: Liberalism, Christianity, and the New Left in America.* The Scranton Commission made a similar point in 1970, locating the main source of campus unrest in the new youth culture, and many others have made it since. It has been emphasized in recent works of scholarship in order to connect the sixties to the previous decade. See the *Report of the President's Commission on Campus Unrest* (Washington, DC: U.S. Government Printing Office, 1970).

13. Beth Bailey, *Sex in the Heartland,* 7.

tation on the student protest movement at Indiana University suggests that "at a local level, the last years of the decade could hardly
be described as a time of decline in university and community protest." Rossinow's study of the student movement at the University
of Texas makes clear that, early on, religion (as well as alienation)
was a significant factor motivating student organizers in certain
parts of the country, and that living the values of the movement was
important from the start. Rossinow began an important reevalua-
tion of the impact of the New Left. While agreeing with many other
scholars about the "cultural liberalism" that is the movement's greatest legacy, he connects it to succeeding movements, especially the
women's liberation movement and environmentalism.[14]

One hallmark of the New Left, and especially of prairie power activists, was that their conception of changing the world was not
simply instrumental in the sense of making America live up to its
ideals; it was also expressive in the sense of demanding personal
liberation, here and now. The latter idea is at one and the same time
the source of much of the criticism of prairie power (and sixties activists more generally) and the explanation for its appeal. While
Gitlin, for instance, sees a turn toward the expressive side as the undoing of the New Left, James J. Farrell holds up "personalism" as
the core of sixties radicalism and Wini Breines sees the strength of
the New Left in its expressive, or "prefigurative" elements.[15] That
prefigurative side of the movement held to an ideal that was easily
co-opted and corrupted. As Osha Neumann writes, the insistence
on "freedom now!" gave energy but undermined form.[16] Yet even
the critics acknowledge that this same ideal, that freedom had to be
part of the struggle, helps account for the power of sixties radicalism,

14. Heineman, *Campus Wars*; Mary Ann Wynkoop, "Dissent in the Heartland: The Student Protest Movement at Indiana University, Bloomington,
Indiana, 1965–1970," 9; Rossinow, *Politics of Authenticity*, chaps. 2, 3, 8. A useful
complement to Heineman's study is Clyde Brown and Gayle K. Pluta Brown,
"Moo U and the Cambodian Invasion: Nonviolent Anti–Vietnam War Protest
at Iowa State University."
15. James J. Farrell, *The Spirit of the Sixties*; Breines, *Community and Organization*. It is ironic that Breines pays so little attention to prairie power activists,
to whom she refers as "prairie dogs" (68), since they underscore her point
about the power of sixties radicalism.
16. Osha Neumann, "Motherfuckers Then and Now: My Sixties Problem,"
71–72.

which lived on in a meaningful way in subsequent movements for social change.

Perhaps the ambiguity of the expressive, personal-is-political tendency is seen most clearly in New Left male views of the women's liberation movement. Virtually all the grand narratives of the sixties treat women's liberation in the context of the fragmentation and decline of the movement. The movement divided in the late sixties, such accounts tell us, as whites were expelled from the black movement and women began to go their separate way. While this is to some extent an accurate picture, it lacks a broader perspective. The women's liberation movement was one of the most significant and successful movements of the sixties and seventies, not simply a disruptive force in the New Left. As Nigel Young wrote in 1977, "[T]he most deeply seated and least recognized attitude of the NL—its sexism—spawned the most important of the movements to survive its demise."[17] While the New Left never professed feminism as an important goal, it did serve as a seedbed for leaders, tactics, and philosophies of the women's movement. Feminist scholars such as Alice Echols have made this point as well, but with a different emphasis, explaining the development of the women's liberation movement not as part of the destruction (or self-destruction) of the New Left but rather as a continuation of some of its basic ideas. While these scholars are also critical of the idea of politics as self-fulfillment, acknowledging the danger of focusing purely on lifestyle and forgetting larger political issues, they are cognizant of its power and particularly of its importance in the origins of the women's liberation movement.[18]

Whether one sees prairie power activists as representing what was best or worst about the New Left—and there is vehement disagreement about this—it is certain that they did have an enormous impact. Not simply at the leadership level (that is, taking over the national office of SDS) but all the way down to the grass roots, prairie power helped shape and define the issues and style of the student New Left in the latter half of the sixties.

The term *prairie power*, as used in this book, is not meant as just a

---

17. Nigel Young, *An Infantile Disorder? The Crisis and Decline of the New Left*, 367.
18. See for example, Alice Echols, "Nothing Distant about It: Women's Liberation and Sixties Radicalism."

contingent of SDS, nor as a precise geographical description. At bottom, it is a metaphor for mass participation in "the movement," a participatory democracy that is not dominated by elites, whether intellectual, political, or class-based. It is intended to capture the character of the student movement at non-elite state universities in the Midwest, any one of which could have experienced the same sort of events that occurred at Kent State, where four students were killed by the National Guard in the spring of 1970 during protests over the invasion of Cambodia. Such campuses had evolved from normal schools or land grant agricultural colleges to large universities in a relatively short period of time, experiencing especially rapid growth in the sixties. Administrators' concerns suddenly went from football and parking to how to house, educate, and maintain control over a large number of students in a "multiversity." Most of these schools were located in conservative areas, although, like Kent State, they often developed reputations as popular places to party as they increased in size. Town-gown tensions were exacerbated by the traffic jams and the bar scenes around the campuses. Growth also meant more bureaucracy and larger classes, causing students to complain that their educational experience was impersonal and dehumanizing. Students tended to identify themselves in terms based on lifestyle, and many of them were touched by such issues as in loco parentis, the sexual revolution, the African American struggle for equality, and the Vietnam War.

Even many students who were not attracted initially by any of these issues became radicalized by incidents of administrative repression or police brutality. As the President's Commission on Campus Unrest (also known as the Scranton Commission) explained: "The high spirits and defiance of authority that had characterized the traditional school riot were now joined to youthful idealism and to social objectives of the highest importance. This combination moved the participants to intense feeling and vigorous political activism and provoked from state or university officials reactions and overreactions that promised to keep the whole movement alive."[19]

Robert Pardun says simply that prairie power was "a mixture of direct action politics and cultural rebellion." When we treat prairie power in these terms, as a description of the spirit of the student

19. *Report of the President's Commission on Campus Unrest,* 28.

New Left in the late sixties and early seventies, down to the grass roots, a number of distinctions stand out. One is that many activists did not draw a clear line between political and cultural activism. For example, rather than the counterculture coming along and disrupting the program of the New Left, as the standard narrative would have it, we see just how blurred the line was between political and countercultural protest. "Gentle Thursday" perhaps is the best example of this blend, a day in which students challenged university rules and traditions (such as staying off the grass) and played Frisbee, blew bubbles, and joyfully celebrated the values of the counterculture, often as an indirect challenge to a university-sponsored event such as a presidential inauguration. The tactic was first deployed by the largest SDS chapter, at the University of Texas, where, according to Jeff Shero Nightbyrd, one of the people interviewed in this book, the aim was to "act out the good society" for one day. The UT administration's response was to warn university staff that if a group of students said they wanted to be "gentle," they should be told to leave the premises and the incident should be reported right away.[20] Hard-core political activists were also skeptical about Gentle Thursday, but it was a successful tactic, even at a conservative school such as the University of Missouri. Political and counterculture types came together on other campuses to protest the war, among other issues, in the late sixties and early seventies. As one SIU activist put it: "The culture and the talk were the same whether you were in George Graham's house or at Hutchins Creek Farm, or at my house, or at a bar. Same subjects were being talked about: the war, the oppressive government, the need for an alternative lifestyle, the need—the great need—for change, especially to democratize SIU. . . . These were all issues everybody agreed to."[21]

Many midwestern activists, then, tended to see the New Left and the counterculture as all of a piece. Sociologist Rebecca E. Klatch explains: "By necessity, political and countercultural communities came together in the face of opposition." She quotes Terry Koch, an SDS activist from the late sixties: "What to me was wonderful about St. Louis was that if you were a poet, if you were a black jazz musician, if you believed in abortion rights . . . it was the same as being

20. Robert Pardun, *Prairie Radical: A Journey through the Sixties,* 2, 185. See also Glenn W. Jones, "Gentle Thursday: An SDS Circus in Austin, Texas, 1966–1969."
21. Author interview with Jim Hanson, July 20, 1997. See also Brent Green, *Noble Chaos.*

in the antiwar movement. You were all in it together because you're in St. Louis and you're surrounded by a bunch of rednecks. . . . It was all one and the same."[22]

Generally, on isolated midwestern campuses, activists tended to focus more on what they had in common rather than on their differences. Political lines were less clearly drawn, factionalism much less evident, and alliances more broadly built. Nonexclusion had more to do with the desire to build coalitions than with concerns about whether or not to work with Communists—Trotskyists, Maoists, or others with the correct line. Several of the oral histories here demonstrate how student government, fraternity and sorority people, the Young Republicans and Young Americans for Freedom (YAF), as well as SDS types, worked together on issues of student rights. A good indication of how much agreement there was between left and right on such issues was that at the University of Kansas, Gus DiZerega was head of both SDS and YAF at the same time. Even the "party people," those who wanted the right to engage in panty raids or to act out on the street, could sometimes get behind the cause of student rights. Some of these people became swept up in the movement as their lives took a countercultural turn; Bill Ebert describes in this book how students who came to KU in chinos and oxford cloth shirts grew their hair long and began wearing bell-bottoms and beads; instead of drinking beer on Friday afternoons, they were suddenly potheads. Larry Vaughn and Larry Bennett were among those students at SIU who went from drinking beer and battling the police on the streets to getting high, supporting free speech on campus, and demonstrating against the war. In other words, some students did make a transition from personal to political, with individual rights at the center in many cases.

Related to this focus on individual rights was the tendency to focus almost exclusively on local issues, such as dorm hours and free speech on campus. Some of the biggest controversies described in the oral histories have to do with the right to sell underground newspapers on campus. In loco parentis, an important issue on every campus, often led students to a sense of empowerment. They were taking control over their lives—living out the ideal of participatory democracy—and having fun doing it. Even the issue of the war was often seen as personal, not only because of the draft but because

22. Quoted in Klatch, *A Generation Divided*, 141–42.

working-class students knew people who were dying. The war was not an abstract issue, but a very personal one. Larry Vaughn says: "I actually had older friends, brothers of friends, sons of my parents' friends who had already died in Vietnam. For me it was a real thing. . . . [W]e knew that we could die, that we could be killed." Pat Harris, an African American woman from Chicago, says she felt more involved in protesting the war, because she knew people who were dying, than she did with the issue of civil rights, which seemed more distant.

Prairie power campuses were no different from more elite universities where students found a local target, a symbol of *their* university's complicity with the war machine. The university's ties with the military became a local issue with a different target on each campus: Kent State had the Liquid Crystal Institute, SIU the Vietnamese Studies Center. At KU the focus was on the Reserve Officer Training Corps (ROTC), specifically on getting rid of military science courses that passed as liberal arts requirements. MU students wanted their chancellor to make a statement against the war that would separate their university from immoral government policies. At the same time that these issues were being translated into local terms, even the most grassroots activists, who knew or cared little about organizations as such, found it important to feel part of a movement, part of something larger.

An issue that needs more careful attention is the impact of drug use. One somewhat surprising conclusion that can be drawn from these oral histories is that, at least in some cases, drug use was not only a means of finding new ways to look at the world, but also a way of becoming more involved in the movement. Young people tuned in and turned on, but they did not necessarily drop out. Jim Adams, a student at SIU in the sixties, says, "There were a lot of drugs and that made a difference. Somehow or other that created an involvement rather than a drop-out" mentality.[23] Ray Lenzi explains that the use of illegal drugs politicized people: "As more and more kids got turned on, that increased their sense of negativity toward the government—'What do you mean they put you in jail for doing this?' That was just another reason to assume there was something evil about the authorities and the government system." The dangers

23. Author interview with Jim Adams, July 28, 1999.

were real, as authorities clearly used possession and use of drugs as an excuse to go after political activists.[24]

In his memoir, *Prairie Radical*, Robert Pardun describes the profound impact of taking psychedelic drugs: "People come away from the experience with a sense that all creation is one thing, that the observer and the observed are not separate, that all people should love each other because they are all one, and that the earth is alive and should be respected." Pardun claims that the use of psychedelic drugs, which erase the boundaries between the user and the rest of creation, led some activists to their concern about environmental issues. He writes, "As a friend of mine once said, 'It's harder to cut down a tree after you've had a conversation with one.' "[25] He describes one of the first environmental protests in Austin (in 1969), in which members of the Young Democrats and Young Republicans joined other students on the main mall of the university to show their displeasure as a number of live oak trees were cut down to make room for an expansion of the football stadium. Pardun was one of many heartland activists who helped plant an important seed of the environmental movement by going "back to the land" in order to live in harmony with nature and set an example of a more peaceful, organic, nonexploitive lifestyle.

While the oral histories focus primarily on student rights, the Vietnam War, and the influence of the counterculture, the significant impact of the civil rights and black power movements should be acknowledged here as well. It is noteworthy that the national SDS leaders have more to say about these issues than do the student leaders or grassroots activists. Jane Adams went to Mississippi for Freedom Summer, which was clearly a life-altering experience for its participants.[26] She was also involved in desegregation efforts in Carbondale. For Carl Davidson as well, the New Left would be

24. In 1967 the *Columbia Free Press Underground* reported on a student spy who had tried to find out whether Rory Ellinger, among others, was guilty of drug violations (October 1967, p. 1; Students for Democratic Society Papers, 1958–1970, microfilm, reel 23).

25. Pardun, *Prairie Radical*, 32, 293. Some of the people I interviewed made a similar point, although they were not all willing to be quoted on the subject. One former activist put it this way: "You dropped acid and had seen the secrets of the universe, met God, yourself, personally, and really feel that you know so much . . . and you still have women's [dorm] hours?"

26. For a discussion of how this experience affected the participants as well

unthinkable without the central impact of both the civil rights and black power movements. Yet the student leaders and grassroots activists seemed to have little direct connection to these issues. Rory Ellinger expresses great reverence for civil rights activists, and some of the others acknowledge racial equality as an issue, but few of them had direct experience with the movement as such.

Some of this difference may be attributed to the generational shift in the New Left that many scholars have noted. Those who got involved later in the decade did not share the experience in the civil rights movement that the early New Left had. It is hardly surprising that following the turn to black power, when white people were no longer welcome in organizations such as the Student Nonviolent Coordinating Committee (SNCC) and could play at best a supportive role in the struggle for racial equality, young white activists focused on other issues. As John McMillian and Paul Buhle explain:

> [A]ctivists of color were potent sources of inspiration for the New Left, and . . . combating racism was a central component of New Left politics. However, the United States in the 1960s was . . . culturally and politically segregated to an enormous degree. As the 1960s unfolded, black and white radicals operated more on parallel tracks than on the same track. . . . The challenge for historians, then, is to present the New Left accurately, as a mostly white and largely patriarchal movement, without writing women and African Americans out of this history and reinforcing the forms of segregation that plagued the New Left.[27]

While many of the oral histories don't say much about civil rights, all of these activists clearly absorbed its influence. The civil rights movement was not only a model and an inspiration for the early New Left, but its spirit and its tactics were still important in the latter part of the decade. SNCC's courage in confronting authority and its use of nonviolent direct action clearly affected New Left activists throughout the decade, and the more confrontational style of some of the demonstrations in the later sixties took its cue from the black power movement.

Black power and the New Left held in common the ideal of liber-

---

as how they went on to influence sixties activism, see Doug McAdam, "Applying the Lessons of Mississippi," chap. 5 in *Freedom Summer*.

27. John McMillian and Paul Buhle, eds., *The New Left Revisited*, 6.

ation, that one's identity was the basis both for one's oppression and also for the struggle to be free. For instance, Gregory Nevala Calvert wrote in 1967 that the basis of radical consciousness was "the discovery of oneself as *one of the oppressed*" (emphasis in original). Calvert was among those who proposed that many middle-class professionals (including students, who would come to play those roles) were members of a "new working class" whose role in bringing about social change was critical precisely because of their place in the knowledge industry. He suggested that "[w]hat has held the new radicalism together, what has given it its life and vitality, has been the conviction that the gut-level alienation from America-the Obscene-and-the-Dehumanized was a sincere and realistic basis for challenging America."[28] The black power movement expressed this idea in different terms, but the point was that radicalism began with an affirmation rather than an apology for one's identity.

The black power movement is also an essential part of the backdrop for understanding the response of administrators, law enforcement, and public officials to student activism. Students in the late sixties were often seen as troublemakers, and one of the nightmares of "the establishment" was that the black power and antiwar movements would join forces, on and off campus.

Campus officials and concerned citizens often sought to blame "outside agitators" for their problems, while government leaders demanded a search for foreign (i.e., Communist) links to the movement and harassed and persecuted black power advocates. But the New Left and student protest was homegrown, both at elite schools on the coasts and in the upper Midwest as well as at prairie campuses. At the latter, student radicals were always a small minority. But it was not so much the numbers of activists as their influence and the issues they raised that concerned university administrators and government officials. As Kenneth J. Heineman points out, institutions that did not have much of a national reputation and where the majority of students (and faculty) were prowar or apathetic are "a more perfect mirror of American society in the 1960s."[29] So what do the activists at these institutions have to tell us?

---

28. Gregory Nevala Calvert, "In White America: Radical Consciousness and Social Change," 127–28.
29. Heineman, *Campus Wars*, 5.

In this book, prairie power activists tell their stories in their own words. In these descriptions of their backgrounds, ideas, and activities we can see plainly how the desire for personal liberation and authenticity came together with the hope of political efficacy in the New Left. The oral histories illustrate as well the importance of cultural influences—music, poetry, literature, mass media—in galvanizing young people to try to change their society. Activists talk about reading Allen Ginsberg's *Howl*, listening to Bob Dylan and the Beatles, seeing graphic images of civil rights battles, and even taking psychedelic drugs as experiences that changed the way they viewed the world. They often seem to have learned as they went along; there is a sense of motion in many of the oral histories, whether it is Carl Davidson and Jane Adams talking about organizing "Interstate 70 SDS," or Ray Lenzi, president of student government at SIU, discussing his attendance at several of the most important national events of the late sixties. Through the media and popular culture, as well as through their own travels, their conception of the world became wider. Some activists flowed easily back and forth from local, immediate concerns to national-level politics; Rory Ellinger, a former student leader at the University of Missouri, describes going back and forth from (radical) student politics to (liberal) national electoral politics.

Part of what is striking about prairie power universities is that any one of them could have been Kent State. There were multiple conflicts on each of these campuses: demands on the part of black students ranging from curricular reform, admissions, and hiring to the university's role in addressing local poverty; in loco parentis issues, especially the issue of women's dorm hours; concerns of both administrators and community members about long hair and drugs; right-wing vigilantes preparing to take events into their own hands; and, of course, the war. Similar to those on the national scene, most protests were nonviolent, and very self-consciously so. Yet by the late sixties, there were also serious threats and incidents of violence, most of which involved damage to property: the Agriculture Building at SIU was bombed in 1968, the Old Main building burned down under mysterious circumstances the following spring, and the National Guard was brought in and the campus shut down after seven days of rioting following the killings at Kent State. The KU Student Union was burned in April 1970 and two people were killed by the Lawrence police in other incidents of violence that summer.

One of the more noteworthy points about the interviews is the difference in the perspective of national SDS leaders and local activists. The oral histories begin with SDS national leaders who were regional organizers in the prairies. These are the people who were self-conscious about using the term *prairie power* to differentiate themselves from the old guard. They had strong ideas about the direction in which the movement should go, and when they took over the national leadership of SDS they carried out their own vision of campus organizing. Jeff Shero Nightbyrd, among others, argues that it was their sense of humor and ability to have a good time that distinguished prairie power activists from the old guard. Nightbyrd tried to integrate the bathrooms at the University of Texas with the slogan "Let my people go." Carl Davidson talks about daring people to attend an antiwar rally at which a dog would be napalmed. Jane Adams remembers one prairie power activist who talked about overthrowing the system with forceful and violent laughter.

Humor was not their only weapon, however. Prairie power activists developed and stood for basic New Left ideas: organizing people around their own oppression, focusing on students dissatisfied with the bureaucratic and authoritarian manner in which universities were run and with the irrelevancy of the curriculum, connecting student power to broader social issues. They emphasized building the new society in the shell of the old, an idea dating back to the Industrial Workers of the World, and connecting the personal to the political, an idea that became the hallmark of the women's liberation movement.

The second group of oral histories, from the point of view of local leaders, gives us a deeper understanding of prairie power activism. Local leaders on college campuses in the lower Midwest were less self-conscious about standing for "prairie power." They share some of the characteristics of the national prairie power leaders—less ideological and more focused on student rights than the old guard—yet they also illustrate the diversity of experience of the local leadership and thereby help us break down the stereotype of the "long-haired, dope-smoking anarchists." Local leaders such as Rory Ellinger, head of SDS at MU, or Bill Ebert, who was elected student body president at KU in 1970, hardly fit the bill.

One point that comes through strongly in the oral histories is that national organizations had little to do with local events. While leaders at the local level seemed aware of, and sometimes participated in, national events, they also felt they were on their own when it came to local organizing. So, while the regional organizers describe going to various campuses and helping organize chapters of SDS around local issues, local leaders describe feeling a strong *lack* of connection with a national organization. This serves as a reminder that the student movement is not synonymous with SDS. To those involved, student organizing and demonstrating about dorm hours or the war in Vietnam often seemed "a very local affair."[30]

The grassroots activists represented in the third group of oral histories give us a rare view. These are students who joined demonstrations on their own campuses but did not necessarily identify strongly with either local or national organizations. While some of them might not have described themselves as New Leftists, much less identified with the term *prairie power,* they are in fact more typical of student protesters than either group of leaders. Their stories are included here in order to indicate the range of students who participated, if only occasionally, in antiwar and student rights protest on midwestern campuses. Again, it is difficult to see the activism of these people as mindlessly expressive or destructive, either of SDS or the university. Trish Vandiver, arrested and suspended from MU for selling the *Columbia Free Press* on campus, and Carol-jean Brune, who raised two children while staying active in the civil rights, antiwar, and women's liberation movements at KU, are good examples of grassroots activists whose efforts do not fit the usual description of "prairie power." Larry Vaughn and Larry Bennett were clearly part of the trend in which "party people" on conservative campuses took a countercultural turn and were swept up in the movement, becoming what Carl Davidson called the "shock troops" of the student movement. (It is worth noting in this regard the reactions of Vaughn, Bennett, Dan Viets, and Wayne Sailor to being pushed around by the police, which echo others' stories of how they were radicalized by a police club and bear out the point that overreaction by authorities helped build the movement.) All of

30. Hanson interview. Former SDS activists Michael Harty (SIU) and Rory Ellinger (MU) echoed these sentiments.

these people had an impact on their own campuses and, cumulatively, on society. They were also profoundly affected by their involvement in the issues, and to a great extent maintain the values they developed through their participation in the student movement.

It is not simply the "yippies to yuppies" generalization that these people's experiences challenge, however. A close look at prairie power forces us to call into question several widely accepted conclusions about the New Left and its development:

1. None of the supposed ending points for the New Left—the SDS national convention in 1969, the accidental explosion of a bomb by Weathermen in a Greenwich Village townhouse in 1970,[31] the shootings at Kent State that same year—are compelling when we recognize the continuities between the New Left and successive movements. The women's liberation, gay rights, environmental, and antinuclear movements all shared with prairie power activists an explicit attempt to link the personal to the political, tackle local issues, struggle with questions about leadership, and so on. If this is our starting point, then we need to rethink the characterization of the late sixties as simply a period of declining activism.

2. The relationship between the New Left and the counterculture is more complicated than much of the scholarship has allowed for. There were some local activists who saw a clear distinction between political and countercultural activity. For example, Rory Ellinger was never interested in drugs and saw himself as a hard-core politico and yet he came to appreciate Gentle Tuesday at the University of Missouri. In any case, one cannot simply argue that the counterculture came along and derailed the New Left, because for many activists the counterculture was their inroad to the New Left, while for others the distinction between the two was nonexistent.[32]

3. The violence of the late sixties was not so much a function of

31. When SDS split in 1969, one faction, taking its name from a Dylan song, formed the Weathermen (later the Weather Underground). The group carried out symbolic bombings of government buildings in an effort to "bring the war home," viewing itself as an ally of third world revolutionaries against the U.S. government. The bomb that blew up the townhouse was reportedly intended to be the first used on human beings, not just property.

32. See Klatch, *A Generation Divided;* and Peter Braunstein and Michael William Doyle, eds., *Imagine Nation: The American Counterculture of the 1960s and '70s.*

the anarchism of prairie power activists, but part of a much larger turn toward confrontation in sections of the student and antiwar movements. Even so, most protests were not violent, and virtually all of the violence perpetrated by students was against property, not human beings. While several writers have suggested that the violence came mostly from the "new breed," there is little evidence to support this claim. Jane Adams argues that on the national level prairie power activists were less likely than the old guard to romanticize third world and African American movements that supported violence. Many of the local activists worked to prevent violence on their own campuses. While part of what shocked people in the late sixties was the extent to which student confrontations with authority had spread to more conservative parts of the country, clearly it was not prairie power that brought violence into the movement.

4. Blaming prairie power for the destruction of SDS or the student movement is problematic. The prairie power contingent is generally charged with insisting upon SDS's nonexclusion clause even after it was clear that Progressive Labor aimed to take over the organization. But the "new breed" was carrying on SDS tradition, not just being naive. They saw the openness, the freewheeling debates, the participatory democracy within SDS as strengths that reflected their experience in the Midwest and at more conservative institutions. The elite schools often had large, factionalized movements, but at more conservative schools grassroots activists saw broad coalitions as the way to build the movement. Their experience affirmed the idea that SDS's inclusiveness was one of its greatest strengths, even as the experience of the old-guard SDSers was teaching them that too much inclusiveness could be debilitating. The student movement's decline can actually be attributed to many factors. While protest did not disappear after Kent State and Jackson State, clearly the student deaths at these institutions brought home the risks of continued confrontations. Many people comment on this as a turning point for the movement. Dan Viets remembers thinking, "[T]hey're killing us," and says, "I identified as one of them." Another host of reasons for the decline of the student movement have to do with its successes: challenges to segregation, in loco parentis, and restrictions on free speech all led to changes on the local level, while the end of the draft and, eventually, the war also defused the movement.

5. While prairie power activists were no less sexist than the old guard, they do help us understand the roots of the women's movement. As Sara Evans explains in *Personal Politics*, the New Left spawned the women's liberation movement not only because it treated women as second-class citizens, but because it simultaneously gave them the space to grow and develop their confidence and abilities. The prairie power emphasis on the ties between the personal and the political, on participatory democracy and community, on local issues and lifestyle concerns—all of these were reflected in the women's liberation movement that followed.

In challenging the old image of prairie power and giving greater recognition to midwestern campus activists from non-elite institutions, my intention is not to glorify these people nor to downplay their foibles and contradictions. But while acknowledging the problematic aspects of their ideas and activities, we can also resist the stereotypes and highlight their diversity as well as the contributions they made to the protest movements of the sixties.

Disagreement will continue as to the successes, failures, and impact of sixties protest—civil rights, antiwar, student rights. Nevertheless, there is fairly broad agreement among scholars, and even among politicians right and left, that the legacy of the New Left was a generalized antiauthoritarianism and a cultural liberalism that gave young people a broader array of lifestyle options. For better or worse, prairie power activists played an important role in passing on this legacy.

ORAL HISTORIES I

National SDS Leaders

CARL DAVIDSON

Carl Davidson was born in Beaver County, Pennsylvania, in 1943. He received a BA in philosophy from Penn State University in 1965, and attended the University of Nebraska in 1965–1966. He served as national vice president of SDS that year, and as national interorganizational secretary the following year. He is currently executive director of Networking for Democracy. He has been a technology specialist in the schools and in the community in Chicago for several years. Davidson is also managing editor of cy.Rev: A Journal of Cybernetic Revolution, Sustainable Socialism & Radical Democracy. *Davidson was interviewed in Carbondale, Illinois, on September 17, 1997.*

The rebellious state of mind that led me to join the student movement started in high school, but the things that instigated it were more cultural than political. I grew up in a working-class rural section of Hopewell Township outside of Aliquippa, Pennsylvania, right on the Ohio River near the West Virginia border. My family had been there for a long time. My dad was an auto mechanic, my mother was a beautician. They were never affiliated with politics, they never had much use for politics or politicians. The main trouble I got into as a teenager was when I crossed the color line. Most of the white kids I associated with grew up in what was essentially a country-and-western culture and in the mid-fifties rhythm and blues started becoming popular. It mainly came from the black kids at school. When Elvis Presley, who represented sort of a marriage between black rhythm and blues and white country and western, emerged on the scene it put a lot of us in conflict with our parents. My dad, who never liked Elvis, saw him as basically a white guy singing black music and didn't particularly care for it.

I started hanging out with a lot of Korean War vets who actually were Beat Generation–type people and they hung out at local bars and pool halls. I can't remember which one gave me a copy of Allen Ginsberg's *Howl*. These were guys who were alienated Korean War vets who worked in the mill and for one reason or another had gotten into black culture and jazz hipster culture and I related to them. I was also a kid who was very into mechanical things and technology. I was bright, I always wanted to know how things worked. Part of it I picked up from working with my dad in his garage, part of it was that I was always inquisitive. I just wanted to learn about things. People started calling me "Sputnik" as a nickname, because when the Russians launched Sputnik I was the only one who could explain why it didn't fall. Nobody in my family or the other kids could understand why it stayed up there and I was able to explain why it wouldn't come down. So I earned that nickname.

When I was in mechanical drawing class I designed a three-stage rocket that could do all sorts of different things and won an industrial arts fair, which is how I ended up at Penn State University. So I went into Penn State being a sort of gregarious type who was space-smart, who loved jazz, hung out with black people, and when the civil rights movement started it was a natural for me to identify with. I took the attack on blacks as a personal affront on my friends and I just got involved in the demonstrations and supported my friends in SNCC [pronounced "snick"].

This led to a lot of questioning of things in general. I became associated with the peace movement on campus. We had compulsory ROTC then and I never liked it. I never liked carrying a rifle or wearing a uniform. So I became Penn State's first conscientious objector to ROTC. I walked off the field one day, refused to participate anymore.

Apart from civil rights activity, the first demonstration I went to was [related to] the Cuban Missile Crisis. There were a bunch of ROTC students who came down and threw red paint at us and called us awful things [for opposing U.S. foreign policy]. The interesting thing is later, five years later, if you could find five kids on our campus who were in favor of the war in Vietnam it probably would have been the exact reversal of what had happened. We had about 1,500 students at that university who took part in the student strike.

I got all kinds of flack from my family for being a student activist. The Davidsons had been in Beaver County before it was Beaver

County. They were among the first settlers, and my family had been associated with every war starting with the Revolutionary War: the War of 1812, the Civil War, the Spanish-American War, the First and Second World Wars, and all of a sudden for a young Davidson kid to be a draft resister was no small deal. They didn't particularly care for it.

My dad's first choice in any election would be a Kennedy because he was an Irish Catholic. If there wasn't any Kennedy running he liked George Wallace, but usually he didn't vote for much of anybody. He said vote for the richest one because they were the least likely to be corrupted, but he was basically wired with this old-fashioned racist mentality. He didn't know how to relate to the black movement at all. My mother was more open. When I went to Mississippi my dad was just aghast. He basically stopped talking to me. My mother was sympathetic. She was concerned and her politics developed. Her friends would argue and say nasty things about me and she would rise to my defense. She went through her own development and she eventually ended up voting for Dick Gregory and Jesse Jackson.[1] Not my dad.

When I was in high school they divorced and remarried to very nice people and lived about three miles away from each other, but I never got much support from any of my relatives except my siblings, my two brothers and sister. We were of the same generation. They basically all ended up on the same side of the political spectrum as me. My brother went to Penn State and became head of the SDS chapter there while I was out in Nebraska. It kind of just passed on from brother to brother. We all banded together whenever we went back home for Christmas or Thanksgiving, to give each other support. But there wasn't much support from elsewhere in the family.

Surprisingly, there were a few teachers who sought me out. They sort of came out of the closet as lefties whom I had never known and they said they really liked what I was doing, keep up the good work, but it was always in these hushed tones. It wasn't because Aliquippa was such a conservative place. It was because it had been a battleground, a very militant battleground for the Communist Party. It had organized there and there was a Communist cell in

1. African American activists, outspoken on such issues as civil rights and peace.

town. I learned all this later. It was where Gus Hall and the steel-workers had based themselves when they first organized the CIO.[2] Jones & Laughlin was the largest steel mill in the country and this local was always one of the most militant. They always went on strike two weeks before everybody else and went back to work two weeks later. So there was a militant class struggle in town. Even though my parents had reactionary values on some issues, one thing I was always taught was that you never crossed the picket line. I remember my dad when the steelworkers went on strike—he had a small business, a gas station—he would carry them all even if it meant he had to go deep into debt. He would sympathize with them. Class issues were very clear in that sense—often turned into class struggles and a kind of trade union consciousness.

One of the first things we did at Penn State was we formed an ad hoc committee on student freedom. It was the group we used to fight dorm hours, and we had another on the Vietnam War, Students for Peace, and SURE, Student Union for Racial Equality. At some point we decided we needed a multi-issue socialist organization. . . . We didn't know what to pick so we sent a letter to everybody asking for their literature. The only ones that ended up showing any interest in us, two of them came through town. One was a guy from SDS. He was associated with the old League for Industrial Democracy.[3] He came to campus and gave us some literature and basically said what we should be doing is organizing graduate students into a union and helping cafeteria workers organize a union. It seemed like he was from Mars—the war in Vietnam was blowing up, kids were being shot in Alabama and Mississippi, and this guy wanted us to organize cafeteria workers. So we kind of dismissed him.

The May 2nd Movement was the other group that came into town, and at that time they all had long hair and sideburns and cowboy boots and they carried this paper called the *Free Student* and Viet Cong films, so we said these are the guys for us. So we took big bundles of their paper and I became a distributor of the *Free Student*, but we never really got a chance to organize a chapter of

2. Hall was a union organizer who later became head of the Communist Party USA; the CIO is the Congress of Industrial Organizations.
3. LID was the parent organization of SDS, which developed out of the Student League for Industrial Democracy.

the May 2nd Movement. As April 17th approached, a different guy from SDS showed up, a guy named Steve Weissman, and this guy was completely different from the other one. He sat us down and we said, "Well, where do you stand on all these things?" and he said, "I don't agree with any of that Old Left stuff, we're the New Left, we identify with the Wobblies and anarchists." This was music to our ears. We thought this was great, so we sat up and talked to him all night long and set up a committee to organize a bus to go to the March on Washington and it was fabulous.[4] I went to that march; they expected about 5,000 people and it ended up being 25,000 before it was done. I was so involved. I had never been in anything like that. I joined SDS on the spot.

I came back and I really thought the next day the war was going to be over. After all this, [President] Johnson just had to end it. So I went and got my *New York Times,* fully expecting Johnson to say, "Okay, guys, well, we've reconsidered now . . ." But we could have had 500,000 people out there [and it wouldn't have made a difference]. It didn't seem like they were budging. That was sort of where we were coming from at the time.

A few months after that I left Penn State to become a graduate student at the University of Nebraska. I went out to Nebraska with a friend. . . . We both went to the philosophy department there and we both founded SDS. We did the same thing. We went and checked in with the philosophy department, got our course assignments, picked our classes, then we went to the student union building, cased the joint, and filled out the application for the SDS chapter. All this in the first two days. We were rolling.

We had a lot of fun. The chapter in Nebraska was like virgin territory; that was the refreshing thing about it. There hadn't been a whole lot [of activism] in Nebraska. We did some research and found out the last group that was there was in the thirties. We put the word out, we put some posters in the student union: "SDS Organizing." Our first project was setting up a committee to organize a teach-in on Vietnam, and the shit hit the fan. It was like all of a sudden reporters from all the papers were paying attention, [including] the *Omaha*

4. April 17, 1965, was the date of the first big antiwar demonstration in Washington, D.C., sponsored by SDS—not to be confused with the March on Washington associated with Martin Luther King Jr. and the civil rights movement, which took place in 1963.

World Herald, which was the biggest paper in the region. We lined up a few liberal-minded professors and we even got some preachers. We got one guy who was for the war, and we picked one guy to be against it. It made a big hullabaloo and hundreds and hundreds of people came. It was plastered all over the papers. So that was the first thing that we did and people loved it.

After all the publicity I met the farmers out there. A guy came to my door one day; he said he was with the United States Farmers Association. I looked at him and I thought he was some kind of redneck coming after us, but it ended up he was with this grassroots organization we knew nothing about. He said the first time they marched on Washington was during the Korean War and that they opposed U.S. imperialism in Korea. So they were a great bunch, and I learned the whole history of prairie radicalism on the long bus ride to D.C. They had been members of the Non-Partisan League in South Dakota. They told us all about the farmers' uprising in the 1930s, and Franklin Roosevelt's strengths and weaknesses. We learned quite a bit, and I think most importantly not to judge people too quickly.

One thing I always found refreshing about Nebraska was how open people were, how uncynical people were. Even people who disagreed with you would respectfully listen to your point of view. We had a great time. One thing we did which was kind of interesting was early on we formed a coalition against apartheid, against the Sharpeville Massacre,[5] and with that one I tried a different tactic. Nebraska was a big football school. Cornhuskers. So I went to the star black players on the team and we got them to endorse the march against the Sharpeville Massacre, and they led the march through the town. We went to every bank in town and stopped off at each one and read off its connections with apartheid. I co-opted the opposition by getting the star black football players.

SDS was heavily into community organizing at the time. We thought we should organize the poor as part of our work, so there we are in Nebraska wondering how do we do it. There was one section of town called T-Town, which was kind of poor. It was about five blocks from the square, twenty-five blocks altogether, and its

5. When police in South Africa shot and killed sixty-nine unarmed demonstrators in 1960, there were protests around the world.

main intersection was 22nd and T. So we rented a house right there, an old shack, for $55 a month. It was a three-room house and we took up donations and put our mimeograph machine in, put out leaflets on different community stuff or antiwar stuff and we started being known. The neighbors and young kids would come hang out. Some older guys would sit on our porch at night and drink beer. Lincoln, Nebraska, is 90 percent white and 10 percent nonwhite, and they [nonwhites] all lived in T-Town and half of them were native Americans. This old Sioux lady used to come and sit on our porch too. The main importance of all that was we were sitting on our porch when James Meredith was shot. We heard it on the radio. A couple of old black guys in the neighborhood had these two old cars and we said, "Let's go," and they said, "Fine." So they got some of their friends and we got a few more students, and we took off to Memphis and joined the Meredith March.[6] Some of them came back earlier; I stayed for the whole thing. I walked all the way through Mississippi. That was an important outgrowth of [my experience in] Lincoln.

The other thing we did which was kind of interesting . . . we learned about the Mississippi Freedom Democratic Party, so we decided to run in a student election. We formed a campus Freedom Democratic Party based on the Mississippi Freedom Democratic Party,[7] and we came up with a platform that challenged university restrictions on student power. Our platform had a lot of anarcho-syndicalist ideas and it caused a big hullabaloo. It was the first real student election they ever had, and one of our guys actually won. The guy who went out to Nebraska with me actually won. He wasn't student body president but he was one of the top officers.

The other thing we did that really paid off was something I'd done at Penn State. The first time I ever had to give a speech was at Penn State when we brought in the Viet Cong film. We had about

6. In June 1966, James Meredith began a march through Mississippi to show African Americans it was safe to assert their right to vote. When he was shot by a Klansman, civil rights activists flocked to Memphis to continue the march. The "black power" slogan was used with great success on this march.

7. MFDP was an offshoot of the 1964 Freedom Summer project, an alternative to Mississippi's regular, all-white, Democratic party. The Freedom Party's delegation to the 1964 Democratic convention in Atlantic City was rebuffed by the national party, an important turning point for many sixties activists who learned that liberalism had its limits.

twelve hundred people fill this room and I had to introduce the guy who was going to show the film. I was supposed to give a brief speech on Vietnam. I got up in front of this sea of people and froze. I had stage fright. I could not speak. Finally my roommate came and dragged me away and got somebody else to go up there and mumble something to get the thing going. I was so shocked that this had happened to me that I said we've got to do something about this. So we got this big wooden crate which we hid behind the music building and we painted "SOAP" on the side of it. There was this one intersection at Penn State, whenever classes changed there would always be five thousand people, and we hauled this crate out in the middle of it. We carried it out from the bushes. We made every member of our group get up there for five minutes every day and talk, on whatever topic they wanted. If nothing else, just reading from the *New York Times* or *Guardian*, whatever—they had to do something, and that's how we learned public speaking, doing that on a soapbox.

We wanted to do the same thing in Nebraska, but the campus was much more spread out and there weren't any good spots except the student union building. There was a spot outside an eating area that was a natural for it, so we waged a little battle with the administration and they ceded it to us every Thursday afternoon. They gave us a little microphone and we said this was our Hyde Park Forum where anybody could get up, that it wasn't just for us, it was for anybody, left-wing, right-wing, antipolitical, whatever, it would be open air, free speech. The only limitation was that you were allowed to talk for only four minutes. They couldn't really argue against that. Some of the right-wingers spoke out, but it was mostly us. So that was a big tactic that was very successful. Some students just always came. Whenever we found interesting speakers we would bring them in, like Allen Ginsberg: we heard he was down in Lawrence riding around in this old van with Peter Orlovsky, all these old crazy beatniks, but we had him come to Nebraska.[8]

We had about twenty-five students in our SDS chapter in Nebraska. For our South Africa thing we turned out about two hundred

8. The author of *Howl*, an influential Beat poem from the 1950s, Ginsberg was an antiwar and counterculture activist in the sixties. Orlovsky was Ginsberg's lover and a poet as well.

people. I think five hundred people attended our Vietnam teach-in. It depended on what the topic was. Later on, after I left, the demonstrations got quite a bit larger and I think they shut down the school after Kent State, during the student strike.

When I was there we had a small chapter. It wasn't like we had hundreds, but we did a lot of things. We had a couple of black kids who had grown up in the Midwest. One guy I remember, Joe Knight, was from Kansas and was part of the Exoduster movement, or his grandparents were. After the Civil War they moved to Kansas. I learned a lot of history of blacks in the Midwest from him. I learned about black cowboys from him; I never realized there were black cowboys. Then the other ones were just farm kids from Nebraska, that's who mainly went to the University of Nebraska. Maybe their parents were teachers or something like that.

I think SDS was like a lot of social movements of intellectuals. It started off in the elite universities where SDS's traditional base was. University of Michigan, Princeton, Swarthmore, these were some of the schools where SDS was anchored originally. Also it was anchored among the children of the Old Left who were in the Communist Party, the Socialist Party, where they tended to go to school. I represented a turning point in the student movement. After that first march on Washington [in 1965], there was a huge expansion of the student movement that reached down to all the state colleges and universities. When it broadened out and grew up in all these schools, naturally the class character changed. It was funny: for all the class consciousness they had where I grew up, since my dad wasn't a steelworker I always tended to think we were middle-class and the upper-class kids were the ones who lived in a section we called "Snot Knob." When I got to the university, [I saw that] those kids we talked about as being from "Snot Knob" were really middle-class, and I ran into kids who were truly from the upper class. So that was a whole different thing. Also when I went to the university I met the first Jews I ever met. I think there was one Jewish family in Aliquippa. Of course, all the kids at Penn State didn't know about the Serbian holidays like I did. . . .

The biggest issues we organized around at the University of Nebraska were the war and racism, and secondarily we would bring up these civil libertarian types of issues, things that had to do with student government, student representation on different university committees. Our tactics were pretty tame: public forums, marches, passing out leaflets. One of the more innovative ones we did was developing the student political party. But in terms of doing anything really outrageous, up until 1966 in Nebraska the most militant thing we did was take a carload of people down to Mississippi.

When I came back from Mississippi I ran into Jane Adams. She was the national secretary [of SDS] and she kept encouraging me. She'd say, "Carl, there are other campuses and they want people to come out and talk to them about SDS." So I would go to one [from time to time] and I really enjoyed it. Especially after I came back from Mississippi, I took to heart Stokely Carmichael's thing about how you have to go back and organize your own people.[9] So I made up a circuit of all the main schools in four states and I traveled to all of them. They decided to have the SDS National Convention at Clear Lake, Iowa. I had to help build support for it, so I traveled to all the campuses in the Midwest and got to know people and help them with their different strategies and tactics. I spread literature and ideas amongst them, and I sort of became the Great Plains regional organizer or campus traveler or whatever they called us, the "outside agitator," and I enjoyed it. I was deeply influenced by the "black power" thing in Mississippi, so back at our little house at 22nd and T we decided that we should write something up for the convention that was going to happen in Clear Lake. We went round and round and I said, "Look, I'll just write it up. I'll write up something about the students in the group, I'll sum up all the things we've done and talked about and put it in some kind of political context." So I sat down and wrote this pamphlet ["Student Syndicalism"] for the students in this movement. I passed it around to the rest of the chapter and people gave some suggestions, but basically people said it was fine, so we cranked up the mimeograph machine and made a few copies. One of the SDS guys had an old Cadillac Hearse and ten of us got into it and went off to Clear Lake.

When I got there this big political battle was going on between the old guard and the Texas anarchists. Jeff Shero was looking for allies, and he and Jane came to me: "Carl, we want you to run for vice president." I said, "What? You've got to be warped." "Sure you

9. Carmichael was an important and early advocate of black power who suggested that white people should organize their own community.

can run for vice president. Everyone likes your paper." I had set them on a table, didn't even think about it. I thought it would just be a background thing for people to look at. So I finally said, "Okay, put my name on. I don't care." The next thing I know I'd won. I had no idea going there that I would ever do such a thing. One day I went to this meeting and the next day I was national vice president of SDS. The paper that I had written . . . everybody was making copies of it. It was spontaneously being mass-produced all over the country. It was being translated into other languages. French students translated it into French. I guess I said the right thing at the right time. So I figured, well, okay, I'll try it out. I'll do it for a year, what's a year? The guy who had the old Cadillac Hearse said to take it, borrow it for a year, just give it back when I was done. So I loaded up my stuff, dropped out of graduate school, and headed for Chicago.

I borrowed the word *syndicalism* from two different documents. The group I identified with the most in American history was the IWW [International Workers of the World]. I liked the romanticism, the fact that they were this roving band of organizers, mixed culture and politics, and had this sort of real clear rebel spirit about them.[10] When I studied the history of the American Left these were the guys I identified with. The other was a document put out by the Union of Students in Quebec. It was a mimeographed paper I had read earlier where they basically talked about forming the national association of all student governments and they used *syndicate,* meaning "union." It wasn't particularly radical, but to me *syndicalism* had sort of a rebellious character to it. It was a word that was loaded. There were criminal syndicalism acts still on the books. I identified with the militant period of trade unionism, so that's why I picked it—it was subversive. And people recognized that.

There were three of us elected as national officers of SDS: myself; Greg Calvert, who was elected national secretary; and a kid named Nick Egleson, who was elected president. Nick Egleson was a Quaker pacifist type who sort of half-represented the old guard but had a base in some of the community organizing, so he was sort of betwixt and between, and he really didn't want to be in the national

10. Syndicalism was both means and end for the IWW—a general strike would lead to an industrial system owned and managed by workers.

office. Greg and I figured we didn't particularly like his politics. We said, "Nick, why don't you go back to Swarthmore and do what you want to do, write a paper or whatever. You can be president, you can make some statements, you can do whatever you want." He was very relieved, and Greg and I said, "Great." So Greg and I basically took over. He and I sat down and hatched a plan. Greg went off to Princeton and gave a speech at a conference there calling white America to revolutionary consciousness, and he said [to me], "You have to start working on a new document that really goes deeper into the question of the university." So we formed a little group and he hooked me up with a number of like-minded people. When I wrote "Student Syndicalism" I was thinking IWW. When I wrote the sequel, "New Radicals in the Multiversity," I was thinking of French Marxism, revolutionary resistance, the new working class, and C. Wright Mills.[11] A much deeper analysis of the U.S. We wanted to find a way of taking SDS, which we basically saw as a liberal movement, to a more revolutionary movement. We felt that it was important that it happen naturally, but that there were roadblocks along the way that we should move out of the way. That's what we saw as our role.

One of the first things I did was try and help SDS discover who it was. So Greg sent me off with the Cadillac Hearse with lots of literature and Vietnam movies, and I just drove from campus to campus. I must have covered a hundred campuses that year and I wrote this long document—I forget what it was called—but basically it told people what SDS looked like. I broke it down into the organizers, the shock troops, and the intellectuals. I did an analysis based on real people, but I didn't give the names. It summed up what was happening in all these various chapters, it was self-critical and refreshing, and it got people interested in trying to redefine the organization.

I saw SDS as the main vehicle of the white student movement, not just one organization among many. But it had to be home for several tendencies if it was going to become the voice of the American student movement. We felt it had to develop a revolutionary stance because that was in tune with the times, otherwise we would

11. Mills was a sociologist who strongly influenced and encouraged the New Left.

not capture the dynamic energy. Probably the most important thing was we felt we had to create an organization that required some kind of personal commitment, the sort where you put your bodies on the line, and we felt one way to do that was around the question of the draft. So we emphasized SDS's uniqueness in developing the most militant revolutionary program of resistance to the draft that existed anywhere, which we did. I was the person in charge. There was an interesting seventeen-hour debate at one of the SDS conventions because I had purposely written in resolutions to violate all the antisubversive laws, because we wanted to make it rebellious. Finally, we said, "What do we need to pass this? Let's just do it," because the organization couldn't quite come to an agreement. We couldn't get a consensus, and the vote I think was actually split. I finally said let's just do it. So we withdrew the resolution after seventeen hours of debate and we just went on to implement it. People said, "Well, everyone agreed they wanted to do it, but why put it in writing?" That was part of the thing—"why put it in writing"—so we did all sorts of things that were legal and illegal in opposition to the draft. We wanted to define SDS because we felt if you really wanted to grow you had to have something about you that was adventuresome, otherwise you were just another branch of the Trotskyist movement or whatever "Heinz 57" variety of ideological soup. You weren't really going to draw people unless you had this spirit of adventure, so we made draft resistance, opposition to the war that we developed, reflect that. If you really wanted to do battle, this is where you would want to be.

The earliest tensions between the old guard and our prairie power people were resolved. Basically, we removed them [from office]. We made an initial effort that [Jeff] Shero launched to abolish the national office in the name of decentralism, which was wisely defeated. But even though it was defeated he raised some interesting questions about SDS as a decentralist organization, rather than a democratic centralist organization, which helped it grow. Later on real tensions developed when Progressive Labor decided to join SDS.[12] We always had representatives of different political tendencies within the organization, but Progressive Labor had launched

12. Progressive Labor was a Maoist group that broke away from the Communist Party USA in the early sixties and later tried to take over SDS.

the May 2nd Movement to do exactly what SDS had become. For instance, the story of how I was initially attracted to the May 2nd Movement but SDS stole it from them. So they [Progressive Labor] had a choice at one point what to do: "Do we continue to build the May 2nd Movement as a rival to SDS or do we recognize the fact that SDS is moving in an anti-imperialist direction and influence that direction?" They chose the latter. They dissolved the May 2nd Movement and all the May 2nd people came into SDS, joined SDS chapters. Some people were very opposed to PL, and for quite anti-communist reasons. I never opposed them for those reasons although I opposed their line bitterly, and I always thought their Leninism was impressive. The fact that an organization of only four hundred people could have the influence that they did—I just marveled at it. And the discipline: They all argued the same line, they concentrated their forces, put out these publications, and did it with only four hundred people. I thought that was great. I admired it.

Sometimes it was frustrating. They would all come in sometimes and put forward their line like automatons, the same inflections on the words. So that began to be a little ridiculous at times. But my main objection to them was the content of their line, not the form of the organization. I didn't mind the mechanics. If we wanted to kick out PL because they're a disciplined cadre then we'd have to kick out a lot of people because there are lots of other groups in here, the Socialist Party, the CP [Communist Party] people have a group in here, so are we going to kick them all out? We can't kick one out on that basis; it has to be something about their political line itself that runs in opposition to that of SDS. So I defended them in that sense.

For a while I got attacked for being a centrist. Some people wanted to kick them out early on for the wrong reasons and I opposed it. So there was tension around that. They managed to elect one of their people to the national office, a guy named Fred Gordon. And we had a small administrative committee that was all Chicago-based people and they managed to get one of their people elected, a girl named Beryl Skidmore. So every administrative decision in the national office became a battle with Progressive Labor. They would try to steer things in different directions surreptitiously. To seize control was the name of the game.

It was interesting, in the midst of that the FBI did its number. The FBI, realizing there were different factions, would use its operatives to send documents from each faction to the other. Sometimes they were real documents, sometimes they were nothing but nasty cartoons about each other that the FBI had written. They actually had their own cartoonist who made these things, and they spread factional warfare. It all came out in the COINTELPRO papers.[13] The FBI put these strains on our national office. If we had made any errors in our views in the organization, it was errors on the side of not being organized enough. We knew we had at least 100,000 members, but we had no way of counting them. People did not even turn in membership lists. We had chapters of two hundred people in places we didn't even know we had a chapter. We had to read it in the *New York Times* that two hundred people came to an SDS meeting somewhere. That's how loose it was. We would read about it in the *New York Times* and send somebody out to find out who they were. Some of them actually filled out a membership card every now and then and sent us the money, but it was a very loose operation.

The shock troops were mainly people who were into the counterculture. They loved to go to demonstrations. They liked being high. They had radical politics in the sense that they were against the war and the draft, but they had no time for organization. They did not like to spend time in meetings. If there was a huge rally with interesting things happening, they would show up. But apart from that only a few of them would come to meetings some of the time. They were not into it. The intellectuals were mainly graduate student types who were writing their Ph.D. theses. They saw the chapter as being the place to debate the finer points of the thesis they were working on. Some of them were very good, but a lot of them were pains in the neck. They tended to be conservative in their politics. On something that really required audacity they would tend to hold things back. But we truly had some of the best and the brightest people, people who went to the New School for Social Research, Harvard University. Some of them took the wrong path, some of them were killed. But some are well-known intellectuals, very advanced in their thinking.

The organizers were sort of the dedicated crew, the ones who carried things from one day to the next. Who saw themselves (a) as

13. The FBI's domestic counterintelligence program aimed at disrupting the New Left, among other movements.

part of the national movement, and (b) [as people who] saw beyond SDS. They saw SDS as one piece of something much broader; maybe it didn't even exist yet, but they saw SDS as one contingent of a revolutionary movement. They had a camaraderie with each other. At one point we organized when we were in a big battle with PL and we needed every vote we could muster. A lot of the organizers who weren't attached to any chapter, who were travelers, formed "Interstate 70 SDS." We had about twenty people. So we managed to get a couple of votes. It was called that because Interstate 70 was one of the roads which connected a lot of the schools.

The shock troops were probably the largest group, the organizers and intellectuals were maybe 10 percent. The organizers were maybe 5 percent and the shock troops were the rest. When I thought about it later on—in one of my other organizations twenty years later I tried to do a similar analysis—I realized that this was not unusual. In fact if you take any mass organization, insurgent organization, and did an analysis of it, this is the kind of stratification you would find. There wasn't anything special about SDS. What I did was put a flashlight on it and put labels on it.

I've always argued and still believe that the main thing that defeated or split SDS was the racism, in this sense: When the black student movement began occupying administration buildings all across the North demanding black studies and open admissions or at least an increase in admissions for black students, hiring of black professors, and so on, those of us who had been through the southern civil rights movement realized that this was a profound advance and this was great. In fact, the black students were taking us to battle [against] the racist structure of the university. The Progressive Labor Party had just gone through a national congress where they had completely changed their line on race and national issues. They came up with the line that all nationalism was reactionary, and so when the black students would demand an increase in admissions for black students, they said this was a nationalist demand and should be opposed, and all these black strikes should be broken because they were reactionary strikes. So you had one faction in SDS taking that position and another side taking the opposite, and then there were those in between. I remember I went back to Penn State and raised the issue. I said, "Well, what are you doing around anti-racism stuff?" "Nothing." "Why?" "We don't have any problem with racism; there aren't any black students here." I remember the guy sort of blinking at me. I didn't say anything, I just kept staring at him. All of a sudden I could see the lightbulb go off in his head. He said, "Oh my God." He just realized what he had said. So I said, "Now we see what the problem is here." So that was the kids in the middle who raised the question about what we called the "my little brother" line: "Well, it's great for all these black students to get open admission, but what about my little brother? I mean, he can't come."

The Brooklyn College black students shut down Brooklyn College, and SDS at Brooklyn College was dominated by Progressive Labor. They were going to organize a march and break through the picket line. So a bunch of us took the minority of the Brooklyn College [SDSers] and other people from SDS chapters around New York City, and we put a line in front of the student picket line and we told the PL, "You gotta go through us before you go through them." We were ready. We had chains and everything. We were ready to fight. The same scene to one degree or another was repeated on about twenty campuses. It was only six months later that the thing finally blew up in Chicago, but the split had taken place at the base and was around the issue of racism and antiracism.

PL wasn't just against the blacks. They came out at the same time with [the line that] Ho Chi Minh was a reactionary traitor, Mao Tse-tung was a sellout. They developed their own weird set of politics. So the split took place, and we just felt that when it came apart at the convention there wasn't much we could do about it. We felt that the split was a good thing to have happened and in this case the opposition to PL was correct. It wasn't because they were Communist that we kicked them out, but they had a white chauvinist line and that's why we kicked them out.

The big difference was almost everybody who had been through the southern civil rights movement had no problem at all understanding the black student movement, even if they might have different views. Some people didn't feel bad about SNCC's position, while other people were very upset about it.[14] Regardless, they all understood the profound revolutionary character of what the black students were doing on campus and wouldn't have any problem as

14. The Student Nonviolent Coordinating Committee expelled its white members when it entered its "black power" phase.

to why it should be supported. A lot of people who didn't [support the black students] were people who had no connection with that movement except at a distance, or who came in mainly for some other reason.

The Meredith March, for instance, was a crucible where you learned things, tempered by fire. People can talk about King's nonviolence all they want, but this march was armed to the teeth. After Meredith was shot, the Deacons for Defense came on the March. They were quiet. You didn't see them too much, they were not flashy, but they were older black guys, mostly Korean War vets or Second World War vets. Every night after we'd stake out where we were going to sleep, they would put up a CB radio, and there were CB radios in the cars, so even if something happened and there were no telephones we would always have a CB radio. All those cars were armed, and all those guys in them were straight ahead and natural as could be. I would ask them, "Well, doesn't Dr. Martin Luther King believe in nonviolence? What about you?" They said, "Davidson, Dr. King's a man of the Lord, he should believe in nonviolence, and we believe in nonviolence too, but we also believe that the Lord takes care of those who take care of themselves." That's why they had these shotguns and rifles and whatnot sitting all over the place. You couldn't see them; it wasn't like the Black Panther Party.[15] These guys were just secure and it was there, and the Klan knew that they were there, and King knew they were there, and nobody said anything and they just did their work. On that march I made the transition from being a radical pacifist to a believer in armed self-defense and saw how it worked in an up-close, practical way. We'd go to these little sleepy hamlets where they'd put us up at night, and as we were driving through I'd ride in one of the Deacons' cars, and he would stop and say hello to some sleepy-looking guy and then I realized the whole town was an armed camp.

A lot of people didn't quite know how to react to black nationalism and were upset that so many interracial things had broken down, but I learned an important lesson on that march. One afternoon I was sitting on a porch—we had walked into this little town, Greenwood, Mississippi, and there was a SNCC project there. There was this young white kid who had been there for over a year and he

15. The Black Panthers carried guns openly, making no effort to conceal them.

was with this older black man. I started talking to the older black guy. He told me he had just registered to vote, and he pointed to this young white kid and said this kid had gotten him out to register to vote. I said, "Well, how do you guys get along?" He said, "This so-and-so has been just like a daddy to me." This really struck me. Here's this guy who must be seventy years old pointing to this young white kid saying this kid has just been like a daddy to me.

I sat down on the stoop and about three young black girls came up and were sitting around me—they must have been five or six years old—and they kept playing with my hair. I had long hair then, and they kept playing with my hair. I finally asked this one girl, "How come you're playing with my hair?" She said, "Because you have such good hair." I said, "What do you mean, good hair?" She said, "Well, your hair isn't like mine. Mine's all nappy and curled up and yours is long and straight." So that night I'm listening to Stokely Carmichael in this black church out in the middle of nowhere with all these sharecroppers and he says, "When your daughters talk about their nappy hair, you've got to tell them they're beautiful." The place becomes electric and it just dawned on me, I mean everything just fell into place. . . . Even if you had the best intentions with some of the older people, a paternalistic relationship would be set up, or just because you were representative of the dominant culture, even if you had revolutionary values, people would still look at you in a certain way. All those structures had to be broken if the real revolutionary energy was to be unleashed, and that's what Stokely and the rest of them understood about the importance of black power and black consciousness. The white SNCC kid had to get out of the way. So that was a very profound lesson I learned.

I took that lesson back, I went around and made speeches on it. I felt that part of the transition we wanted to make in SDS was that in the past student movements had always been adjuncts to other movements. They were sort of suburban allies to the labor movement or they were not even so much allies as adjuncts, helpers of some sort. What we argued is because there were changes in American education, because students of the working classes, middle classes, were being brought into education in a mass way—and this was nothing temporary, this was going to grow—that students were a constituency in their own right, and that our job was to organize that constituency not just as an adjunct to some other struggle but around their own interests, develop their own consciousness as a new sector of the working class. That was the change we wanted to make from the type of old-fashioned, Old Left–type student movement to what we saw as a new one that was more related to, say, the black movement or the labor movement. It was a mass rather than just this small adjunct of intellectual helpers.

I'd always seen "Student Syndicalism" as incomplete. I saw it basically as a working document, and there was a deeper analysis that I wanted to get at about the nature of American higher education. I wanted to describe the university as the place where the new working class was being shaped and created and was tied to advances in science and technology. I basically wrote [the new paper] off of discussions I had with Greg Calvert and a lot of study I did while I was on the road. I wanted to finish in time for a certain national convention, so I took a month off and hung out at a bar at Columbia University in New York. There was a group there called the Praxis Axis which I became a member of. It was a faction of SDS that was into theoretical work. Teddy Gold was in it, who's now dead. He was one of the Weathermen that blew himself up. Terry Gilbert was in it. He's now in prison. He's one of the Weathermen who did the Brinks robbery. Bob Gottlieb was in it, and we'd get together at his apartment in SoHo. It was a little scroungy place next to the Port Authority Bus Terminal, and so we wrote a draft of a new paper we called the Port Authority Statement, as opposed to the Port Huron Statement. We wanted to do a new analysis, and it turned out be a very seminal document. It was the first time, and this was in 1967, that we put out the term *underclass* and we put out the term *new working class*. We talked about the shrinkage of the blue-collar sector of the labor force and the rise of science and technology, the problems of technological elites.

There was a companion piece I wrote afterwards that got me in trouble with the Senate Internal Security Committee. [Senator James] Eastland was very upset with that paper, put it in the *Congressional Record*. He said my name should be added to the list of one hundred people who should not be invited to college campuses to speak, a list which they circulated to American university professors, to chancellors of American universities. Naturally all the student governments got hold of the list, so I got a lot of speaking invitations.

The term *prairie power* came from me. It was after I came back from Mississippi when the black power thing happened and Jane [Adams] referred to the Texas anarchists and how we had to get rid of the old guard. I said, "Well, okay, we'll form an alliance with the Texas anarchists, we'll call it prairie power, and we'll use it to displace the old guard in the national SDS." That's where it came from. Later on it came to mean more things. Kirkpatrick Sale popularized it in his book and it took on a life of its own. It came to mean radical grass-roots democracy, a sort of stance and ideology.

The difference between the old guard and the prairie power people was mainly politics. Old-guard people had roots in the old social democracy. Even though they were rebels against it, it was still kind of an anchor for them. They cared about what people like Bayard Rustin said.[16] Most of us didn't give a shit and we didn't know who Bayard Rustin was, let alone why we should care about what he had to say. They were into this whole thing, they understood these debates about YPSL [Young People's Socialist League], Socialist Party and Pop[ular] Frontism from the Old Left. They had lived with that from the early years when SDS was a branch of the League for Industrial Democracy. They had rebelled against it, but they were still schooled in all these things. Even after their break from it, they were still held back by it. They were still what you would call left social democrats, and we had a different politics. Ours was more undefined, more insurgent. There was something brazen about it. Then later on we called ourselves Communists. They would cringe at calling themselves Communists. Even if we weren't Communist, we called ourselves Communist because the other side opposed that. We would just throw it right back at them. So they did not have that kind of spirit. To them these things still served as brakes or limits. We had made a much more decisive break with the Old Left than they had, maybe because we were never a part of it.

I used to organize kids to sing the Mickey Mouse Club jingle at student government meetings. . . . Sometimes I thought that the only appropriate way to expose things was to use these provocative tactics. We would do something which was black humor. We'd circulate on

16. Rustin was one of the main organizers of the 1963 March on Washington, and an important figure in the history of both the civil rights and pacifist movements.

campus that at such and such a time we were going to napalm a dog at the center of campus. We had a recipe for homemade napalm; it was a certain amount of cups of Ivory Flakes along with so much kerosene. You could make homemade napalm, and at such and such a time we were going to napalm a dog to protest the war in Vietnam. People would go bananas, just go bananas with the thought that we would go and do something to this poor little innocent dog; then once they would get there we'd have all these pictures of Vietnamese children who had been burned. It was kind of black humor in a way.

One of my favorites was I used to get people's attention at one of the Hyde Park forums with the Playmates of the Month. The fraternity guys were into the sex thing so much, we'd try and liberate them from it. We'd hang up Playmates all over, then we would try and get everybody talking about it. What does it have to do with maleness? What does this idea of manhood have to do with why you think you have to kill in Vietnam? We would do things like that—provocative, confrontational. We would get people's attention. Most of the time they would work. Sometimes they would backfire. You never knew ahead of time. The masters of it were Jerry Rubin and Abbie Hoffman.[17] They were tremendous. Jerry Rubin showed up at that HUAC [House Un-American Activities Committee] meeting as Santa Claus and they were forced to be on national TV and in newspapers as carrying out Santa Claus. Jerry Rubin explained that he wanted to expose to every American little kid that HUAC was against Santa Claus as a way of desanctifying authority. It was brilliant, and HUAC was never the same again. It dissolved after that. Jerry Rubin dressed in a Santa Claus outfit had destroyed HUAC. All the shit the Old Left went through, all the fear and trembling for years that institution had created, [and] he just with a provocative anarchistic tactic blew it away.

I don't want to put down the old guard. I think the old guard's problem was that they were limited by the framework of their politics. It wasn't that they were less decent people or less opposed to the war in Vietnam or less antiracist then we were, but they weren't

17. Two of the organizers tried for inciting a riot at the 1968 Democratic convention in Chicago. Rubin and Hoffman were known for their provocative actions, such as throwing money onto the floor of the New York Stock Exchange, where traders scrambled to pick it up.

as audacious as we were. We didn't give a shit what the press said about us. They were very concerned with what spin would come on. In fact, we used to ban the press. We didn't want them to come in. At one Ann Arbor meeting we set up a workshop on making bombs or something and attracted all the press and police we could at that one. Then they would leave us alone [at the other sessions].

I never stopped [being an organizer]. So in that sense it never ended for me. There were some periods where things were a little darker than others and a little more strange, but even when I was on the road selling truck lumber across eighteen states I carried on a nuclear freeze campaign and organized nuclear freeze rallies. I organized for Jesse Jackson out in Iowa and Nebraska. I had to go to truck stops and sell lumber by day and talk to farmers at night about Jesse Jackson. Not everybody's done this. I'm one of the minority of people who just never stopped.

It cost. It cost me two families. It's hard to say in retrospect if I should have had a family if I was going to live this lifestyle, because it put an unequal burden on the women in my life. There are some things that maybe I could have done differently to make the burden a little less unequal. But there's no way in this society that you can be a full-time activist or insurgent organizer and have a family and have a full-time commitment to family. People can say they can work it out, but unless you're independently wealthy it can't be done. That's one lesson I learned the hard way.

JANE ADAMS

Jane Adams was raised on a farm in the Southern Illinois hills. Her parents had been active members of the Socialist Party in the thirties. She attended Antioch College from 1961 to 1963 and Southern Illinois University in 1964–1965 and 1976, when she received her BA in anthropology. She received her MA and Ph.D. from the University of Illinois, where she went to school from 1979 to 1987. Adams became interim national secretary of SDS in 1966. She is currently professor of anthropology at Southern Illinois University at Carbondale. Adams was interviewed in Carbondale, Illinois, on January 26, 1997.

I was born May 12, 1943, in Murphysboro, and I grew up on a farm about twenty miles north of there, near Ava, except for a couple of years during the war when we were following my father around. He was in the navy when I was a baby.

My parents had been members of the Socialist Party, which is how they knew each other. My father had gotten a job with the [Department of Employment Security's] Unemployment Compensation division, which brought him down here. He'd gotten very tired of the sectarian infighting of the Socialist Party. So they came down here and bought a farm. He'd always wanted to farm. I guess by the time they moved here the Socialist Party was pretty much dormant, so they were left-wing Democrats, liberal Democrats.

My dad was irreligious. He had been raised American Baptist and lost his religion when he was around twelve, but he knew the Bible very well. He loved to debate people, like neighbors who were Seventh Day Adventist, I think, and they would debate the fine points of biblical interpretation. My mother's father was supposed to have been a rabbi, and he became an atheist, a fairly devoted atheist, but kept the High Holy Days. My mother was also very nonreligious. They would have been members of the Ethical Society if there'd been one here. They became Unitarians, joined the Unitarian Fellowship in '56. They had deep morality but it was a secular morality.

The community was "backward" Southern Illinois. Many of the people had no more than an eighth-grade education. They didn't read very much and didn't have much knowledge of the larger world. So our family were sort of oddballs. We were decent people, good neighbors, but we weren't Christian, we didn't go to church. Not being Christian was a very difficult thing, and we weren't related to anybody, that was the other thing. Everybody in the neighborhood just about, except for renters, was related to half the other people in the neighborhood, so we were kind of socially unconnected.

But my parents were really active, and I think they were well respected. My dad served on the school board, after consolidation. During the process of consolidation he was specifically asked by neighbors who liked him not to run for the school board. They told him that everybody knew he was a Communist, and if he was in the public eye the consolidation wouldn't happen. We had very warm relations with the immediate neighbors, lots of help and support. My mother was active in starting the school library and the 4-H Club and home extension, and then having the farm extension demonstrations on the farm. People came. There was no ostracism. The culture of the community was one of not being snobby. We were clearly different, but we were respected.

I think the worst thing we had was that my folks played bridge with the banker and kind of local elite, and there were feelings that they were sort of being uppity. Ava, 750 population. When they first moved down, my mother had kind of an urban view. She was in a drugstore having a Coke and somebody was talking and saying so-and-so was a climber, and my mother said, "Where's there to climb in Ava?" She quickly learned that there's this ethic of egalitarianism; everybody is common and treats each other common. Once the cliques started happening in sixth grade, my friends were the Catholics and the people on welfare. We were sort of the collective "out" group, the very poor kids on welfare and the Catholics and me.

The big political issues in my childhood were school consolidation, public health, those kinds of issues. One of my early memories, this of course was family stuff, was that the AFL-CIO merger was a big deal. I remember being quite young and being at the dinner table, and you know, this was really a big deal. I don't know how many other people in the world saw the AFL-CIO merger as a big deal. It was sort of like the end of an era.

The other thing that made a real impact on me was our farm was used as a demonstration farm for a lot of conservation practices, so conservation and all those kinds of issues were important, to take this ruined, worn-out farm that was full of gullies and to reclaim it. Then I was active in 4-H. My mother was a 4-H Club leader, and she was also in what was called home bureau, now it's home extension. In 4-H I learned clothing construction, cooking, interior decoration, all those kinds of feminine [skills] . . . how to dress, how to adjust for all your defects. I didn't have a critical eye on it; this was just what one was doing. Now that this is part of my scholarship, I look on that and see it as part of the integration of rural people into mainstream America.

There were several little vignettes that stuck with me all my life. One was when I got on the school bus one morning, there weren't many places left and I looked for a place to sit. I must have been in grade school, I don't know how old. I sat down and everybody started laughing, and I looked, and I was sitting next to this kid my age, a year older than me maybe, who was a renter who lived back down on the creek. His family lived in a shack, and he was reputed to have lice, and they were dirty and real scummy. You know, they were real poor white, and I quickly got up and moved. And I felt just, well, I was mortified, I was embarrassed, I was humiliated, and at the same time I knew that my reaction was snobbish, and so it tore me.

Then when I was in I guess eighth grade, or maybe freshman year, there was another event on the school bus when this little girl from down the road got on the bus and nobody would sit with her because she was a bastard. Her mother had borne her out of wedlock, and this was in '55 or '56. She was illegitimate and nobody would sit with her on the school bus, this little six-year-old girl. So that always stuck with me, and I didn't do anything. I was already seated. She got on after me. And I didn't do anything. Those two things really, you know, somewhere in me I had some sense of injustice and I don't know where those came from. I thought from my parents in some way, but it made me kind of understand the underside of a community.

Around that time I was really, really getting into folk music. When I was little we had Burl Ives and some other stuff on records, but when I got into high school I listened to a lot of Woody Guthrie, Pete Seeger, the Weavers. I owned a Weavers album, and I'd sit at the piano and pick out folk music tunes. I guess Woody Guthrie and Pete Seeger were probably my biggest influences. Then when I was in high school the Beats, reading *Howl* and Kerouac. In high school I was also reading Sartre and Alan Watts.[1] Those were real influences my junior and senior year in high school.

We started going to the Unitarian Fellowship when I was thirteen, and that was the first time I was around people I could talk to. That was wonderful, having people to talk to and having all these religious youth conferences and singing folk songs. The civil rights movement was beginning to happen and there were some incidents in the high school. I got involved in civil rights stuff my senior year, partly because my parents were involved, but also through the youth group, which was college kids as well. The Unitarian Fellowship was sort of the center where a lot of civil rights activities happened. I remember John O'Neal, who was probably the only person I knew who really had a profound impact on me. His parents taught at Attucks School in Carbondale [an African American school] and John was one of the founders of the Free Southern Theater. He came back from Mississippi. . . . He was maybe four years older than me, and I remember being at the fellowship where he talked about satyagraha, which was the first time I'd run into the concept of non-violence. He was really sort of a hero. He's the only person who served as a role model for me during those years that's a real human being, not some kind of public figure.

There was an incident here, it must have been my sophomore year because that was the only year I was in the band. There were two black kids in the band and we took a trip to a roller rink in DuQuoin, and they wouldn't let the black kids in. The rest of us were going to turn around and come home, but they didn't want to ruin it for us, so it was one of these complicated things where they didn't want to be the cause of the rest of us not having fun. So we all

1. Jack Kerouac was the Beat writer of *On the Road* fame; Jean-Paul Sartre a French existentialist philosopher who wrote about anticolonial revolutions, among other subjects; and Alan Watts one of several writers on eastern religion who heavily influenced the counterculture.

ended up, except for the two black kids who sat in the bus, going in and skating at the roller rink. When we got back, another girl who was a member of the fellowship, she and I wrote a petition with our parents' assistance, and circulated it among all the students in University School. That was my first political thing. Then the principal did not want us to send it [to the roller rink] because it would reflect badly on the school. He pulled us in, had a long talk with us, and I don't remember what we ended up doing. But that was my first political act.

Then I was part of the group that desegregated Carbondale. There was a college Unitarian youth group which I was part of although I was in high school, and they'd gone around, and all of the white restaurant owners said, "Well, I don't mind serving Negroes but if I do I'll lose all my white clientele." They all said it. So then we did testing. First a black couple would go into a restaurant, and then a white couple would go in. I was one of the white couples that would go in, and there weren't very many restaurants. There was the Hub Cafe and there was some place out on Route 13. Anyway that was the official end of Jim Crow in restaurants. [But] the schools were still segregated, and this was where the Jim Crow cars went on the railroad, so this was the official start of the South, here in Carbondale.

There was a black man who worked at Unemployment Compensation with my father in the 1940s, and he was a friend of the family. My mother worked in the garden in a halter top and shorts, and then they had this black friend. I know they really scandalized the neighborhood. The first black people I knew were from the Laundromat and dry cleaners in Murphysboro where my mother worked—in '58, maybe? Pressers and dry cleaners were always black; that was a black job. My mother's office was right next to where the presser did his job, so when I went to help her out I'd talk with the man. My mother drove him home one time and he sat in the front seat with her, and I sat in the back seat. And I remember feeling that I hoped nobody saw me, or saw her with him, because he was in the front seat, and I knew we were violating some sort of a taboo. This was really, for a young adolescent, humiliating. And I hated myself for feeling those sort of things. I knew it was wrong and I felt it, and I've always wondered where that came from, because I grew up in an all-white community.

When I graduated from high school I joined the Student Peace Union, which was a ban-the-bomb group. While I was still in high school, I would go up to the university cafeteria to eat lunch, and there was this really interesting guy in a wheelchair, a really big, kind of red, dark-skinned man who ate there. He was just really interesting looking. So I would go and sit down across from him, and after a while he started talking to me. It turned out that he was Hawaiian and had been a longshoreman, and he'd gotten put in a wheelchair in a labor battle. He'd been beaten up and broke his back, so he was in a wheelchair. His name was Al Nakanah. We'd talk about all kinds of stuff. He lived with another fellow named Jim Peake, who was a farm boy from Illinois who'd been hurt in a farm accident. And there was a blind black guy, and then there was another white guy who'd come down from Chicago. Jim Peake did anti-ROTC stuff and he later became the head of the Du Bois Clubs.[2] I didn't realize it, but that little group was the local CP cell. I had found it as a senior in high school. Somehow the only Communists in Southern Illinois, I found. I didn't know it. They didn't tell me. They sort of adopted me. I think I was sort of a mascot or something. I was politically active and I was reading Sartre, and I was reading *Howl*. I was into all that kind of stuff. When I went to Antioch, people knew Al and I still didn't think about the Communist connection. It was just astonishing to me that somebody knew him. Now I look back and I understand why.

I think I joined the Student Peace Union because it was YPSL. When I went to Antioch, there was a big peace movement there. I got real active, and that was my first real experience with those kinds of politics, because the Trots tried to take it over and there was a big fight among the different factions of YPSL. There was a big pacifist group, and my first real organizing I did then. We went into Dayton and we went door to door distributing literature and talking to people about banning the bomb, and then had a vigil. And the vigil felt pretty dorky, but the going door to door talking to people was great. I really enjoyed that.

When I was in New York,[3] the people I ended up hanging out

2. The Communist Party's youth clubs, named after leading black intellectual W. E. B. Du Bois.

3. Adams worked at the Brooklyn Children's Museum for six months as part of Antioch's work-study program.

with were these black jazz musicians and poets. For the life of me I can't remember how I fell in with these guys. Through some friend I guess, or a friend of a friend, I don't know. But we just talked philosophy and art and stuff. Lots of talk. That was '62, '63, I guess. And when I was in Cleveland, the folks I hung out with there were an older group of anarchists, and I remember going to a meeting that must have been left over from the Garveyites.[4] This was a kind of militant, urgent, very angry kind of black thing. It was very different from anything I'd experienced here [Southern Illinois], which was the only other place I'd lived other than Antioch. I also went to my first, my only burlesque. I was with this interesting group of Beat kind of people who were anarchists. A couple of them were also in New York, which was the first time I'd smoked dope. I got really seriously disoriented. I mean it was very powerful stuff. It was like hash, and I would get real paranoid because I didn't know what direction I was going, and I didn't know what was going on. I didn't like it very much really. So I started smoking cigarettes because I wanted to learn to inhale. I was with all these people who smoked dope, and I couldn't inhale. I would cough and I just felt like an idiot. My roommate smoked Kools so I started, practicing to learn how to smoke. And I got hooked on cigarettes. Dope I could always take or leave, it was never anything I was deep into, but I got hooked on nicotine. I always felt that was a real irony. Yes, children, it [marijuana] will lead you to hard drugs.

The Student Peace Union died in '64. They tried to recruit me in the summer of '64 to be international secretary. It was like I was going to be international secretary of the Student Peace Union or go to Mississippi. My folks said, "That's a no-brainer, Jane. Go to Mississippi." They saw the Student Peace Union as a dying organization. It just didn't have anything, and what was happening was the freedom movement. That's where the struggle was. If you were going to do stuff, that is where you had to be.

My folks did a lot of support work up here. They were real active helping organize the first NAACP in Murphysboro in the late forties or early fifties. My mother had been down with her first husband when the Southern Tenant Farmers' Union was organized in

4. Marcus Garvey, the leader of the black nationalist movement in the 1920s, urged black people to return to Africa.

the Missouri Bootheel, so she'd been out in the swamps and had gone around talking—well, she didn't talk, her husband did. But she knew what that kind of frontline organizing was and had done it. She had a real sense of struggle; both of them did. Dad had slept in the same bed with Walter Reuther and organized the UAW. When they were traveling around, there'd be three people in bed in a cheap hotel. So they had a real sense of the struggle and the importance of it, and they knew where it was happening, that it was really important to be in Mississippi. Actually, my roommate in [the] Harmony community, where I was sent in Summer 1964,[5] was practically disowned. She was from Iowa, and my folks went and visited with her folks to try to reassure them, let them know that it was a good thing, respectable people's kids did it. It wasn't because we wanted some black ass. That was the only reason she ever wanted to do it, they thought; it was because she wanted a black man. People were calling up her parents and saying this stuff to them. I expect the kind of support I had from my parents was unusual. The sense of social justice and being in the struggle and that kind of stuff— that was our moral core.

I've really always been upset with myself: I missed the March on Washington. People at the Brooklyn Children's Museum, where I was working, encouraged me to go. I just missed it. I did go in '65 to the march on Washington against the Vietnam War. I went to that from here. I'd come back here to finish up some courses, Spring of '65. A bunch of us went to that.

I think I'd joined SDS by that time. I had hitchhiked with another fellow from down here up to a conference that they held, somewhere in central Illinois, and Robert Theobald[6] was there and Jesse Prosten of the [United] Packinghouse Workers was there, and I was really impressed by them. Theobald was talking about postindustrial society, and Jesse Prosten of course was real labor, and I was real taken with this. First time I'd heard political people really talking about

5. Adams was sent to Mississippi by CORE (Congress of Racial Equality). CORE and SNCC, the organizers of Mississippi Summer, worked in different parts of the state, with an umbrella organization, COFO (Council of Federated Organizations), coordinating their efforts.

6. Later considered a "futurist," Theobald was an author who argued that fundamental change in human patterns of thinking and living were necessary, beginning with the industrial system.

the world I was engaged with, on the left, so I joined SDS. There was a sensibility of labor, of the potential of technology to liberate us, and yet it wasn't being achieved. This was a period when there was a lot of concern about people being displaced by automation. I think about a utopian tradition, "The Big Rock Candy Mountain" and "Oleanna,"[7] and the tradition of utopian community which I'd read about and knew about, and the technology was there that could allow it to happen. And it was just causing us massive social dislocations. Theobald was talking about all that, and he was the first person I'd heard really talking about what was sort of out there in the air.

Then there was the larger program of SDS. It wasn't a single-issue organization. And I was really hungry for something that addressed the whole range of issues that seemed to be facing us—World War II and the concentration camps and the Holocaust were of course part of it. That was the other thing I was reading in high school, was stuff about the concentration camps. There wasn't a lot of literature at that point, but there was some. That was very important. That was my link to a Jewish identity, was through the Holocaust.

I went to Mississippi in the summer of 1964. I was with the second group who went in. That story's been told over and over. We went to Oxford, Ohio, and I was with the second group, so while we were there we knew that Chaney, Goodman, and Schwerner had been killed.[8] Then I went by car—a lot of people went in a bus, but I went in a car—to Canton, which was the CORE district rather than SNCC. Then from Canton I went over to a community in Leake County called Harmony, which was an old black community. It turns out that there had been a very, very large landowner—an ancestor of Ross Barnett, the virulent segregationist who was governor of Mississippi in the early sixties—and he had a white family and a black family, and he acknowledged them both. He divided his estate between his families, and the Harmony community were his black descendants. I stayed with the [biracial] Hudson family, and

7. Humorous songs about an imaginary utopia.
8. SNCC recruited hundreds of volunteers—many from elite schools—to come to Mississippi in order to help register black voters and draw attention to their cause. The federal government refused to provide protection, so volunteers came at great risk. James Chaney, Andrew Goodman, and Michael Schwerner were brutally murdered after being released from jail late at night in Philadelphia, Mississippi.

passed for a member of the family frequently. When we'd go into town in the black community, people knew the Hudsons. They had four daughters and people who knew them, but not well, would think I was one of the daughters. Mr. Hudson was dead by the time I had got there. When he had a heart attack, he was put in the white section of the hospital until his wife came in, and then they realized they'd made a horrible mistake. So they moved him over to the black area of the hospital, because she was brown.

The program I was associated with was called Federal Programs. What you hear about Freedom Summer is the Mississippi Freedom Democratic Party and the Freedom Schools, but there was another small program which was trying to tap federal programs and bring them in to the communities. That included the cotton allotment, because blacks had been squeezed out of cotton allotments and the Farmers' Home Administration for housing loans. Those were the two big ones. And blacks had just been squeezed, not let in at all. So what we were doing was researching those things and trying to make that information available. We also did a lot of work for the Freedom Democratic Party, going around and canvassing and that kind of stuff.

I was really struck when I went back there [for a reunion years later], because I hadn't been able to remember what I did. But Winson Hudson had this really handsome home that was built with a Farmers' Home Administration loan. Throughout the community there were all these homes that were Farmers' Home Administration–financed homes, nice, modern—you know, plumbing, the whole nine yards—and I thought, I helped make this happen. There were very few of us who were from the rural areas and non-elite schools. So I think that is why I got put into that, because we were country people. I had a big fantasy about people going to Washington, that we were going to do a small-farmers' union. That was a fantasy.

In the fall of 1964, I went to work at the COFO [Council of Federated Organizations] office in Jackson. One of the things that SNCC people, particularly the Mississippi SNCC people, had been really worried about with Freedom Summer was that whites would come in and start taking over everything, and it was a legitimate concern. You know, here I was going down to the office and spitting out all these big schemes about organizing this farmers' union, and I was going to organize a conference and everything, but I sort of got carried away with the visionary kind of thing. Ivanhoe Donaldson, I think it was, gave me a little lecture about "you educated northerners" coming down, you know, and he was absolutely right. He was just right on target. You know, this was going to happen [without the help of outsiders]. It had come up from the bottom, and it couldn't be people sitting in Jackson organizing. It had to be something that came up from the bottom.

There were a bunch of us from Carbondale. There were two sibling pairs and several other people. For a school like this, that was a lot to go. My roommate, Connie Jones, who was black, wanted to go and her father wouldn't hear about it. And he was right. It was much more dangerous to be black than to be white. Especially after the three guys were killed. But because SIU was on the main line of the Illinois Central Railroad—plus Chuck and Chico Neblett, Freedom Singers who were from here, John O'Neal was from here— there was a long history of people stopping here on the way north, up to Chicago, and we'd sing all night and all that kind of stuff would go on. Carbondale was sort of a way station. It was a little unusual that way. I think we probably had more people go than any other non-elite school. I don't know that, but that's my suspicion.

I was not a pacifist. I had decided because of what was going on in Guatemala and Cuba, and the guerrilla movements that had started—I was thinking about doing agricultural development or something like that—it wouldn't be my role to be violent, but how in the world could I tell people under those kinds of oppressive regimes not to take up arms when all other political dimensions had been excluded? So I was never a pacifist. I like the idea of pacifism and as a personal philosophy I've always tried to live it in my personal life, but as a political commitment I think there are times when it's appropriate to take up arms and fight.

What I understood there, that summer in particular, the really powerful thing that I understood was the power of a social movement. Before that, I'd been really despairing, caught up in the throes of existential angst. I thought that if I got to be thirty-six and still felt as despairing as I felt that I would kill myself. You know, that suicide was an option because the world as I saw it did not look wonderful. I'm not sure I would have—it was sort of adolescent angst—but it was genuine enough at the time. And in Mississippi I really felt the transformative power of a people's movement, and that it was really possible, there was real utopia. It was real millennial and profound; it had all those qualities. Bernice Reagon[9] talked about being born again in the freedom movement, the civil rights movement, and it was that kind of a transformative, redemptive quality that the movement had that was extraordinarily powerful. That's what I got; that was the profound thing that happened that summer.

And then there was the philosophy, Bob Moses's philosophy,[10] organizing the grass roots, which was right in line with what I wanted to do. That genuine kind of populism. But I think the really, really powerful thing was exemplified by one transforming incident: We were canvassing for the Freedom Democratic Party, and I was with one of the girls I lived with. We went up to this woman's house. It was a shack, and I guess she was a sharecropper. I'm sure it was on white man's property, and she had a couple of kids. I don't know if she had a husband, but she came out, and it was "yes'm" and "no'm" and "yes'm." We were asking her just to sign the petition for FDP, and she was looking down at the floor. And as we talked to her, all of a sudden, it was like something just turned over in her, and she straightened up and she looked us in the eyes, and she said she'd sign, and she signed. Now, she could lose her home. She could lose everything by that act. That action of signing that petition was risking, probably not her life, but certainly any modicum of security that she had. And you know, that's powerful. When people are going to do those kind of things, and know what they're doing. I mean, kids don't know what they're doing, but she knew what she was doing. That's powerful stuff.

I came back here [to SIU] in January '65 to finish up some course work. So I was up here for a quarter, and then went back down. And when I went back down, they [CORE] asked me to go down and work in Amite County, which was in the southwest, and I was the first white woman to work there. It was tough, and it was where Herbert Lee was assassinated and Louis Allen was killed.[11] But by

9. Civil rights activist and singer.

10. Moses was an important figure in the early civil rights movement, an inspiration to many young activists because of his courage, commitment, and philosophy. A prime mover behind the Freedom Summer project, he insisted on interracial and nonviolent coordinating strategies.

11. Lee was a black man who in 1961 was shot and killed in broad daylight by Eugene Hurst, a local white official, for attempting to register to vote. Allen was killed several months later when word got out that he might testify as an eyewitness to the crime.

that time, the big breakthrough had happened. The back of Jim Crow had been broken and nobody knew what to do next. There was a lot of black-white tension, there was a lot of sexual tension, and basically nobody knew what to do. What got to me was I was trying to organize a quilting co-op, and I suspect that there was some factional stuff going on in the community that I didn't know about. Everybody would say they would come to the meetings, and these were women who had been schoolteachers, and they had master's degrees, they were well-educated women. And it was "Yes, Miss Jane," "No, Miss Jane," and then they wouldn't show up for the meeting. And I'd "Yes, Mrs. So-and-so," "No, Mrs. So-and-so" right back to them, but I could not get past that, you know, being white. And I knew I can't do this organizing job in this community. I can't get past this; I was a child and they're deferring to me. Black power was beginning to happen, and I thought it just seemed like it had to happen. It just had to happen, because I certainly wasn't going to be an agent of that change. The structure of that system was too powerful, and I couldn't overcome it by my own volition.

That was in the summer of '65. Then in the fall, the Vietnam War was heating up, and so I went north to work against the war, and I was going to do grassroots organizing. So I went up to Chicago, and I was either going to work with SDS in Chicago or the Committee against the War that was organizing in Madison. Of course Chicago was first, so I stopped there. The offices were on 63rd Street, and Jeff Shero was there and D. [Gorton] and Paul Booth, so I ended up staying there for a while, and then folks from Iowa City came in. D. had been working with the folks out at Iowa City and they wanted somebody to come out and do organizing, organize a region in Iowa, Nebraska, Kansas, and Missouri. D. knew that I wanted to do that kind of organizing, and so he and Jeff put me together with the folks from Iowa City. So I went out there, to Iowa City, and did campus traveling. That's where I learned a lot about the war, read all the books that were available at the time, which wasn't that much. And then I did organizing. I organized conferences and tooled around, first in a VW Bug some people loaned me and then in this little TR3 that some people in Ames loaned me, with a "Make Love, Not War" bumper sticker on the back. And when I was doing that, it was one of the high points. That was probably one of the best times of my life then. I was just tooling around from campus to campus, the or-

ganizer, you know, coming in and dropping off literature and organizing conferences, and it was just a lot of fun. Real free-spirit kind
of thing.

I was living in Iowa City, and I would go to Drake College in Des
Moines. The campus ministry was the center there. There were just
a few people, so I'd stop in there and then I'd go up to Ames, and
there was a good group at Ames. Greg Calvert was at Ames. He was
a real charismatic guy. He had this cadre of disciples around him.
Then I would go on to Lincoln, Nebraska, which is where Carl
Davidson was; there was a good group there. Then I'd go down to
the University of Kansas—that was an interesting group. There
were a bunch of libertarians there, along with the SDS types. Then
I'd go to Kansas City, and there was a little group there. The black
woman who was there was the only black person, I think, in all of
the SDS chapters. Then I'd go to Columbia, Missouri, and there was
a little group at Stephens College. And then I'd go to St. Louis, and
there wasn't much happening in St. Louis. There were some individuals, but nothing quite jelled there. Then I'd go back up to
Chicago and get literature. I'd go wherever there were people. I
would get lists, like if people called into Chicago, then I'd seek them
out. And I would organize conferences. I'd go into the national office in Chicago and we had a press, and I'd print up the program.
That would get mailed out to everybody who was on the list in
those states, and then we'd pull the conference together. I think we
had one in Columbia. I know we had one at Lawrence, and I think
we had one at Kansas City and one at Lincoln. It was like one a
month, seems like. That was in the spring of '66. That summer I was
elected national secretary.

People didn't expect to see a woman traveling alone. I would go
in at night, be headed somewhere, like back to Iowa City, and I'd
stop at a truck stop along the way to get gas and some coffee, and
they wouldn't serve me. Because they expected a man to be coming
in, because he was gassing up the car and I was coming in, right?
And I would have to finally call somebody over and say, "I'd like
some coffee, please." Because it was so unusual. You just didn't see
women driving around alone, and especially at night you didn't see
them driving around alone. It just didn't happen. And with my
"Make Love, Not War" bumper sticker, all these truckers would try
to get me off the road. They thought I meant it.

That summer, there was a convention and Paul Booth was stepping down as national secretary and they had to have a new one. The organization had just gone through some big changes. It had just opened up to becoming this mass movement. It had been sort of a club before that, that came out of these elite schools in the East, with a few chapters here and there. And that year, in '65–'66, it just burgeoned. Just mushroomed everywhere. And we were thinking about how to organize all this energy among young white people, and we were somehow trying to be responsive to it without any clue what to do with this incredible energy. You know, everybody was joining. These chapters were forming and nobody knew what in the world to do with the energy.

It was antiwar, it was the inspiration of the freedom movement, it was the cultural revolution beginning to happen. Also, in loco parentis was being challenged. You know, kind of throwing off the traces. It was the baby boomers just getting into college, and all hell was breaking loose. The Vietnam War was the crucible. And the sexual revolution. The Midwest had become a big locus of it. SDS moving from New York to Chicago had been symptomatic of that. When they moved there in '65 they were really following a current, and they happened to be positioned right. I'm not sure why SDS became the center rather than some other organization, but SDS became that center. And the old guard didn't have a clue really, because there was a whole cultural dimension. These were not red or pink diaper babies,[12] but people who came up without any sophistication about politics. They were much more anarchistic and much less realpolitik. The old guard was glued to that sense of Washington being where things happened and that's where you focused your organizing. But this thing that was welling up was where you lived, you know. It wasn't "the personal is political," but that was where it was going, in that direction. It was schools like SIU, the kind of kids that are accepted here. It was middle-class, but first generation in college, and Christian background. A lot of the organizing was around the student Christian ministries. That was really the center in most communities, and an awful lot of what happened in the Midwest focused around that.

In ERAP,[13] there'd been a lot of women out of the East. There'd

12. Children of the Old Left (Communists or Socialists).
13. Economic Research and Action Project, an early SDS project in which women played important roles organizing poor people in urban areas.

been a lot of women out of women's schools who were doing stuff. But women had never been the public face of SDS. It'd been a sort of club. That was where things happened, through interpersonal relations, so the women had a lot of power as it became more of a national organization. But when I came in [to the national office] there were virtually no women visible. Virtually none visible.

I saw myself more as "prairie power," which was what we were called, but there were significant ways that I was a bridge. It makes sense structurally that I was elected [interim] national secretary at that particular juncture. Everybody could agree on me. They twisted my arm. I did not want to do it. It was the last thing in the world I wanted to do, but . . . I was part Jewish, you know, had enough of that [experience] to integrate culturally; none of us talked about this or understood it at the time, how important that Jewish/Gentile divide was, but I think it was a big part of it. And yet I'd grown up here in Southern Illinois, went to church; my sensibility was really the rural kind of Midwest, but at the same time I understood this other "pink diaper baby" Old Left kind of heritage. It was part of my heritage. So in that sense I straddled . . .

We had a sense of a people's movement with the romance of the Wobblies and the labor movement, that whole kind of romance of the working class and the people. And then later, the people who came in a year or two later, when it was flower children and the cultural revolution was really happening, many of them didn't have that strong sensibility of romance of the labor movement. It was different for the East Coast folks than for the midwestern folks, anyway. I think midwesterners look more to the Wobblies than the easterners do. The easterners looked more towards the UAW and Flint, the sit-downs and all that stuff. Our little red book was the Wobbly songbook. After we had all these fights and the political wrangling was over, at the end we'd all put our arms around each other with our Wobbly songbooks and sing old labor songs. The office trooped down at one point, after we moved up to the West Side [of Chicago], and we all joined the IWW. The men had to vouch for me.

Prairie power meant . . . I remember one instance when Dick Reavis from Texas got quoted by the press [saying], "We're going to overthrow this country with forceful and violent laughter." There was that kind of sensibility of, you know, just thumb your nose at them.

Laugh at them. Different from the East Coast approach, which was very, very serious. Very academic as opposed to this wide open throw-open-the-gates approach, which is the thing that Todd [Gitlin] is reacting to [with] this "anarchist" kind of thing. Underneath it there was a lot of smarts, and a lot of understanding. But it wasn't the same kind of understanding and the same kind of schooling, especially their tactics—I mean Texas humor. They [the easterners] just didn't appreciate it. Now, everybody loves Ann Richards and Molly Ivins, but back then I think people just didn't have a clue about that kind of humor . . . which is the style, you know, it was a performative style. It was really wonderful, but it could do outrageous kinds of things, like have Gentle Thursday.

And this was just not politics, in the eyes of most of the old guard. It was a real cultural divide. Really was. Wasn't an ideological divide, it was a cultural divide. When Booth was national secretary, this report came in that folks in Oklahoma had been busted for dope. And there was a picture with all this stuff that had been gotten, and oh, the national office just went into conniptions. You know, you shouldn't be smoking dope and getting . . . dah, dah, dah, dah. Well, it turned out that in fact the cops hadn't found any dope. They had dog shit. They had oregano, you know, they had the herbs in the kitchen. There was no dope. But the national office was going to expel the chapter for smoking dope. They were like Progressive Labor in that [in] politics you stay legal. You stay completely legal and very straight, very, very straight. Well, the prairie power folks were experimenting with the cultural revolution right along with everybody else, so that was part of the cultural divide. It gets characterized as a sharp cleavage, but in fact part of it was the fluidity with people moving in and out and some of it was [the old guard] disliking what was happening.

I was there when SDS broke up in 1969. I was up in the balcony. I watched it and cried. I don't know how much of it was COINTELPRO. I think COINTELPRO had a piece of it. Debrayism had a piece of it.[14] PL [Progressive Labor] had a big piece of it. One way to tell

14. A significant part of the FBI's COINTELPRO operations were aimed at disrupting the New Left. Régis Debray was a French scholar and journalist who had been jailed in Bolivia. Debray was admired by many New Leftists who wanted the movement to follow his theory of guerrilla warfare, laid out in his 1967 *Revolution in the Revolution?*

the story is that when PL was first in the organization, I actually was fairly pleased to have them there because they were sort of hard-edged labor folks, and we had all these kids who were real mushy, upper-middle-class, didn't have any sense of class anything. And so despite the fact that they were sort of puritanical jerks, they injected, I thought, a useful kind of thing into the discussion and they just participated. They weren't moving on the organization. At East Lansing, which must have been '67, '68, they moved to having an organized presence as a caucus, and they started chanting. We started doing our singing at the end. We sang "The People's Flag," and they squared off and started chanting, "Don't use the red flag against the red flag." They'd been pretty obnoxious throughout that conference, they'd been offensive. But this was our ritual of unity at the end, when you set aside differences and you embrace and you sing the old labor songs, and they refused to honor that, and that is what I saw as the beginning [of the end].

The response of the people around the national office was not helpful. It was to replicate the discipline, the secretive methods that PL was using, to outcaucus PL. And PL would come with a very organized group, and they operated of course sub rosa. So they were very hard to call, because if you tried to call them then you were being paranoid, and they had their line, they knew how to deal with it. But the national office was doing the same fucking thing. I think that there were some key people in the background instigating that kind of sectarian response, but it fed into people who were there.

The other thing was that PL had a very strong line and were very rigid, and the thing about an open, democratic kind of organization like SDS had always been [that] nobody had a line. And so you didn't organize. I mean, if you have a line then you can organize your troops strategically. You can plant them here and here so that when the vote comes you have this groundswell. When you're an open kind of organization you don't do that, because you don't have that kind of discipline. You don't have that kind of line. The response was that we have to have a line. So then you start wrangling over lines, and we get into correct linism, which had always been anathema. It's not something that we do. With a generational shift, what's important was that the old guard knew the dangers of correct linism. If they had a line, it was that that's not going to happen. That's not what we're going to do. We're going to wrangle, but we're not going to do it in those terms. The new people didn't have that Old Left experience, most of them, and were not committed ideologically against that. So some Old Left types began to move in, who saw the opportunity to come in and bring the correct line to us.

Things were getting pretty wild anyway. I don't know if the organization could have survived. I think it would have survived as a charismatic center, as a magnet, if it hadn't gone into this really destructive kind of thing. I don't know that it ever could have survived as an organizing center. Take '68. SDS didn't support the demonstration at the Democratic Convention, and that wasn't purely sectarian. It was that they couldn't get their shit together to figure out whether or not they supported it or how to go about supporting it. All the Cleveland folks went, and we were marshals there. We were keeping cops and students apart and we were in the thick of things. So a lot of SDSers were there, but the organization as a national organization couldn't get their shit together. I think if it hadn't been for PL and the response to PL, that the organization could have persisted where it was a symbolic center of the movement. Some people think PLers were provocateurs—I don't. I think that they were absolutely typical of the Old Left. I mean, they function like the Old Left. You don't have to be a cop to function like that. But I think there were people around the national office who were pushing a counterresponse that fed that. And those of us who weren't doing that couldn't figure out where to intervene or how to intervene. There were a bunch of us opposed, but we couldn't figure out what to do.

My first experience with the growing violence was the Motherfuckers. Terry [Roberts] and I were out in Oklahoma. We were trying to bring together the cultural revolution and the political revolution in Norman, Oklahoma. Hardly a bastion. We started getting these reports about the Up Against the Wall Motherfuckers[15] and about Molotov cocktails, and it was all rhetoric. They weren't doing this stuff, but they were using this wild and inflammatory adventuristic rhetoric. We were going, "My God, these guys are going to get us

15. Taking their name from a poem by LeRoi Jones, this group of Lower East Side activists saw themselves as cultural revolutionaries and were proud of their tactics, which shocked not only "the establishment" but much of the political left as well.

killed." We were trying to organize against the draft, demonstrating at the draft board and stuff, getting beat up at night by the jocks, by the frat rats. So I was not thrilled, seated in the Midwest, with the kind of wildly adventuristic rhetoric that was happening. I thought that it was really way out of touch, really self-indulgent. If you're going to do violence, you do violence. I wasn't against violence, but I certainly was against the romanticization of violence. I never liked the romance of violence, which Weatherman was infected with. Terry Robbins's[16] model and maybe some of the others' model was the resistance in Europe during World War II. Their analysis was that the U.S. was like Nazi Germany and that the white working class was bought, and that the only thing a white radical could do was to function as a saboteur, and in alliance with third world people. That meant black people, which meant the Panthers. Somehow the Panthers are the only true voice of black people, which we white people get to choose. As white people, we get to choose, and they [the Weathermen] didn't see the irony in that particular anointing of leadership.

I don't know how many other people shared Terry's particular analysis, but I disagreed with it. I thought white guilt was not particularly useful. I could see how the analogy of resistance on some level was compelling given what was going on in the country at the time, but I believed we were not at that point. You know, we really hadn't gone over the edge. There was still room to organize. We were not being forcibly repressed in that way, there weren't Brownshirts. There were things that were happening, but they certainly weren't on the scale of Nazi Germany. And the alliance with the third world wasn't the way to do it. And the Vietnamese didn't even want us to do it that way. People who were working with the Vietnamese didn't approve of this kind of adventuristic stuff. So I didn't agree with them on any number of points despite the fact I had lived with most of the leadership at one point or another.

The people I felt sympathy with, that I liked, that I got along with, were the midwesterners and southwesterners. There was a working-class sensibility that I definitely felt. There were all these kids from Swarthmore and Harvard and those kinds of places who had no

16. Not to be confused with Terry Roberts, Robbins was one of three people who died in the 1969 townhouse explosion.

sense of class. It wasn't on their radar screen, any kind of class system. And they had this feeling like they really had a direct pipeline to the Kennedy administration and all these high and mighty people, and I didn't even like Kennedy. I certainly didn't feel any relationship whatsoever. I mean, Washington was what we were trying to get rid of in important ways. It was the enemy. So I didn't have any of that being-groomed-for-power kind of stuff. When I read the beginning of Gitlin's book [*The Sixties*] I was really nauseated by that sense of empowerment and access. It was an illusion anyway. They were no closer to power than I was, but they had the seduction that they were, and it created a really different consciousness, I think.

There was a group of people from the Midwest who were energized and moving as friends and who were a network, who worked together, who had reached into chapters and who had a different sensibility than SDS had previously had. The Praxis Axis was doing the same things in New York, working on similar issues but in a different way. They were real educated, reading neo-Marxism and all that stuff. But there was the same kind of current that they were plugged into. It was part of the cultural revolution, but was politicized in a way that the "tune in, turn on, drop out" or the "Summer of Love" kind of stuff wasn't politicized.

Prairie power had its roots in populism. We had a little newspaper in Oklahoma called *The Jones Family Grandchildren*. The Jones family were some folks who were part of the Green Corn Rebellion, and I read up on a lot of the Populist viewpoint at that time. One of the things about the East Coast folks was they never thought of the United States as agricultural. They were very urban. They came from the turn-of-the-century immigration to the city, and they had no sense whatsoever of the U.S. as a place with an agrarian movement. And that's where the Wobblies are different than the UAW. The Wobblies were miners and lumber workers and agricultural workers. Those were the big centers of Wobbly work, aside from the mills in the East. In the West, it was Joe Hill and the mines and the wide open spaces . . . that sense of the agrarian roots, that thread, that notion of grassroots democracy that goes back to Jefferson and the notion of the yeoman farmer and mechanic as the foundations of democracy. There was a premanufacturing, preindustrial vision of agrarian democracy. And I think that went directly into the back-to-the-land movement and underwrote it, and that was deep in the midwestern prairie power sensibility. The old guard really didn't have their finger on that pulse at all, as the Old Left didn't. What went into the environmental movement was in many ways organically attached to the prairie power phenomenon. But not to the ERAP—that was an urban thing.

After the watershed, the breakup of SDS at the '69 convention, Terry and I went out to California. We ended up getting work in San Francisco. We either had to have money for a deposit on an apartment or tires for the car. Tires were bald, so we got an apartment, got jobs. I got a secretarial job and he worked at an envelope factory. We got more involved with counterculture and guerrilla theater; there was a lot of cultural stuff going on. And a little bit of the women's movement stuff. I'd been real involved in the women's movement stuff in SDS and then lived in communes, and that was seen as political. It was all people who were politically active. It was seen as the political thing to do, for some reason. I don't know why it was. I tried to figure out what to do. And this was the period where there was massive burnout, and a lot of people were getting into religious stuff and all kinds of different cults and meditative practices. Hare Krishnas were all over the place, and lots of people were getting into that. A lot of people I knew were getting into those kinds of things, trying stuff like Buddhism.

My daughter Dawn was born in '71, and then in '76 I decided it was finished. We weren't going to create a new society. So I went back to school to get a degree so I could make a living. I had started out in anthropology at Antioch. My first major was anthropology and then geography and then Latin American studies when I came here. So there's a real profound continuity in my life and commitment.

SDS was the magnet around which the white youth movement coalesced and named itself and knew itself, and that was very important. It was a symbolic center. A structural weakness was that there was a profound discontinuity with the older generation. When I think about SNCC, there were some older people, like Ella Baker,[17] who was critical in being somebody with wisdom and

17. Baker, of the Southern Christian Leadership Conference, encouraged young civil rights activists to form their own organization, and SNCC was the result.

knowledge and networks and who understood and was able to work with the militant young people. She provided a kind of wisdom and insight, for a few years anyway. We never had anybody like that, as far as I know. It was the LID [League for Industrial Democracy] people and then, when we cut ourselves off from them . . . Dave Dellinger[18] was the closest. Highlander Center[19] was very important in the Southeast, but we had nothing like that really. People tried to link into it, but it was too far away. So we were really just a bunch of kids who didn't know what in the world we were doing, and didn't have a fund of knowledge or contacts. The problem was that the anticommunist crusade was so deep and thoroughgoing that it really had pulled the teeth of the noncommunist left. I don't quite understand why that generational discontinuity was so profound. Some of the biggest demonstrations that were organized by adults, the peace coalitions that existed in every city, were Old Left coalitions. They were based in those old labor-Communist networks, all those folks, but there was practically no structural connection between them and us, which is pretty mysterious. I don't know why that didn't happen, but that was a profound problem. They didn't understand the cultural revolution.

The old guard did, to a much greater extent, end up working with those groups, but the newer generation, the second wave, really didn't. We were really a youth movement, with all the weaknesses of a generationally based movement. COINTELPRO was also important. For some reason we were incredibly naive about that, and we should have known better. Because we knew about provocateurs, we knew about that stuff. And I can't figure out to this day what that particular blindness was about. I think partly it came out of an ideology that we are public, that we have nothing to hide, and the notion that we would be infiltrated was funny, you know? But we didn't understand the kind of sabotage that COINTELPRO did. In that way we were ignorant.

SDS gave people a name and a way to organize themselves. It was critical. Now, if SDS hadn't been there, very likely something else would have done that. But we were certainly the first that

18. An older pacifist leader of the anti–Vietnam War movement who worked closely with the New Left.
19. Highlander Folk School in Monteagle, Tennessee, had been a center for training organizers since the thirties.

named the war, that named the system in some coherent way, that said: This is a result of the system. This is not a mistake. It is not an aberration. SDS had a thoroughgoing critique that hit people's hearts in a way that nobody else was doing. Nobody else was saying that the war was a product of the system, and that system is corporate liberalism. And once you get corporate liberalism, you get into everything else, mass-produced out of universities and the economic side of racism, all those kinds of issues. And SDS was really the only organization that was doing that. That was a real strength.

JEFF SHERO NIGHTBYRD

Jeff Shero Nightbyrd attended four universities, and, he says, "gradu-
ated magna cum laude in demonstrations after being expelled from the
University of Texas." He served as a national officer of SDS for three years.
Nightbyrd was a national leader in the movement against the Vietnam
War, and was arrested by the FBI for draft resistance. In more recent years
he has been a vigorous opponent of the "war on drugs," which he views as
an attack on civil liberties, and he is a nationally recognized expert on drug
testing. Currently he owns a talent agency in Texas that has the largest
Latino/Hispanic talent division in the Southwest, and he helps young film-
makers produce independent digital films. He is "one of the few activists
not writing his memoirs." Nightbyrd was interviewed in Carbondale, Illi-
nois, on September 17, 1997.

I went to high school in Bryant, Texas, where I was popular because I had lived in other places, including Japan. I had different
ideas, I was an agnostic. The only one. I was the "nigger lover" in a
segregated school, a school where Hispanics were definitely not to
be dated. If I had any politics at that time they were probably ultra-
right, military politics. My stepfather was an Air Force officer. I
thought *Time* magazine was a font of wisdom—anticommunism was
clearly the right thing. Basically I was a right-wing American kid.

I wasn't a racist. My mother had always accepted people however they are, and she had always taught me that people should be
judged on how they act. The civil rights movement started in the
deep South. . . . I graduated high school in 1960 and went to Texas
A&M, which was a military school. I was in a kind of West Point
military environment which I didn't care for. With a shaved head
and all, I was still the "pissiest fish" in the corps. Then I went to Sam
Houston [State University], which is in East Texas and segregated.

That was my first deep experience with, say, southern fascism. The valedictorian of the black high school in that city, Huntsville, couldn't get into college there, because she was black.

The center of progressivism was the Methodist Student Center, which had one of those young ministers who cared. We had secret meetings that we would get to by different directions. It was a real risky deal. The end of that story is a story about liberalism. The administration got a whiff because we had done some other things, like we had run a write-in candidate for student body president, Dee Segregate, which got the police out and everything. We put up signs at night and they thought, "It's the NAACP down here from New York." That literally was the conclusion: "These agitators from New York [are responsible for this]." Anyway they got a whiff of this and told the Methodist minister that if we continued then they wouldn't be able to teach any Bible classes for credit at the Methodist Student Center. That was a big enough threat that he backed down. I was utterly disillusioned. Then the president of the college actually called me into his office and told me he didn't think I was Sam Houston material and that I would be better off searching for another college next year, which I did.

I went to the University of North Dakota and basically the same thing that was happening with blacks in Texas was happening with Sioux Indians there who were used as migrant laborers. At the end of the season when they had money they couldn't try on clothes in the department store because somehow [it was assumed] they'd make them dirty or something.

I came back to Texas. We had a big sit-in movement—despite its reputation, Austin was segregated well into the sixties. It was educational because the chair of the Democratic Party, LBJ's big buddy Frank Irwin, was also the chairman of the University of Texas and an ardent segregationist. So we were having sit-ins in the university and the central city to integrate facilities, which the university administration and the Democrats were opposing, and then I joined SDS. It offered a new participatory democracy. So I joined.

This was Fall of '62 and we had hardly any members. I mean there was maybe four or five kids. SDS was an idea; they had one national convention, at Pine Hill [New York]. Robert Pardun is one of the people who got me involved. Somebody would call us from one of the Mississippi Freedom Centers: "We need a lot of people down in Macomb because the police are trashing us. . . . [If] we don't get a lot of white people down here, they're going to kill people down here." So we would all jump in our cars and start driving to some-place in Mississippi, which was profound, utterly profound. The supposed dregs of society—black, uneducated teenagers—were doing heroic things and it was inspiring.

Then I went to the second Pine Hill SDS meeting. I was over-whelmed—the best people I had ever met in my life. I had never been around a group of people like that. In fact years later when I got out into the regular world and was working, I kept expecting people to be that sharp, and I kept being surprised. To this day I would say that's the best group of people I ever worked with. Incredibly bright, savvy people. So I decided this is it, this is great, and I debated Tom Hayden and got elected to be one of the officers on the National Council.

We had a workshop called "Agents of Change." We're sitting out on this grassy knoll in Pine Hill, and Todd Gitlin was the modera-tor. We all were debating who were the agents of change—in other words, which groups in America were potentially progressive forces and who should we spend our time organizing. There was a book by Michael Harrington called *The Other America* and at that stage SDS was kind of wedded to liberal democratic politics and we thought we would organize the unorganized. Blacks would get a vote, the poor whites would be brought into the system, and it would be the fulcrum by which the progressive wing of the Democratic Party could take office. So in this argument about agents of change, Hayden argued a kind of classic social democratic line, which was that we should organize workers. I sat there listening in disbelief because I wasn't educated in left politics but I knew something about the culture, and I said, "I really disagree with your ideas. First of all, I think students are about to go into motion. I observe it everywhere I am. It was students that helped in the southern civil rights movement. We stuck our necks out; it wasn't the workers."

Clergy obviously helped, but we weren't going to organize the clergy. I also realized even at that time how arrogant it was for nineteen-year-old kids to be going into factories telling workers what to do when we didn't know diddly-squat about the world. I mean, you can be smart but that doesn't mean that you can tell some guy who's in a manufacturing plant how to run his life. I said,

"We're students and we should organize where we are and who we understand: students."

So this workshop couldn't come to an agreement. Hayden was considered a god because he had written the Port Huron Statement, but I really didn't understand that he was a god so I wasn't that impressed. That night in the plenary, in a barn sitting on hay bales, we were supposed to debate. I got up and gave a rap about what we should do, and Tom got up and said, "Well, I don't basically disagree with that," which stunned everybody because all day they had said, "You're a really nice guy, Jeff, but you're really going to get creamed tonight." I kind of had the attitude if I get creamed I get creamed, but I think I'm right. Tom basically made a ten-sentence speech and sat down. So my star started rising, plus I was a blond-haired Texas neophyte and I think for the East Coast [people] they thought, "We're really onto something, look! These innocent peach-faced idiots like Jeff are coming to our meetings."

I went back to Texas and said, "Let's build SDS," and so before [course] registration I got everybody together and we made this table and put up signs all over. We sat there for five days of registration—it was the old days when people had to sign up with cards and stuff. It was a five-day process and we signed up basically every alienated person we could get of every kind, which was perfect for SDS's kind of politics. That year we had an alliance between the guys that rode motorcycles, the kind of bohemian artist-writer types, the integrationists, the early vegetarian peacenik types, even people who hated fraternities and sororities, which ran the school. So it was an interesting coalition that year. We had two hundred people in SDS, which was by far the largest [chapter] in the country, and did lots of actions. I always believed that the way people learned things was to go into action.

I understood in those early days a fundamental lesson that I think some of the old guard doesn't understand in what's been written afterwards, and that is about action. If there are contradictions in a system, direct action that is correctly thought out will usually set up a cycle of action/reaction and expose the contradictions. For instance, one of the issues was in loco parentis at the time. The university was taking the place of parents. The student movement was saying we should take care of ourselves. In loco parentis corresponded to a huge number of issues, from dress code to where you could live, curfew hours, etc. Carefully conceived actions that were responsive to some local issue really exposed the administration because usually they would overreact and threaten arrest over something like dress code or dorm curfew.

In some of the southern places I organized, an issue would be a black [male] student came to one of the dorms to see a white woman student, and this would set off this whole chain reaction. Maybe the old house mother in her sixties would call the local campus security because she thought the young girl was going to be raped. Maybe the black student was coming to talk about the history final, but he's talking to the security guard who's asking what he's doing there though he's a registered student. All those kinds of issues would spin out. So I understood action and I realized that by making direct actions you're organizing a base.

A year later I'm a campus organizer. I thought just like the IWW we should put people out on the road, visit everyplace. My goal as an organizer was you'd hit a campus, you'd have a couple of names, you'd spend two or three days meeting everybody that you could, you'd have an SDS meeting called, you'd tell them about it. Twenty or thirty people would come to the first SDS meeting and you would by then know what the key issue was on that campus. It could be anything. Later it was things like the draft, military recruitment on campus; earlier it was things like racism or multiversity issues.

My job as an organizer was to explain SDS and its decentralist nature, which appealed to people. "You're not getting controlled by some distant office, you're going to run your own affairs." It was very appealing to people because we were still in the lingering aftermath of anticommunism and people didn't want to be controlled from someplace else. If you were any good as an organizer you would kind of prod and push people in a subtle way to make a demonstration around that issue. In the course of that week everybody has told you that "this is a very conservative place. This may be one of the most conservative campuses in the country." Literally, you'd hear that everyplace you went. "You just don't understand, this place is one of the most conservative . . ." You'd say, "Yeah, but you know, they're doing stuff in Oklahoma, so hey, maybe let's take a shot." You'd suggest a demonstration and usually people would want to do it. You'd stay through the demonstration and what would happen is there'd usually be a huge crowd.

I remember at Texas Western University in El Paso we put up an antidraft information table. SDS had literature on how to resist the draft. We were surrounded by maybe a thousand or so people, the majority irate, screaming at us. We'd get up and stand on a chair and scream back. People threatened to beat you up, it was back and forth like that. At the end of that, an enormous number of people in the crowd that you didn't know existed, thirty or fifty people that you didn't know, would come out of the woodwork. The next meeting, you'd have sixty to eighty people because you had done something that struck a nerve, and SDS would then start rolling.

Usually if you were traveling in the Midwest or South you'd get a name at the next campus. You'd call this person and the next Sunday or Monday you'd hit the campus and crash on that person's floor. They'd tell you it's the most conservative campus . . . you'd start that process again. I was a catalyst for maybe twenty chapters or so. I believed like the Populists and the IWW that we should put our resources, which were mighty meager (we kept looking for those vast sums from overseas but they never quite arrived), into organizing. One of the issues of prairie power was "What do you do with your resources?" and the old guard felt that you should have a top-down organization. Some of them wanted to have positions that you argued in a national context, which I thought was ridiculous because we were such a small organization it didn't make any sense. It didn't matter what our fucking positions were; we had to build up our base. So I wanted to spend our resources on campus traveling and literature, have stuff to give out.

SDS had been focused on domestic policies up until we were confronted with the war in Vietnam. We came out of the civil rights experience and we decided we should be organizing; we had about six or eight projects organizing white underclass people. As the war in Vietnam started, SDS had a big national debate, because we knew that if we stood out against the war we'd be attacked as Communist, and that whole issue, which was still in the culture, would skew our organization. At that point, before the war, we were on track to be an alternative radical union of students. We were probably on the trajectory of being the left-wing National Student Association. But we began taking on the war, and we organized the first march on Washington [to protest the war].

Early on we had voted to throw out the Communist exclusion

clause, which meant a lot to the Old Left kids on the East Coast. It meant nothing to me because I didn't understand the history. All I thought was that you had an open debate of ideas and then you had to trust people's ability to think through issues. I didn't think it was a good idea to have an exclusionary clause because it was kind of like damning witches. I felt if the Communists wanted to come and argue we ought to listen to them and see if they had good ideas or not. I wasn't too impressed with the CPUSA because it was such a moderate organization. So for a kid out of the prairie, Communist exclusion seemed not very American in the land of free speech and open debate.

When we started organizing against the war we got lots of pressure—for instance, when we organized the first anti-Vietnam march—to have an anticommunist clause for participation. We refused. No other organization in the country would join us, and we had a national telephone poll. I was on the National Council, so I was called down in Texas. "How do you vote on the question do we want to have a Communist exclusion clause in the march on Washington?" "No, we don't want that." At the last moment, our march was developing so successfully everybody wanted to join in on it. Then we had another vote: Are we going to [allow them to] do it? My attitude was "Hell, we organized the damn thing, we should do it. We don't need these other organizations," and we didn't take them.[1]

That first march on Washington, for the Texas [and] Oklahoma chapters, it was hard to truck everybody to Washington; we didn't have much money. We did a sit-in at LBJ's ranch, which was pretty interesting because the Secret Service just didn't know what to make of us. Somebody from Johnson's place came out and brought us coffee. Of course I was aghast. We were almost like flat-earthers. The Secret Service at that time barely understood what Vietnam was, and suddenly all those marchers! I remember [chanting] "No troops in Vietnam" and people saying, "Where the hell is Vietnam? What is that?" So we were into organizing against the war early, but we knew it was going to skew the organization and it clearly did.

1. Other groups did not want to join the march unless Communists were excluded, but, according to Nightbyrd, when it became clear that the march would be a big one these groups wanted to join at the last minute.

I had read the history of how Populism had been divided by the issue of race and how splitting the white farming/working class on race ultimately destroyed the whole movement. So we knew that lesson, not only in race but you could apply that to the anticommunist cause too. If you get into these kinds of litmus tests you're going to destroy the organization or undercut your work. It's interesting that the decentralist and action wing of SDS—you could probably draw a map over the chapters that were like that—was basically where the Populist Party [had been] strong. Texas had a number of people whose great-grandfathers had been part of the Populist Party. One guy who joined our chapter had a family story that his great-great-grandfather had sat on the stage when Sam Houston had come to Waco. His great-great-grandfather sat on the stage with other farmers with shotguns so if somebody tried to come and shoot Sam Houston while he was campaigning against joining the confederacy, the farmers would defend him. So there were those kind of historical stories in people's backgrounds. Sometimes members had cultural roots. My grandfather used to play jazz in the black clubs. Or you'd have other kinds of things, but it was not usually left parties. The other part of the nation that was into direct action was the West Coast, which was always sort of out there but kind of separated from SDS. They had their groups, but they didn't come to meetings that much.

For a while we [Texans] had a lot of influence in SDS, for several reasons: one, we were the biggest chapter in the country for two or three years; two, there was a package of appealing ideas that came from there that's labeled "prairie power"—decentralist, anarcho-syndicalist—and it was appealing to a lot of people who didn't want a top-down, centralist organization; three, Texas represented a blending of culture and politics which later became larger and larger. As the sixties played out, the people with academic backgrounds were out of touch with youth culture. The Texans and more generally the midwesterners tended to go to be-ins, drop acid, put out the underground papers, wear love beads and SDS buttons. They were part of the cultural flux going on. There was this kind of hedonistic breaking down of taboos of the fifties. People in our chapter would skinny-dip all the time. That was just natural; everybody would take off their clothes and go swimming. The kids from Brown or Harvard I don't think went skinny-dipping. So prairie power people were those comfortable with the cultural flux going on, and fit into it.

A turning point for me was Woodstock. I was in New York publishing [the underground newspaper] *RAT.* I was still relating to the SDS office in New York City. I had helped recruit some people like Jeff Jones and Mark Rudd, who was a guy I liked who was [a member of the] Action Faction. They always attacked him for not being an intellectual, but he really got this takeover movement going at Columbia [University]. I was there when it all happened. So I was immersed in the SDS world of New York and I was putting out *RAT* and we were involved with Woodstock. Abbie Hoffman and I went and threatened the organizers—we had the idea that it was going to be big—that they were ripping off the people's culture and all this verbal garbage, and that they only had to give us $100,000. And they called us pirates and rip-off artists. Abbie was a genius—he went into an apoplexy and said he was going to jail anyway, he didn't care, he was going to sit in. There was not going to be a Woodstock. They were nervous enough that they huddled and basically gave in. As I recall, they gave us $60,000, which funded the medical aid system at Woodstock.

We had visited the Hog Farm [commune] up there and they basically had two bags of brown rice. We could tell that it was going to be a big, big thing; at the street level everybody was talking about it. The organizers didn't know it was going to be giant and we said, "We're going to need buses to take people to Woodstock." We bought I forget how much food to give to the Hog Farm. I took a printing press. Abe Peck from the *Chicago Seed* and I printed survival bulletins. During the rainstorm somebody climbed up and patched into the telephone pole, ran us a line, and we got the printing press chugging. After the rainstorm there was a big sea of mud, and we were putting out bulletins with survival tips. There were 500,000 people—you couldn't get in to Woodstock, and the roads were clogged so the ambulances couldn't get through. So we were on our own. We had births and marriages and everything. Finally the governor declared it a disaster area and the National Guard brought in helicopters.

We also funded something called Movement City, which consisted of a big tent [where] all the various groups had literature. After the rainstorm, it was very interesting to me that a lot of the traditional left groups sat in their tent in Movement City complaining about the people, saying they had no consciousness, and others like Abe Peck and Abbie Hoffman worked, went down to the bad trips tent, got things organized. The Hog Farm was doing the food; people in the cultural area of the movement got out there and did what was necessary. If there ever was our constituency, there it was, and the theoretical neo-Marxists sat there and complained about low consciousness! "Gee, they're listening to Richie Havens and they're not reading our leaflets," etc. On the trees there were these Meher Baba signs: "Don't Worry, Be Happy." They were all over the place. All the lefties would complain about these, but "Don't Worry, Be Happy" was more of a contribution than sitting in your tent complaining. That was kind of late in the game, and from then on I wasn't much interested in SDS.

SDS was being assaulted by the Progressive Labor Party, which I think was basically funded and infiltrated by the United States security establishment. SDS didn't deal well with having a disciplined faction. We were used to having open debate and reasoning out issues, and to have a disciplined cadre inside that didn't reason on issues but were told how to be a voting bloc kind of destroyed the idea of SDS. By then SDS had lost its leadership of the antiwar movement and couldn't answer the basic question "What do we want?" It was just another player in the field, and some violent politics became more and more important, but even more important were headlines. For instance, I was in New York at the time, and I was very good friends with Jerry Rubin, but Jerry didn't represent anything other than the guy who played the media in New York City. So at that point the politics became headline politics.

Earlier, a lot of SDS groups started alternative papers. We started one in Austin called the *Rag*. There was one in Michigan called *The Paper*, and one in Madison. We said, "Jesus, if they can do it in Ann Arbor or Madison, we can do it in Austin." There was a really nice paper in Lawrence, Kansas, with news the local papers and media weren't going to give. We had some national meetings of the underground press, and as we got more organized we had a news service known as LNS, the Liberation News Service.

The faction that kind of dominated LNS was the old Marxist or neo-Marxist faction. They started sending out packets and it became easier to start underground papers because you could reprint a lot of stuff from the LNS packets, but because they were in New York their politics was really unimaginative. Soon everybody's paper was filled with solidarity with the freedom fighters of Namibia, solidarity with the freedom fighters in Angola, we're one with the Aboriginal freedom movement in Australia, etc. All of which may have been well and good but in the Midwest doesn't have much relevance to some kid off the farm who's nineteen and trying to figure out what life's about. The early underground papers were very powerful because they were generally started locally and dealt a lot with what people knew, that electrified people. Later on they became these turgid mouthpieces, with rhetoric of the worst sort, the most boring sort, and it was one of the things that started to ossify the SDS chapters as an organization. Marxist rhetoric never was really part of the American psyche. It didn't work, it wasn't captivating like our earlier stuff was, and our influence waned.

At some point we might know how much infiltration was part of the demise of all these chapters. . . . Agents provocateurs would get up and say, "If you really want to be against the war, we'll burn the American flag at the next demonstration." I've been in meetings where guys got up saying, "Look, the Vietnamese are dying . . . people who want to do the heavy stuff, sign up on this list and we'll have our own meeting." Some of the old hands would say, "Now, everybody, it's not such a good idea to sign up for this. Just because it sounds more militant to be talking about bombing, it doesn't mean it's more effective." Well, that's a hard sell to eighteen-year-olds who are all fired up with the revolutionary spirit. In that anarchic meeting structure, people would literally advocate bombings and pass around a pad and pencil and all these people would sign. I think a lot of that was government agents. To what degree we don't know. I don't think that's why SDS ended, but it did skew the organization at some point.

When you're young, you live 100 percent in the moment. Every day you do everything that you can. On the other hand, you are trying to gain knowledge of some historical antecedents that will help you operate in an intelligent way. Prairie power, almost by definition, didn't have precursors to tell us what we were, where we stood. East Coast kids coming out of old Socialist and Communist families knew how movements moved, knew how they developed, knew how government infiltration worked, knew lots of just organizational questions. We prairie power types talked to some progressive Democrats, some union organizers, but generally the fifties had wiped out the direct action. So as a twenty-four-year-old white boy I didn't have any forty-four-year-old white man to tell me anything, so you had to harken back to earlier things like the IWW, or listen to Woody Guthrie songs. I remember I sat down and read the three-volume *History of the Russian Revolution* by Trotsky, and the one that fascinated me was volume two, which is always left out of the compendiums of his works because it's all organizational stuff. It's how they go out and organize, and most people consider it very boring, and I thought it was just fascinating. So on one level I had an awareness and wanted to push ideas I thought were sound for SDS. On the other hand, I was woefully naive because I was a young man without any antecedents trying to learn what I was doing as I was doing it. By '66 or '67, SDS and students took on the role of national opposition. The Republicans and Democrats were on one side, and here was a national student movement calling into question the fundamental policies of the United States government. I was twenty-five or twenty-six years old and vice president of SDS. I had to articulate national policies when I had no older generation to guide me. It was a very difficult position.

How consciously was I pushing ideas? I very strongly believed that an organization functioned best if it were decentralized. We had a motto, "Let the people decide"—the idea was that the closer to home you can make decisions about any kind of policy, the closer to the people affected, the more workable and better those decisions will be. That's almost as much an ecological idea as a political idea. It was the opposite of the Communists, Socialists, Republicans, Democrats, all the top-down parties. I read about the IWW and the idea of anarcho-syndicalism. How you would transform the country was that there would be organizations in various work-related areas that would act as spokes of a wheel that had a representative at the hub. The IWW talked about one day we'll have one big strike and shut it all down. It wasn't that they were going to go to war with the U.S. Army. They said, we're going to have one big strike and shut the whole system down, and we had in the universities one big strike and we shut the universities down. So that was like an anarcho-syndicalist model that was successful for us in the universities. Prairie power at its core had an anarcho-syndicalist idea that you decentralized organizations, and your strategy for change is that as you and your allies organized you would be able to make the machine stop. The war effort was going to stop because at some point the bus drivers weren't going to drive the buses, clerks weren't going to do their job sending out the notices. You could make the machine stop.

If you were an East Coast member of SDS, which started out as a social democratic, liberal left organization, and you went to help the civil rights movement in the South, and your family was Old Left, they were happy. If you were in Kansas, your family was probably mainstream Protestant and they were appalled. When the war came along it was a real cutting issue in the heartland of the country. To go against your government, to say you should burn your draft card, to call into question the whole military and foreign policy of the United States government, to accuse the United States government of flagrantly lying was so out of step with your parents' generation that you were generally disowned. You weren't patted on the back. You were an embarrassment to the family, especially if you came from a small town, and in the worst cases, which were frequent, you didn't go home at Christmas. If you were in college, everyone goes home at Christmas, but we'd sit around and there'd be like twenty-five people who weren't going home. It was like, we'll have our own Christmas here. This is my new family. That process tended to bond the prairie people together more in the chapters. So we were more likely to lay around in one of these big old houses that are common in the Midwest, and a bunch of people would be sharing the rent, you'd all smoke pot, you'd groove together. You were much more bonded in a family kind of sense than people from the East Coast who were doing something that was in the tradition of their families.

What it did is make people politically stronger in the sense that they would take risks. They weren't so easily threatened. All those kinds of places that I organized in, you were really making sharp breaks with your family tradition, and to do so meant very major personal steps. It also made it very alluring. It gave you lots of power because alienated kids, of which there were many in college even if they didn't come the whole way, thought, "Those are really powerful people." There was a lot of magnetism to being a very self-confident outsider with great confidence attacking the insider. A student attacking the president of the university in a public forum as a blowhard, a fool, and a liar—that would be common in those days. You could say those things with absolute self-assurance. It was incredibly magnetic, and to other people who were alienated . . . the orbit around SDS was huge.

Also, the prairie is interesting because it has less class awareness.[2] There's some very rich farmers but their kids never felt upper-class, and so typically in a chapter you would have people from different social and income backgrounds all thrown together without much sense of class, which is a much more democratized situation. This was another characteristic that distinguished prairie [power] from the Ivy League people. America in this century has not been conceived of as that place on the East Coast, but something like this big heart of the country. In novels and literature we've always been trying to get at the essence, the root of it. In between the East Coast and San Francisco and LA was something like the great American character, and everybody was trying to figure out what it was we were. So within national consciousness it gave us a special kind of power being all-American kids. A big, psychedelic festival in the middle of Lawrence, Kansas, resonated much, much more than the same event in New York. New York is a thousand traditions, whereas we were getting at the very kernel of what it was to be an American and what our society was about.

The midwestern culture experimented with acid, pot, and stuff, and looked in part to the tradition of not only the IWW and the Populists, but to the American Indian, who had ideas about the land and the interconnection of all living things. That led to a whole environmental movement, a different way of seeing our relationship to who we were and to the land. The other view, say, the Tennessee Valley Authority, was we're going to conquer nature, we're going to build dams, we're going to subdue nature much as we're going to subdue the Vietnamese. After that realization we argued, "Jesus, righteous people in Vietnam can't be subdued," just as nature can't be subdued. In the Plains Indians sense, it's something you live with, you don't dominate, and you could take that analogy into the family. The family is not something to be subdued and dominated

2. See Jane Adams's oral history, pp. 71–72, for a differing view.

by the father; it's some sort of partnership still up for definition. So if organizationally what came out of the Midwest was more or less a failure, in other ways, in the power of ideas, it was enormously influential. When people give their lives to ideas they resonate over time. Organizationally we left nothing, but in the dialectic of ideas we were tremendously successful. When I say "we" it's that big orgasmic collective "we" that kind of shot up just as we went into the next decades.

The movement presented a fundamental challenge, and one reason a lot of ministers moved was they could see morally that it was correct. The whole question that came about from television was, "What right do we have to slaughter peasants with some vaguely defined foreign policy in Vietnam?" It ultimately really bothered huge numbers of American people, so that by the end of '69, probably, in Iowa we had carried the day, we had a majority of the people thinking it's wrong. Five years before, they didn't know where Vietnam was. They thought our presidents Nixon and Johnson were disgraces now. We couldn't stop the war, but fundamentally the consciousness was changed. What had been the post–World War II American machine came to a smashing stop against the barricade of morality and in that process and out of what we started was a dialectical whirlwind that changed fundamentally other parts of the consciousness of our country. For instance, the dialectic once in motion changed people's diets, it changed the relationship between men and women (who clearly weren't getting an even shake, and a lot of SDS women were some of the first feminist leaders who raised those basic questions), and it changed ecological awareness.

At some point we had the majority of Americans against the war in Vietnam. We couldn't stop the war. Nixon got elected with the secret plan to end the war, which he didn't have. He began to destroy Cambodia, which *was* his secret plan. People, students, began being shot. Well, students had been shot before but at Kent State it was the first time whites had been shot and that sent up quivers.[3] People went back to the land and said we'll make alternative societies, which was a wrongheaded idea. We turned inward and began attacking and devouring ourselves, which is common in movements.

3. White people were shot—and one was killed—at People's Park in Berkeley in 1969, prior to Kent State (1970). Still, Nightbyrd's point about the effects of Kent State on the movement is supported by several of the other oral histories.

The feminist movement, which largely started in SDS, turned on the male leadership. It's not that in SDS things were so equal, but SDS went further in regard to women's roles than other institutions at the time. We weren't great, but certainly women had leadership roles. Jane Adams was the national secretary, etc. My impression was that in general women leaders were listened to. I don't remember lots of sexism, but the women generally have different accounts. I got denounced as a horrible sexist guy by my girlfriend and others and had a nervous breakdown. Actually a lot of the male leadership did. There were a lot of suicides in the mid-seventies among mid-western male leaders. Not only did men not end the war, but the women they cared about attacked them. If you were really sexist you don't give a shit, but if you think, "Jesus, I like women; God, they're telling me I've been really bad," that really is devastating to some men who are ideologically and spiritually committed to some sort of progress. So there were lots of nervous breakdowns and some suicides. We men watched this big thing come apart and didn't know our role. It is a very difficult place to be. You have to reinvent your life.

In the good Texas way, I picked myself up again and started another newspaper, worked at a station that was bombed twice by the Ku Klux Klan in Houston. I did lots of things. I started a big anti–drug testing movement. You have to find yourself again after your defeat. The media like to tell us about all the sellouts. What I found was that most everybody who was active was basically not doing flashy stuff but by and large doing pretty good things. They weren't sellouts. They were good.

I still believed in confrontational tactics. Take an issue like parade permits for marches against the war. I believed the Constitution gave you the right to peacefully assemble, we had the right to march. The parade permit issue heightened the contradiction. Boy, that's all the better time to march. The police are going to come and it's going to really make the issue. So on one level I liked aggressive confrontational action, and on another level I came up with the idea of Gentle Thursday. We in SDS would always ask, "What do you want? What kind of society?" I thought of having this day where we for one day act out the good society. Picnic on the grass—nobody sat much on the grass—bring your children to school, invite the teacher or somebody you've always wanted to meet. This was the day you could say, "Okay, come and have lunch with me on the grass." The first time we did it we put out leaflets, but our university, like most of these midwestern campuses, were run by the sororities and fraternities. They would literally stand on the edge of the grass—because at that point people wore kind of nice clothes and didn't want to mess them up—five and six deep, staring. But we were having so much fun that [they said,] "Gee, maybe next time I'll wear my jeans, my cut-offs, and sit on the grass too." So we put out a leaflet [saying] since this was a success we'll be having Gentle Thursday next month, and the next month, and then we might do it two Thursdays a month and finally every Thursday, and when people get used to acting this way we'll start doing it every day of the week, and then that's the revolution.

What was interesting about Gentle Thursday was it offered a positive way of imagining society. Because if you just say, "We're against the war and we're against the imperialist lackey-dog military industrial complex, we're against racist, fascist pigs who run the university," that rhetoric takes you only so far. Ultimately, people want to live in a more pleasing way. The hippie acid culture offered alternatives all the time. I found in organizing that ultimately people need some utopian vision about where they are going, why they are putting in this effort. My politics and my tactics were as much as possible confrontations to accentuate and make clear the contradictions in the society. And novel. I tried to do original kinds of utopian things to reach out to different constituencies.

Music and politics in Texas were inseparable. We used to have folksinging night. Janis Joplin came to it in the early days. . . . We'd all gather in this place and sing. Music, drugs, and politics were inseparable, too. Most of the music was better understood if you were stoned. It was written by stoned people for stoned people, people who were alienated from the real American middle establishment that was an alcohol culture. It was the first time you had a clash of drug traditions. The drug tradition in the great heartland of America was alcohol. It's so inculcated into our culture we don't even see it as a drug. Marijuana was identified with the underclass and blacks. You can use it as an equalizer, and most people tend to use pot in that way.

What became separable in the later sixties was SDS from the cultural movement. In the earlier stages they were inseparable, but singing freedom songs is a very different experience than Jefferson

Airplane doing "White Rabbit." I walked the picket lines and I
know a million verses of "We Shall Overcome," "We Shall Not Be
Moved," and so on. There's a whole cadence and at a point, especially if you're tired and a whole bunch of people are singing songs,
for people like me who don't sing well but can fit into the har-
monies, it's uplifting, it's transcendent! But that era of freedom
songs ended as the youth movement started developing. The music
changed and SDS was still singing folk songs. They were comfortable (I'm making a generalization) with the East Coast and Pete
Seeger, and in the Midwest they were more comfortable with Country
Joe McDonald and the Jefferson Airplane.

I always felt very centered with my politics. When I was a child I
had some mystical experiences, like knock-you-on-your-ass religious kinds of experiences, not church-based. I felt very solid, connected to life, very grounded. It was like having a near-death
experience. You're both humbled and feel grounded. One reason I
could take what seemed to society very extreme positions was because I felt very confident and secure. When I was in high school in
Bryant, Texas, they called me "nigger lover" and I was still popular.
I got elected the wittiest guy in the school. So I was a popular guy,
but I told people what I thought, and I was absolutely certain that
they were wrong. There was a real strength in that conviction of certainty. I don't think a lot of people feel that. I think they feel discon-
nected and discombobulated. But the key to certainty is knowledge
and wisdom.

I think humor is a tremendous weapon because humor is based on
throwing up a contradiction. If you can't attack directly, you can find
ways of making jokes to bring out the ridiculous level of things. So
humor is the guerrilla tactic of the powerless. One thing I liked about
the Yippies was that they made fun of the establishment.

Dancing. Ask people how much they danced. In the sixties, dances
didn't have steps. The music kind of whirled around and anybody
could do anything. It was cool, and everybody could dance because
all you had to do was get out there and move around. But there
were still people who didn't dance and some of them were old-
guard leaders of SDS. In an era when anybody could dance and anything that you did passed for dancing, whether you had natural
rhythm or not, some people still didn't get up out of their chairs.

THREE PRAIRIE POWER CAMPUSES

So I have been sitting here for a while in the green tweed chair, watching Kansas burn on the TV screen. . . .

In the name of God, what has happened to this country? If this were Columbia or Cornell or Berkeley, the flickering image might not sear the heart. Scar tissue grows. But this is Lawrence, Kansas, heartland America.

—James Kilpatrick

The oral histories that follow this chapter represent three campuses in the heartland: the University of Missouri (MU), the University of Kansas (KU), and Southern Illinois University (SIU). All three are large state institutions in isolated, conservative areas that experienced turmoil in the sixties and early seventies. They offer some variety, as discussed below: There was a relatively large amount of activity at KU, MU was more quiet and students were determined to keep their activity nonviolent, and SIU was one of the hundreds of schools nationwide that shut down in the midst of riots that followed the killing of four students by the National Guard at Kent State University. Still, the three campuses also have enough in common that they make possible the generalizations about prairie power activists and their impact that are discussed in the introduction to this book. Moreover, the long-term effects are still evident on all three campuses, for example, in students' expectations about free speech on campus and in problematic town-gown relations. The story would be much the same, with some local differences, at Nebraska, Oklahoma, and other institutions that fit the profile of "prairie power" campuses.

They may not have called it "prairie power," but activist students and faculty in the lower Midwest were aware of the fact that their protests came as a shock to many observers. From different perspectives, administrators who feared the New Left, student activists, and their opponents all compared activities on their own campuses to the Free Speech Movement at Berkeley, in which nearly eight hundred students were arrested in a 1964 demonstration. While a handful of student activists might have seen Berkeley as a model, others agreed with their opponents about the need to avoid creating "another Berkeley." Students in the heartland wanted to raise some of the same issues—and free speech was particularly important— but in general they did not seem to relish the turmoil and threat of violence that resulted from their efforts.

SDS was a rather loose affair on all three campuses. When the Missouri SDS chapter was threatened with loss of university recognition because it failed to list its complete membership, the chapter secretary told the administration: "I should explain that membership of a local chapter of SDS is a very nebulous thing. You could come to a meeting, take part in the discussion, make motions, vote, and even give the treasurer money—this would not make you a member unless you chose to call yourself one. This is a very strong point about SDS. As secretary I do not have a membership list, I have a mailing list. I could not point out a name on that list and say whether that person is a member or not, unless that individual so designated himself."[1] The administration at KU saw SDS in a similar light. A confidential memo on student unrest from Chancellor W. Clarke Wescoe to the board of regents in May 1968 included this description: "We have had on campus, ever since its inception nationally, a chapter of Students for a Democratic Society. . . . On campus, that group has been relatively ineffective: they operate so democratically that they cannot elect a chairman or leader and as a group cannot commit themselves to any action. It is difficult to deal with them, of course, for they are individuals, not a cohesive group."[2]

All three local chapters felt somewhat distant from, and took pains

---

1. "Emergency SDS Meeting," flyer, 1967, folder 189, Rory Vincent Ellinger Collection, Western Historical Manuscript Collection, University of Missouri, Columbia.

2. W. Clarke Wescoe to board of regents, May 13, 1968, Student Protest Files, 1969, University Archives, Spencer Research Library, University of Kansas, Lawrence.

to distinguish themselves from, the national office. The KU chapter's response to a question from the national office about its impact on the local group was: "Largely negative affect [*sic*]—our gains, sadly, are more in spite of, than because of N.O."[3] In his oral history, Rory Ellinger, the leader of the MU chapter, says: "Our relationship to national SDS was really nothing. We were off on our own. In fact, we'd be very suspicious of people [from outside]; we'd think they were agents provocateurs." Carbondale activists also stress the independence of the local chapter. Larry Bennett says he saw the national organization as "dominated by Chicago and Michigan people, and Southern Illinois has a real complex about Chicago. . . . Our SDS actually called itself Coal City SDS because we wanted to make it clear that we thought differently than Chicago."

Despite its ultrademocratic style, looseness about membership, and distance from the national office, SDS was perceived as the most left-wing, and often the most effective (in the eyes of the students) or the most threatening (in the eyes of administrators), campus group. The local chapters shared the national organization's discomfort with leadership; only at Missouri, where the movement was so small, could the leader of SDS be viewed as a "legend" by those that succeeded him. At both Missouri and SIU, a leader of student government could also be a leader in the antiwar movement (see the oral histories of Dan Viets and Ray Lenzi), while at KU, where the movement was much larger and more active, there was less of an overlap between student government and the New Left. (Even so, by the late sixties and early seventies, student body presidents took strong antiwar stances.) In any case, SDS did not lead the largest demonstrations on every campus, although, as in the *Free Press* incident at Missouri, SDS activists might have been at the center of events that provoked demonstrations. When students rallied on behalf of free speech or dorm visitation rights or against the war in Vietnam, there was little leadership, SDS or otherwise, to be seen. In some sense, this seemed a logical reflection of the antileadership attitude and rhetoric of SDS on the national level.

Although events did get out of hand at KU and SIU in the spring of 1970, organizers at all three schools were firm in their encouragement

3. Chapter report, n.d., Students for a Democratic Society Papers, 1958–1970, microfilm, series 3, reel 22.

of dialogue and insistence on nonviolence. In May 1968, KU activists called off a sit-in they had planned when students agreed
they should hold a dialogue with administrators first. In May 1970,
campus groups came together to organize an extensive series of
public lectures and discussions called the Action for Peace Movement Calendar, which was intended to dispel violence and provide
means for students to express discontent with Nixon's foreign policy and educate themselves on the issues. On all three campuses,
activists organized events at which people were encouraged to discuss issues and at which a variety of viewpoints were represented.
Typical of such events was a convocation at MU during the October
1969 moratorium, with "all points of view to be expressed."[4] The
threat of "another Berkeley" always seemed to be lurking in the
background.

University of Missouri

We didn't have enough people to have a faction. If there was anybody committed to violence it was one or two people perhaps.

—Trish Vandiver, quoted in John Beahler,
"Something's Happening Here"

Students at the University of Missouri–Columbia seemed the most
determined to keep events nonviolent; perhaps the fact that the
SDS faculty adviser was a longtime pacifist had something to do
with this. A regular peace vigil that began in the sixties as a protest
against the war in Vietnam continues in Columbia to this day. The
local observance of the national antiwar moratorium that took
place on October 15, 1969, also exemplified the nonviolent character of the movement. A flyer encouraging students to skip class and
attend special "Peace Day" observances pleaded: "If you wish to
burn buildings or riot, please choose another day. October 15 is not
a day for extremists . . . but rather the people's day, 'Peace Day.' On

4. "Take the Day Off for Peace," leaflet, 1969, Student Attitudes toward Vietnam Conflict Collection, Western Historical Manuscript Collection.

October 15, everyone should try to smile and put down their ha-
treds."[5]

Founded in 1839, MU was the first public university west of the
Mississippi. Located just off Interstate 70 in the center of the state,
Columbia is the flagship campus of the University of Missouri
System, which now has branches in St. Louis and Kansas City (each
about a hundred miles away) as well as in Rolla. Of the three institutions represented in this book, Missouri was by far the most
conservative in terms of traditions and administration. The student
movement was small, yet even here—or perhaps especially in places
like this—after the sixties things were never the same. Students
gained representation on university committees, became involved
in community politics, played a role in alternative institutions created by the counterculture, and raised larger issues such as the university's role in society, particularly its relation to the military. They
also touched on issues of race relations, a sore spot in the Columbia
community and the university, and these issues continue to be raised
today. The lives of individuals were affected dramatically, as students
from small towns around the state received an eye-opening education that went far beyond the classroom.

The University of Missouri was not a hospitable place for black
students in the sixties. Historically, the university had resisted the
admission of African American applicants, routinely referring them
to Lincoln University in Fulton. If black students could not find the
courses they wanted at Lincoln, they were paid to go out of state.
When Lloyd Gaines, an African American, applied to MU's law
school in 1936 and refused to leave the state, his case went to the
U.S. Supreme Court, which ruled in 1938 that Missouri had to provide equal education within the state. But it was not until after the
Brown decision in 1954 that African Americans were admitted on a
more equal basis. By the late sixties, the campus still had fewer than
two hundred black students. The Confederate flag was carried
around the football stadium at the beginning of every game and
after each touchdown, and the band played "Dixie" at halftime.
Students for a Democratic Society was the major organization raising civil rights issues on campus until the founding of the Legion of

5. "*You* Can Be the Difference between Idealism and Realism," flyer, n.d., Vietnam Conflict Collection.

Black Collegians in 1968. (Black Marxists had formed a chapter of the Du Bois Club in 1966, but it was never officially recognized because it had been labeled "Communist" by the Justice Department.) LBC became a recognized student organization in 1969, the same year as the election of the first black homecoming queen and the hiring of the first black faculty member.

In 1965, the Young Democrats were the largest political group on the campus; other groups included the Young Republicans, New Fabians (a democratic socialist discussion club founded in 1961), SDS (which the student newspaper reported was formed to protest U.S. involvement in Vietnam), Young Conservatives, and Young Americans for Freedom. One activity that year was a debate cosponsored by SDS and YAF on American intervention in the Dominican Republic. Students complained about large classes and restrictions on visiting members of the opposite sex. "Students under age 21 may not be guests in rooms or apartments of the opposite sex, whether or not the housing is University regulated," reported the student newspaper, *The Maneater.* One young woman wrote a letter home about the "dippy rules and regulations" in her dorm, but from the administration's point of view the restrictions were already beginning to loosen.[6] Exchange dinners could now take place on all weekday nights, not just Wednesdays; men could remove their suit coats in hot weather during Sunday meals, and women could now determine for themselves whether it was cold enough to wear slacks (in the previous year, it had to be 10 degrees or colder before women could wear pants). The student government, the Missouri Student Association (MSA), was working on a student bill of rights.

The issue that gained the most attention was freedom of expression, which was not unusual for a midwestern campus. The chancellor restricted sale of the *Columbia Free Press,* an underground newspaper that began in the fall of 1966, to one campus location. City officials restricted sales locations as well. *The Catalyst,* a CORE (Congress of Racial Equality) paper critical of university policies such as segregation in dorms, had a similar fate in the early sixties. Such free speech issues would galvanize the campus a few years later.

6. " 'Exchanges' Now Allowed Every Night," *Maneater,* September 22, 1965, p. 2; see also September 29, 1965, and October 6, 1965.

In 1967, the year the first black MSA officer was elected and SDS began the Free University (a series of classes on topics not addressed by the regular university curriculum), the *Free Press* was among the papers that reported on a "brain drain" from the university. The story was that top professors were leaving because of the lack of academic freedom on campus. William S. Allen, associate professor of history, was among those who left after being harassed for his politics. He was not the only one denied raises several years in a row because of his outspoken opposition to the war in Vietnam. In 1968, political science professor David Wurfel, whose experience was similar to Allen's, wrote in his letter of resignation that "[t]he status of academic freedom is poor at Missouri." The *St. Louis Post-Dispatch* editorialized that excellence was built on freedom for the clash of ideas and opinions, and that MU had hurt its reputation in the case of Bill Allen and the others who were leaving.[7]

The character of the student movement in Columbia—decidedly nonconfrontational and inclusive—was evident in the Gentle Tuesday that took place in the spring of 1967, attended by about eight hundred people. It was a day when classes were dismissed because of the inauguration of a new university president, so no one had to worry about missing class. As a flyer advertising the event suggested, it could be viewed as a celebration for the new president or "a protest against the necessity for having a president and all the other trappings of an overly bureaucratic, undemocratic administration." As at other universities, "Keep Off the Grass" signs were ignored, and the event took place near the historic columns in the center of campus. What struck observers, however, was not the broken rules, but the variety of people who participated in Gentle Tuesday. The flyer had suggested that people share lunch with strangers: "Sorority chicks should share their lunches with beatniks. SDS chicks should share their lunches with fraternity guys," and so on. People were instructed to "bring babies, puppies and kittens," "be nice to policemen," and "no matter who you eat lunch with, pick up all litter. It's our university and we should keep it clean." The student newspaper reported that "[n]ot just SDS, which

7. Wurfel's letter appeared in the *Maneater*, May 15, 1968, p. 3; the *Post-Dispatch* editorial was reprinted in the *Columbia Free Press Underground*, October 1967, Ellinger Collection, folder 214.

started the idea, turned out. So did Dr. William Bondeson, philosophy professor, and Chuck Murray, former YAF state president. So did Robert Dickeson, director of student activities, and Cecil Phillips, MSA presidential candidate. So did some Greeks and some dormitory residents. Gentle Tuesday was for everyone."[8]

Yet by this time, things were beginning to heat up on campus. African American activist James Rollins had been arrested for possession of marijuana, and while SDS raised money for his defense, he was kicked out of school even before his court trial. When a group of teaching assistants in the history department dismissed their classes, encouraging them to support the striking workers of Local 45 (nonacademic university employees), the board of curators tried to have them fired. A YAF guest column in the student newspaper, "Left Crumbling under Pot," turned out to be mere wishful thinking, as students, with the inadvertent assistance of the administration, became more rather than less politicized.[9]

The next fall, six SDS members were arrested for handing out leaflets to high school seniors and their families attending University Day. A few dozen students immediately marched from a Gentle Saturday event to the student union to protest the arrests. No charges were filed against the six students who had been dragged off campus by the police, but the university administration, making good on its promise to take disciplinary action, put SDS leaders on probation for distributing antidraft and antiwar literature on University Day. The punishment prompted the MSA president to speak out in opposition to the university's action, while eighteen professors issued a statement about freedom and a Student Activities Forum committee sponsored a speakers' corner to encourage open discussion of the issues. An editorial in the student paper claimed that blocking the free exchange of ideas was a proud tradition on the Missouri campus, and warned: "As it stands now, [university administrators] are looking down the barrel of 'another Berkeley.' "[10]

8. Gentle Tuesday flyer, Spring 1967, Ellinger Collection, folder 140; *Maneater,* April 19, 1967, p. 7.
9. "Rollins Reported Dismissed," *Maneater,* May 17, 1967, p. 1; Rory Ellinger, "Reflections: Local 45 Strike," *Free Press Underground,* September 1969, Ellinger Collection, folder 217; "Left Crumbling under Pot," *Maneater,* October 18, 1967, p. 16.
10. Tom Wellman, editorial, *Maneater,* October 18, 1967, p. 16.

As at other large midwestern state universities, issues of student rights brought people together to take action. In a typical statement, *Free Press Underground* columnist Steve Fuchs wrote in 1967: "The repressive power that University administrators wield permeates campus life. Students are treated as objects to be manipulated and are not allowed to participate in the decision-making processes of their university."[11] This kind of language could be heard on campuses across the country, but it was only at heartland universities such as Missouri that one could see a mixture of front-page headlines like the following in the fall of 1968: "Equal Rights for Women—In MU Panty Raids That Is!" "Racism Dominates M.U.," "[Governor] Hearnes Answers Charges, After SDS Confrontation," "Angry Students Sit-In Read Hall to Protest Dress." The "angry students" had attempted to gain admission to a meeting of the Single Student Housing Committee in order to request the abolition of Sunday dress regulations in the dorms. While the students were denied admission to the meeting, their request was honored a week later.[12]

It was not just the coexistence of different issues and groups, often brought together around student rights, but the strong opposition to them that was a noteworthy factor on large midwestern campuses. When some teaching assistants and professors called off classes to observe the October 1969 moratorium, YAF demanded that they be fired immediately. At the large free speech demonstrations the same year, a group of students carried signs reading, "For Free Speech, Not SDS." Some confrontations were more violent. For instance, when SDS protested the university's policy of prohibiting unrecognized groups, such as CORE, from using the facilities of the student union, arguing that the students should decide, there was a strong reaction. Agriculture students formed a counterpicket with signs such as "Sloppy Dirty Socialists," and they threatened and beat up SDS members. New Left activists were aware of the fact that what they looked like made a difference. When the Committee of Concerned Students was organized in 1968 to supplement the

11. Steve Fuchs, "What's to Be Done?" *Free Press Underground,* October 1967, p. 2, Ellinger Collection, folder 214.

12. "Housing Committee Votes to Abolish Dress Rules," *Maneater,* December 17, 1968, p. 1. The other front-page headlines appeared in the *Maneater* on November 5, 1968; November 1, 1968; November 5, 1968; and December 10, 1968, respectively.

activities of SDS, a student editorial commented on the fact that these students wore coats and ties and didn't have beards. Since they were also politically knowledgeable and had done their research, "They will have to be listened to."[13]

Students put the issue of free speech to the test in 1969, laying the groundwork for the so-called "intervisitation crisis," when men and women insisted on freely visiting each other's dorms. In the free speech case, four students were arrested for selling an issue of the *Free Press* on campus that allegedly had obscene content. The arrests and the university administration's suspension of the students created a huge stir, a perfect example of how such crackdowns helped build the movement. A leaflet headed "U. of MO. Bust" thanked the administration for helping focus the issues, suggesting, "It was one of those rare instances when stupidity and constitutional contempt combined to create the SDS organizer's dream; [an] overnight politicalization of hundreds of students." The incident spawned the largest demonstrations to date—a rally of approximately 2,500 faculty members and students called on the administration to back down—and the *Maneater* urged the dean of students to resign. Even the Young Republicans policy committee supported the arrested students, urging the administration to reevaluate its procedures for determining obscenity and its premises for restricting free speech. The chancellor removed SDS's recognition, even though a faculty-student committee recommended no disciplinary action. The case went all the way to the Supreme Court, where the students were finally vindicated.[14]

The largest demonstrations in MU's history took place the following year, after the killings at Kent State. Evidence of the student movement's local concerns appear in a flyer calling for a rally against the war: "Here, on this campus, free speech has been outlawed, inter-visitation barred, and the ABM missiles are still being built in mid-Missouri."[15] On May 11, three thousand demonstrators on

13. "Don't Support Oct. 15 March," *Viewpoint*, October 1969, pp. 1, 3, Vietnam Conflict Collection; "SDS, Aggies Clash in Union Protest," *Maneater*, May 10, 1967, p. 1; "Clean Cut Activism," *Maneater*, September 27, 1968.
14. These events are discussed at length in the oral histories. See also "2,500 Students Hear Pleas for Free Speech," *Maneater*, February 28, 1969, p. 2, and "University Sees Activism Reborn," *Maneater*, May 16, 1969, p. 1. A draft of an article for *New Left Notes* called "How Administrators Helped Build a Movement" is in the Ellinger Collection, folder 108.
15. Peace Coalition flyer, 1970, Ellinger Collection, folder 150.

Francis Quadrangle called on the chancellor to make an official state-ment condemning the war in Vietnam. Officials responded by lock-ing the chancellor's office. Thirty-two people were arrested for trespassing when they staged a sit-in outside the chancellor's office; they were released without being charged. Chancellor John Schwada refused to speak out about the war, and instead issued a set of strict emergency regulations, including prohibitions against people con-gregating in groups of three or more and using loudspeakers or bullhorns on campus.

Some faculty members had canceled classes so that students would feel free to participate in the antiwar demonstrations and memori-als for Kent State. On May 12, faculty, students, and administrators reached an agreement on how students and faculty who had missed classes and participated in the sit-in would be treated and how grades would be assigned. (Their suggestions were similar to what actually transpired at KU, where students were given a variety of options for taking finals and receiving grades.) But a few weeks later, the board of curators repudiated the joint agreement, insisting that faculty and students be disciplined and grades and degrees withheld for those who had missed classes. The chair of the sociol-ogy department, Daryl Hobbs, was suspended for not complying with university requests to submit names of faculty who had dis-missed classes and given grades for work completed.[16] The curators dismissed another professor, and these actions led to the university being censured by the American Association of University Profes-sors (AAUP). (The censure was finally lifted in 1981.)

The next fall the *Washington Post* reported that before school opened the curators had laid down the law on behavior. Calling Columbia "Missouri's equivalent of Berkeley," the *Post* claimed that James Weaver, the president of the four University of Missouri campuses, had written one paragraph of the communiqué him-self: "Students, faculty, administrators and employees who are not in sympathy with the basic philosophy expressed herein and do not intend to abide by the rules and regulations of the university should not attend the university nor become associated with the institution nor continue to be associated with the university."[17] While students

16. "Curators Reject Student-Faculty Pact," *Columbia Missourian*, June 3, 1970.
17. Edward P. Morgan, "Campus Crackdown at the University of Missouri," *Washington Post*, October 30, 1970.

found such guidelines objectionable, dubbing this the "love it or leave it" clause, Weaver found support among the general public. Among the letters of support to the administration following the events of May 1970 is one addressed to the president of the board of curators that says, "My personal opinion is that all the troubles in all the schools in the country are fomented by the Communist movement."[18] Several letters suggested firing professors, expelling students, and generally taking a hard line against "Communist activity."

Administrators also were caught between student demands and public opinion on the issue of having men and women visit each other's dorm rooms. In his oral history, Dan Viets describes the rallies conducted by students demanding the right to visit with members of the opposite sex. These events point up an important and often overlooked piece of the story of midwestern student activism: while the protesters carried out nonviolent activities, they were sometimes met with violence. In this case, the Committee of Concerned Students reported that four students were beaten and two hospitalized after a rally at the dorms. The president of the Association of Women Students, writing to parents in March 1970, said: "The 'intervisitation' controversy on the University of Missouri–Columbia campus has become an explosive and misunderstood issue in recent months." The dean of students warned the president of the Inter-Fraternity Council against a plan to break the regulations on intervisitation, and a concerned citizen wrote to the administration opposing intervisitation in the name of Christ, arguing, "I'm sure that the majority of Mo. Citizens do not approve of this."[19] Over the next few years, the regulations were revised dramatically to comply with student desires and changes in the culture at large, and to avoid violations of Title IX. By 1977 some dormitories were coeducational.

Activity did not cease after 1970, although it did diminish in size

18. Les Bauslin to William H. Billings, May 27, 1970, Student Unrest papers, University Archives, University of Missouri, Columbia.

19. Committee of Concerned Students leaflet on the intervisitation crisis, c. 1969, Ellinger Collection, folder 144; letter from Association of Women Students president to parents, March 20, 1970; dean of students warning to Inter-Fraternity Council president, January 9, 1970; Hazel R. of Eldon, Missouri, to Judge William Billings, September 29, 1970, Student Unrest papers.

and intensity. In 1971, MSA called for a May 5 moratorium in memory of the students killed at Kent State and Jackson State. The interim chancellor, Herbert Schooling, announced that classes had to meet. The Student Mobilization Committee called on students to boycott classes and march to commemorate those who had died. The march, which began with a prayer service, ended with the renaming of McAlester Park as Peace Park, as described by Dan Viets. More than fifteen hundred people participated in the march. The following year, a much smaller group of students disrupted an ROTC review on Francis Quadrangle. Photos of the protesters in the university archives have notes on the back about the participants, many of whom are labeled "YMCA frequenter." It was the National Student YMCA that sponsored the first Women's Liberation Conference held in Columbia, in February 1970. The previous year, an article in the *Free Press Underground* had raised issues of women's rights in the name of SPECTRE: Sisters to Promote the Ends of Cultural Terrorism, Revolution, Emancipation.[20]

Another issue that began in the early seventies and dragged on for most of the decade, again due to the university's intransigence, was the recognition of a student gay rights group. The university finally lost the case in 1977 when an appeals court overturned a district court decision in favor of the curators. The 8th U.S. Circuit Court of Appeals cited a 1972 Supreme Court decision that said a college could not restrict the free speech or association of an organization simply because it found the group's views abhorrent. In 1978 the Supreme Court refused the board of curators' request that it hear the case.

What stands out is not only the hard-line stance of the administration at MU and the strong opposition to the student movement on the part of the public and some of the other students. These are unsurprising, given the conservative climate in towns such as Columbia. More interesting is the fact of the movement itself, the odd mixture of issues, the intensity of protests not only about the war but also about free speech and intervisitation rights, the strange coalitions that formed around these issues, and the consciousness of activists that their efforts had to be broad-based if they were going

20. "Not Exactly Penis Envy," *Free Press Underground*, February 1969, p. 5, Ellinger Collection, folder 213.

to be effective. Even the underground press tried to reach a wide audience, interpreting "the movement" broadly to include "cultural as well as political radicalism" and running a regular column by "an unorthodox but unrepentant Rightist." The editor of the *Free Press* wrote, "We see ourselves primarily as troublemakers, not bearers of the Word." As politicized as some activists were in Columbia, it is difficult to imagine them being able to relate to, for example, Bernardine Dohrn writing in *New Left Notes*, "No class today, no ruling class tomorrow!"[21] The aim was not communism per se, but a more authentic life, a more free university, and a more peaceful and just America.

University of Kansas

There was an unusual attraction to Lawrence. People came here and found it very fertile ground to disrupt.

—Frank Burge, director, Kansas Union

The University of Kansas differs in some ways from MU and SIU. Despite its open admissions policy, the university sees itself as a more elite institution, sort of a Harvard of the Midwest, and its experience in the sixties is comparable to such campuses. In contrast to SIU and MU, for example, KU had a larger number of political groups and Lawrence had a longer history of activism. Among the groups active in the early sixties were the Civil Rights Council, the Student Peace Union, the Congress of Racial Equality, the Lawrence League for the Practice of Democracy, and, in the mid to late sixties, Students for a Democratic Society, Student Voice, and the Student Mobilization Committee. There was a lot of interaction between campus and community activists. Lawrence is nearer to a large city than either Columbia or Carbondale, so Wayne Sailor, for instance,

---

21. *Free Press Underground*, October 1967, p. 2, Ellinger Collection, folder 214; *New Left Notes*, October 18, 1968, Ellinger Collection, folder 215. The *Free Press* added *Underground* to its name in 1967 "because we think it implies resistance—to hypocritical officialdom, to empty politics, to deadening styles of living" (Gordon Burnside, "The New Free Press," *Free Press Underground*, October 1967, p. 2, Ellinger Collection, folder 214).

developed ties to the Black Panthers in Kansas City. Black power was supported not only by SDS types, but also by the "freaks" in Lawrence. The presence of street people was a big issue in the summer of 1970, when Lawrence experienced an intense period of violence that resulted in the deaths of two people. When the President's Commission on Campus Unrest sent an investigative team to Lawrence, many people informed them that the street people were the real source of trouble.

The town of Lawrence, located just off Interstate 70 about thirty miles from Kansas City, was established by abolitionists in 1854, and the University of Kansas opened there in 1866. The first black students were accepted in 1870, but despite the abolitionist origins of the town, segregation and discrimination persisted on campus and in the community. James Michener's description of Kent State in the post–World War II growth years fits KU as well.[22] Football and parking were big issues, soon to be overtaken by concerns with civil rights, gaining students a greater voice in decisions about academic and social issues, and the war in Vietnam.

In contrast to the experience of SIU and MU activists, who felt their activities were a strictly local affair, activists at KU clearly felt more of a connection to national organizations, and people from larger groups did come through, SDS organizers and Weathermen among them. The core of activists at KU was serious enough that some expressed impatience with focusing on such issues as dorm hours, which seemed somewhat frivolous.[23] Finally, there was a thriving counterculture and drug trade, symbolized by the Kaw Valley Hemp Pickers, a "loosely unified band of hippies, outlaws and freaks" who saw themselves as "the Midwestern partisans of the counterculture struggle against mediocrity, conformity and war."[24]

At the same time, in many ways KU was still rather typical of large midwestern state universities, where stories about protest coincided

22. James A. Michener, *Kent State: What Happened and Why.*
23. The November 30, 1965, newsletter of the Student Peace Union said, "So here is our responsible student movement—preparing to protest closing hours while over a thousand Americans and God knows how many Vietnamese have been and are being killed in Southeast Asia" (Student Peace Union Papers, Spencer Research Library, University of Kansas, Lawrence).
24. David Ohle, Roger Martin, and Susan Brooseau, eds., *Cows Are Freaky When They Look at You: An Oral History of the Kaw Valley Hemp Pickers,* back cover.

with those about panty raids and where the local SDS chapters were somewhat anarchistic. There was a significant overlap between the politicos and the cultural radicals, and the counterculture had a long enough reach that fraternity members, student body presidents, and even some ROTC cadets argued with their parents about the way they dressed or the length of their hair and lived in communal houses with members of the opposite sex. There was a sense of humor and creativity about the sorts of actions people took, even in protesting serious issues of war and university ties to the military. For instance, in 1967 SDS members led a protest against Marine recruiters at which they shot rose petals out of a tank built of old peace posters, an incident that one activist said demonstrated the strength of "flower power."[25] There is levity in Wayne Sailor's accounts of breaking up a police meeting and disrupting the ROTC review. Former KU activists also express a sense of admiration for activists on the coasts; their acknowledgment of how well-read, intelligent, articulate, and committed such activists were implies that they did in fact see a difference between Berkeley and Lawrence. KU is like SIU and MU, moreover, in terms of the issues that captured students' imaginations. The issue of student participation was central to the movement there. Beyond the usual in loco parentis concerns, there was a concerted and successful effort to gain a stronger, more representative voice for students in decisions about university policies that affected their daily lives.

Also similar to other midwestern institutions was the emphasis on dialogue, and activists organized many events with the intention of presenting more than one side of an issue. The same sorts of coalitions were common, with SDS, YAF, and other groups with a variety of viewpoints often getting together to work on a particular issue. The strong nonviolent tendencies of many students were expressed often, which perhaps encouraged administrators and townspeople to believe that "outside agitators" were responsible when there was violent turmoil on campus and in the community. But of course the conflicts were not due primarily to outside agitators; as in thousands of other communities across the country, they were a result of generational conflicts expressed in local arenas around local

25. "SDS Bombards Marines," *University Daily Kansan* (hereafter cited as *UDK*), December 14, 1967.

issues. At KU, as elsewhere, administrators found themselves caught between student demands on the one hand and the board of regents and the taxpayers on the other.

In the early sixties, the activist tradition in Lawrence took the shape of protest against discrimination in the community, particularly in housing and in the lack of an integrated municipal swimming pool. There were also several on-campus, religious-based, multi-issue organizations, but these drew less attention than SDS, mainly because of the latter's national reputation. The Lawrence SDS chapter took pains to distinguish itself from the national organization on occasion, but this had little effect on those who were hostile to it. Before SDS was organized—it was a presence on campus by the fall of 1965—the Student Peace Union had been active, sponsoring a regular antiwar vigil and protesting the presence of ROTC on campus.

In 1965 there was already a fair amount of political activity on campus. The Civil Rights Council held a sit-in at the chancellor's office to protest the university's tacit approval of discrimination in campus housing, fraternities, and sororities. Challenges to in loco parentis were under way, a struggle increasingly framed in terms of rights and responsibilities.[26] The Student Peace Union sponsored antiwar activities, protests that one observer wrote expressed "the real voice of Kansas." An editorial in the *University Daily Kansan*, the student newspaper, commented on the seriousness of the "spring of discontent," while a Topeka publisher charged that one of the most active Communist cells in the United States was at KU.[27]

By the next school year, the first attempt at establishing a free university had begun. Women protested dress codes and dorm closing hours, restrictions that were loosened considerably over the next few years. SDS sponsored a "Vietnam speakout" to protest the presence of Marine recruiters on campus. The organization enhanced its credibility by getting involved in what many students saw as a far more pressing issue on campus: keeping the library open at night

26. One example among many is a 1968 leaflet titled "The Non-Existent Majority" that states, "OUR RESPONSIBILITIES ARE THOSE OF ADULTS, IT IS ABOUT TIME OUR RIGHTS ARE TOO!" (Student Unrest papers).

27. Letter to the editor, *UDK*, March 30, 1965, p. 2; "Spring of Our Discontent," *UDK*, April 30, 1965, p. 2; "Publisher Claims Reds on Campus," *UDK*, September 27, 1965, p. 1.

and on Sundays. When the administration announced cutbacks in library hours, SDS took up the cause and, while other groups were still talking, took action to get the hours restored. But the top story of 1966–1967, according to the *University Daily Kansan*, was the continuing protest against the Vietnam War. Among other issues, university compliance with the draft concerned many students.[28]

After the 1968 presidential election, students marched in a "Funeral for the Democratic Process," part of a two-day "Vietnam Days" protest.[29] That spring the issue was generalized to university relations with the military. Students abandoned plans for a sit-in and instead organized a public forum at which faculty, students, and university officials could discuss military recruiters, military research projects, ROTC, and university cooperation with the draft laws. "We shouldn't picket and then say, 'Let's talk.' We talk, and then if we have something to protest, we protest," one student was quoted as saying.[30] At the dialogue that took place a few weeks later, the acting provost handed students "something to protest" when he told them they were transients who had no voting voice in university decisions. When, a few months later, some members of Student Voice walked out of a campus convocation to protest university relations with the military, they stirred up a lot of controversy within the student rights movement.[31] Nevertheless, the question of the role of students in decision-making came to a head, and students gained an important voice with the creation of a faculty-student committee. "This is a very radical thing—something which even Berkeley and Columbia don't have," said Joe Goering, student body vice president, about the student voice in university affairs.[32] People's Voice broadened the struggle to encompass issues that went beyond student rights, again with an explicit commitment to nonviolence. Other breakthroughs that year included the first "Negro" pledg-

28. "KU 1967: It Was a Very _____ Year," *UDK*, December 14, 1967, p. 1.

29. "Students Stage Death March," *UDK*, November 6, 1968, p. 1.

30. "Sit-in, Planned for Today, Canceled," *UDK*, April 2, 1968, p. 4. A leaflet titled "April 2: For a Decent School" had called for a sit-in to demand the banning of all military recruiters and military research projects from campus, abolition of the ROTC program, and noncooperation with the draft (Student Unrest papers, 1968).

31. "KU Military Debated," *UDK*, April 24, 1968, p. 1; "Convocation Walkout Splits Peoples Voice," *UDK*, September 18, 1968, p. 1.

32. "'Voice' Explains Position," *UDK*, July 5, 1968, p. 1.

ing a white fraternity and recognition of the Black Student Union, an event that filled Chancellor Wescoe with trepidation. In his report to the regents on student unrest, he said, "Our black students are likely to become more militant."[33]

The school year ended with a be-in on campus, the culmination of Delight Days, a weeklong celebration of spring inspired by the Yippies.[34] In May, the *Lawrence Daily Journal-World* commended students and administrators for working together on student rights while "Columbia and Northwestern" were going through "sit-ins, disruptions of important schedules and even violence."[35] But the *Journal-World's* sentiments primarily reflected wishful thinking, for the disruptions at KU were about to begin in earnest.

In 1969, while the student newspaper was still reporting on panty raids, there was a firebombing in the military science building. That same year, a graduate student who challenged the need for campus police to carry guns, "especially at a quiet midwestern campus, not a Berkeley or Columbia," received the support of student government but not the university administration. Instead, the chancellor issued a ruling that prohibited persons not authorized by the "chancellor or his designated representative" from carrying firearms on campus; violation of the rule would result in immediate dismissal from the university. The ruling came after two students asked permission to carry firearms for protection from "campus police pigs." The two were members of the First Artaud Romantic Tautological Society (FARTS), a group whose "revolutionary theater" got people's attention but irritated some potential allies on the Left.[36] Meanwhile, the free university achieved some success, increasing its own

33. In his report, Wescoe singled out Leonard Harrison, leader of the newly formed Black Student Union, as "the leading Black voice in the community and the University," and ended with these remarks: "The situation must be handled exceedingly carefully for Mr. Harrison can manage both the Black students in the University as well as the young Blacks in Lawrence. Literally he has the power to burn the two communities" (W. Clarke Wescoe to board of regents, May 13, 1968, Student Protest Files, 1969).

34. "Student Be-in Is a Success," *UDK*, April 29, 1968, p. 4.

35. A copy of the *Journal-World* editorial is in the Student Protest Files, 1967–1968.

36. "ASC [All-Student Council] Defeats Gun Bill," *UDK*, February 5, 1969, p. 1; "'No Pistol-packing Students—Please,'" *UDK*, February 10, 1969, p. 1; "Rehorn Rebukes Student Group," *UDK*, February 6, 1969, p. 1 (Rev. Thomas Rehorn was the director of the Wesley Foundation at KU).

course offerings as well as those of the College of Liberal Arts and Sciences. (The first black history course was offered that year.) The University Christian Movement offered a course on institutional racism that culminated in a sit-in at the Holiday Inn Restaurant to protest its "racist management." The fall moratorium was observed in earnest, with several faculty members scheduling open classes or participating in teach-ins and three thousand people marching against the Vietnam War.[37]

The most controversial event in 1969 was the disruption of the chancellor's review of ROTC in the spring, which led to its cancellation. While two thousand students signed petitions denouncing the protesters, the student senate resisted pressure to impeach its vice president for her participation in the event, defeated a resolution to reprimand the protesters, and asked outside law enforcement to stay out of university affairs. The controversy was heightened when the administration suspended thirty-three of the seventy-one students charged with disruption of the review, put on probation or postponed graduation for several others, and released the names of fifty students who had public hearings.[38]

An editorial in the student paper sought to refute the "alarmists" who were convinced by the disruption of the ROTC review that "the University of Kansas is a seething hotbed of incipient radicals bent on destroying the institution which harbors them." The writer, arguing that KU students were not radicals or revolutionaries, pleaded:

> We only ask for an education that will equip us to handle your world of war, urban blight, pollution, mechanization, mobility and decaying values.
> We can escape the burning, if we want to, for we don't want to see our lovely Hill racked by bombs.
> We don't want to be tear-gassed or imprisoned. We don't want the police to invade our quiet sanctuary of learning.
> To escape the burning, however, the Kansas Board of Regents on their thrones must be willing to support changes instead of merely lashing out at ROTC demonstrators.

37. "Group Pickets Inn," *UDK*, March 17, 1969, p. 1; "Colleges Observe Moratorium," *UDK*, October 15, 1969, p. 1.

38. "'Peace' Demonstration," *UDK*, May 12, 1969, p. 1; "Unrest Nothing New," *UDK*, October 2, 1969, p. 16.

If changes did not take place, funded by the legislature and supported by students and faculty, the writer said she would not be surprised if KU were "besieged by frustrated students, led by one of KU's few 'radicals.' Their fire will be well-fueled."[39]

Not surprisingly, the spring of 1970 was a tense time. A short-lived student strike took place when the board of regents delayed the promotion of two radical professors. (Both promotions eventually were granted.) The Black Student Union was active, its chair urging black students and community members to arm themselves in self-defense. Perhaps the most shocking event that spring was the burning of the student union on April 20. One faculty member said: "The Union fire touched me the most. It was sort of the high point of unrest. I think it touched more people here than did Kent State." To the dismay and outrage of Chancellor Laurence Chalmers, Vice President Spiro Agnew publicly blamed the million-dollar fire on student agitators.[40]

The university stayed open after the killings at Kent State, as students supported Chalmers's institution of the so-called Rhode Island Plan, which gave students a choice about whether to continue attending classes and whether to take their finals or not; they would still receive grades for work completed. While the compromise plan was criticized heavily by the board of regents and the public, who seemed to feel the chancellor had given in to antiwar radicals, students thought he had done the right thing, managing to prevent violence and keeping the university open. Supporters gave out bumper stickers and badges saying "Kansas Needs Laurence" and circulated petitions that read, "We feel that Chancellor Chalmers, especially in his handlings [sic] of the situations arising on the campus during Spring, 1970 semester, has helped to PREVENT the University of Kansas from becoming 'another Berkeley.' "[41] Despite the show of support from students, Chalmers was forced out soon after these events.

39. Joanna Wiebe, "Fuel for the Fire," *UDK*, September 16, 1969, p. 4.

40. Charles Chowins, assistant professor of journalism, quoted in the 1980 University of Kansas yearbook, *Jayhawker*, p. 81; "Chalmers Refutes Agnew's Speech," *UDK*, May 1, 1970, p. 1. See also "Union Burns," *UDK*, April 21, 1970, p. 1.

41. "Bumper Stickers Boost Chalmers," *UDK*, September 2, 1970, p. 6. See also "Thousands Back Chalmers," *UDK*, May 11, 1970, p. 1.

Two people were killed by the police in Lawrence that summer, one a young black man shot in an alley, the other a white KU freshman who was shot outside a bar. Lawrence had become a battleground by this point, with protests taking place not only on campus but also in the community. At Lawrence High School a firebombing and student strike was followed by a group of black students locking themselves in the office to call attention to their demands, which ranged from having a black cheerleader to hiring more black teachers. In the wake of a series of fires and firebombings in town, state police and National Guard troops were called in and the governor ordered a dusk-to-dawn curfew.[42]

The President's Commission on Campus Unrest sent an investigating team to Lawrence, but chose not to include the team's findings as part of its report. According to Bill Moyers, black people refused to talk to the investigators, who therefore missed a significant part of the story. While some observers thought the revolution had come to Lawrence in the spring of 1970, others held fast to their nonviolent views. At commencement that year, student body president David Awbrey offered his definition of revolution: "I do not conceive of our revolution as typified by throwing rocks at tanks. That is not revolution; that is power madness. I do not envision our revolution being founded on guns or bombs, but on ideas and concepts of what it is to be alive."[43]

In the early seventies, activism of all sorts scaled down at KU, but antiwar protests did not disappear. For instance, a coalition of antiwar groups backed by the student senate asked the chancellor's permission to hold a peaceful demonstration at the Kansas Relays in the spring of 1972. At the same time, other issues came to the forefront. A group of women who became known as the February Sisters took over a building in 1972, a unique event described by Caroljean Brune. This protest led to many changes on campus such

42. See "Summer Brought Tragedy to KU," *UDK*, August 27, 1970, p. 1, and "KBI's [Kansas Bureau of Investigation] Report on Disturbances," *UDK*, August 27, 1970, p. 13. For chronological accounts of the events of April and May 1970, see "Bringing It All Back Home," *Jayhawker*, Spring 1970, and "Doin' It in the Road" in the underground newspaper *Vortex*, 1970, p. 5, Kansas Collection, Spencer Research Library, University of Kansas, Lawrence.

43. Bill Moyers, *Listening to America: A Traveler Rediscovers His Country*, 121; Gus diZerega, "Others on Issues," *UDK*, April 30, 1970, p. 4; David Awbrey, "Revolution without Much Time at All," *Jayhawker*, Commencement 1970.

as university funding of a child care center, the hiring of more female administrators, and development of a women's studies program. The Gay Liberation Front sought recognition, and, as at MU, its quest to become a recognized student organization was a lengthy one.[44]

Wayne Sailor suggests that students currently at KU are aware of the activist tradition and the events of the sixties. If that is the case, Kansas is different from Missouri or SIU, where the subject of student protest is for the most part studiously avoided and where its history is just beginning to come to light.

Southern Illinois University

"When writers for *KA* are harassed, when the act of driving a car is grounds for expulsion, when a student's housing must be approved before he may register for classes, then one begins to realize, and resent, his position within the University 'community'—a community unlike any other in this nation."

  —David A. Wilson, quoted in "Administrators Do Not Understand the Sources of Student Unrest," *KA*, May 3, 1967.

"I think it's important to note that there were no red diaper babies at SIU, or if there were I never knew them."

  —Mike Harty, former SDS chair

In many ways Carbondale is an unlikely place for a major university. Located on the boundary line where the prosperous farmland that makes up most of Illinois gives way to rugged and forested hills, the area around Carbondale and southward differs from the rest of the state both culturally and economically. The economy of Southern Illinois historically has been based on mining, and the region is marked by numerous small towns and a history of violent labor struggles and frequent depressions. Chicago is three hundred

44. "War Protesters Plan Peaceful Relays Rally," *UDK*, April 21, 1972, p. 1; "Sisters' Terms Include Day Care," *UDK*, February 7, 1972, p. 1; "KU Year Marked by Demands," *UDK*, May 9, 1972, p. 1.

miles away from "downstate" Southern Illinois, and the closest city to Carbondale is St. Louis, more than a hundred miles away. The late novelist and SIU professor John Gardner wrote that "nobody arrives at and nobody escapes from Southern Illinois University at Carbondale by accident."[45]

Southern Illinois University began as a normal school in the 1860s, with two African American students in its first graduating class—a point of honor for the institution, which prides itself on the number of black students it graduates. (For years SIU has been in the top ten among predominantly white institutions in its numbers of African American graduates.) The small teachers' college was transformed into a major multiversity between the end of World War II and 1970, mainly due to the efforts of its visionary president, Delyte W. Morris.[46] Morris initiated a massive building campaign, but more importantly, under his leadership the university became a pioneer in several fields, from handicap accessibility to the first U.S. program in ecology. His sense of mission included a deep commitment to using the university to combat the region's poverty and keeping costs and admission standards low enough to ensure accessibility to the area's population. The sense of openness and experimentation extended to the hiring of professors who had been blacklisted elsewhere in the fifties and support for students who engaged in civil rights activities.

At the same time, Morris was a paternalistic ruler whose leadership style became increasingly untenable in the sixties. As Robert Harper explains, Morris "loved being considered a father figure by them [students]. This concern for students and desire to support their interests in a paternalistic way was a major obstacle to his understanding of the militant demands for student rights in the late sixties. He felt betrayed by those he had always strongly supported."[47] SIU students faced the problem then, as they still do, of

45. John Gardner, "Southern Illinois University: 'We Teach and Study and Raise All the Hell We Can,' " *Change*, June 1973, p. 43. For stories of the bitter labor wars in the region, see Paul M. Angle, *Bloody Williamson: A Chapter in American Lawlessness.*

46. See Robert A. Harper, *The University that Shouldn't Have Happened, But Did! Southern Illinois University during the Morris Years, 1948–1970,* and Betty Mitchell, *Delyte Morris of SIU.*

47. Harper, *University that Shouldn't Have Happened,* 38.

being part of a large university in a small town in the middle of nowhere with limited sources of entertainment. With the rapid increase in the student population in the sixties, SIU developed a reputation as a party school, which often placed students in opposition to university and city administrators. The first major confrontation occurred during finals week in June 1966 and entered local lore as "the Moo and Cackle riots," so named because much of the action took place in the parking lot of Carbondale's first fast food restaurant, the Moo and Cackle. The police broke up a late-night water fight and a panty raid on the following night using excessive force, according to the students involved. On the third night the students returned, spreading into downtown Carbondale. State police dressed in riot gear joined local and campus cops, firing tear gas into the crowd as students built a bonfire in the street, threw rocks at police cars, and chanted, "Cops eat shit." When police arrested thirteen students, the crowd marched to the police station and staged a sit-in on Main Street. On the fourth night, police arrested twenty-three more rioters and President Morris expelled all the arrested students, the first mass expulsion in SIU's history.[48]

The Moo and Cackle riots were merely the first in Carbondale's long history of impromptu street demonstrations that frequently turned into clashes with the police. While the origins of the event were apolitical, overreaction by the police created resentment on the part of students and that then became the issue. Students arguing "We have a right to be out here" began imitating tactics from the civil rights movement and engaging in a mass sit-in, yet the overall atmosphere was not exactly nonviolent.[49]

Even as the party culture developed, it became transformed by the counterculture. Carbondale became known as a place to score drugs, although its geographical isolation meant it would never get the sort of traffic that went through Lawrence on I-70. The countercultural turn meant not only a shift from beer drinking to pot smoking,

48. H. B. Koplowitz, *Carbondale after Dark and Other Stories*, 14–15; "Students Romp through Streets until 3 a.m.," *Southern Illinoisan*, June 7, 1966, p. 1; Richard Carter, "Police Stop New Student Uproar," *Southern Illinoisan*, June 8, 1966, p. 1; D. G. Schumaker, "SIU Expels Students Arrested during Student Riot," *Southern Illinoisan*, June 9, 1966, p. 1; author interview with Ray Lenzi, July 15, 1997.
49. Ben Gelman, "Few Riot, Many Cheer," *Southern Illinoisan*, June 9, 1966, p. 3.

but also a broader exploration of alternative ideas and lifestyles, all of which created a strong sense of community. Jim Hanson, a graduate student at SIU in the late sixties, remembers: "There was a lot of socializing in those days. Most of the houses around Carbondale, you didn't even knock on the door, you just walked in. People laid down real cool, 'Hey, man.' . . . It was a neat time, especially this kind of public part of living in Carbondale."[50]

The term *student rights* was used at SIU as early as 1960. That year, Bill Morin ran for student body president pledging to "stand up for student rights for everything from segregation to cars." Morin had no problem with students demonstrating to express their feelings—which they did on the issue of having automobiles—as long as there was no violence or mob action.[51] But it was not until 1965 that student rights became a significant movement on campus. That spring, the Rational Action Movement (RAM) appeared on the scene with a petition drive and mass rally focused on such issues as student control of the student center and the administration's censorship of the editorial page of the student newspaper, the *Daily Egyptian*. One RAM supporter was quoted as saying the movement "is not going to be another Berkeley." Drawing the support of a broad cross section of students, RAM's coordinating committee included representatives from the Student Peace Union, Young Republicans, and Young Americans for Freedom. Out of this activity grew the Action Party, a student party that fought for student rights issues for the rest of the decade. Morris was not sympathetic to such developments; digging in his heels, he refused to abolish women's dorm hours and in 1967 banned *KA*, a student-edited insert in the campus newspaper, after it published an anonymous article encouraging students to violate dorm visitation rules.[52] Morris also temporarily refused to allow *KA*'s editors to reenroll.

The SDS chapter at SIU, a small part of the overall student movement, grew out of the Student Nonviolent Freedom Committee (a

50. Hanson interview.

51. *Daily Egyptian*, May 6, 1960, p. 1.

52. Frank Messersmith, "Student Protest Group Distributing Petitions," *Daily Egyptian*, May 1, 1965, p. 1; Ric Cox, "Dissatisfactions Stirred Rational Action Move," *Daily Egyptian*, May 1, 1965, p. 1; Koplowitz, *Carbondale after Dark*, 16. See also "Students at SIU Seek Policy Voice," *St. Louis Globe-Democrat*, May 4, 1965.

local chapter of SNCC), which picketed local businesses that practiced discrimination.[53] In 1965, a small group of students who were active in the local civil rights movement formed the Socialist Discussion Club, which soon evolved into a chapter of Students for a Democratic Society. Mike Harty, who was the first chair, describes the founding of the chapter, which became a recognized student organization increasingly focused on protesting the war: "One of us got a hold of the Port Huron Statement. We all read it, we all pretty much agreed with it and felt, well, hell, here's something we can affiliate with and still have fun. . . . The irony was that from '65 through '68, SDS was in technical terms quite conservative. We were sort of serious, we weren't interested in game playing, we weren't interested in drugs."[54]

The local SDS chapter was completely autonomous from the national office. Harty says, "We tried to have contact, but nobody ever wrote back. Seriously." Jim Hanson echoes Harty: "It seemed a very local affair. . . . I didn't see any coordinated national leadership. . . . As far as national SDS people coming in [and] holding rap conferences with us—'Here's what we're doing here, what are you guys doing here? We'll assist you, we'll send you money, we'll help you get out posters, we'll do this, we'll do that at Carbondale, we'll help you if you'll help us'—I never heard [of or] attended a meeting like that. It was all local insofar as I knew."[55]

Organizations such as SDS served as the left wing of the student rights movement, viewing in loco parentis issues as valuable for educating students about their lack of power. Yet despite the efforts of SDS to pull the student rights movement leftward, RAM continued to represent a broad cross section of students for several years. It was not until the 1967–1968 school year that student rights, counterculture, and New Left concerns (especially about the Vietnam War) began to come together, especially under the leadership of student government president Ray Lenzi. Lenzi had been elected with Richard Karr, his conservative and prowar fraternity brother, on a straight student rights platform of the Action Party. The two cooperated on student rights issues, publishing an open letter in the

53. Koplowitz, *Carbondale after Dark*, 12, 14.
54. Author interview with Michael Harty, November 24, 1997.
55. Ibid; Hanson interview.

campus paper in April 1968 that called on students to engage in mass civil disobedience by ignoring university rules and determining their own dorm hours. By this time Lenzi also had become a featured speaker at the growing number of antiwar demonstrations. In a self-conscious effort to pull together the various strains of the student movement, he introduced a bill in the student senate titled "Legalization of Marijuana: Pot Is Groovy." Recognizing that many students were becoming politicized through their participation in the party culture, Lenzi called on SIU police to "take the most relaxed attitude toward enforcement" of the marijuana laws.[56]

In May 1968, a bomb caused $50,000 worth of damage to the Agriculture Building, which presumably was targeted because of its use by ROTC. After the bombing, the administration canceled a scheduled speech by national black power leader Stokely Carmichael. In response, two hundred students, most of them African American, entered the president's office to carry out a peaceful protest. When the actions of security officers led to a scuffle, eight students were arrested. The next day, President Morris announced: "Some are in jail. Some are in the hospital. And all are expelled." Lenzi and other student leaders were not the only ones to speak out against Morris after this incident; he was also criticized by the press (locally and in St. Louis), the Inter-Greek Council, the teaching assistants on campus, and the local chapter of the AAUP.[57]

In June 1969 the Old Main building burned to the ground. Old Main was the campus's most recognizable landmark, and while to this day no one really knows the cause of the fire, at the time it was blamed on antiwar radicals.[58] Despite such events, it was student rights issues that brought together and provided a focus for the different strains of the student movement in the late sixties. Sometimes

56. Ray Lenzi and Richard Karr, "Senate Writes Students," *Daily Egyptian,* April 5, 1968, pp. 1, 9; "Senate to Consider Marijuana Bill," *Daily Egyptian,* April 30, 1968, p. 2; Lenzi interview.

57. Harper, *University that Shouldn't Have Happened,* 235.

58. Ibid, 259. Harper points out that despite popular mythology, "the cause of the Old Main fire has never been determined. The building was over seventy-five years old, had a wooden frame and somewhat suspect electrical wiring. It was an insurance risk, and except for its historic significance and the shortage of classroom space on campus, might have already been torn down." See also Mitchell, *Delyte Morris,* 168–69, and Koplowitz, *Carbondale after Dark,* 19–20.

this happened in odd ways. When three hundred women staged an after-hours walkout from their dorm in April 1969, chanting "Hour power" and "We shall overcome," they were greeted by the old-fashioned party culture in the form of a crowd of men chanting, "We want pants!"[59]

A more serious disturbance took place in late February 1970, when a thousand students engaged in a campaign of civil disobedience and the dean of students responded by suspending six leaders of student government, including Dwight Campbell, SIU's first African American student body president. Student leaders reacted by calling for a boycott of classes, and Campbell proclaimed, "Students are niggers and it's time to break the chains."[60] While these events appear on the surface to be typical of the student movement of the late sixties and early seventies, in fact they reveal some of the movement's peculiarities in the Midwest. In this case, a black leader defined himself as a "nigger" not because he was African American but because he was a student, and the issue was not black power or the war in Vietnam, but rather the hours in which men and women could study together in women's dorms.

Campbell and his running mate, Richard Wallace, who was white, had won a landslide election based on a twelve-point Unity Party platform, most of which focused on student rights. The other points included hiring more black faculty and increasing the university's involvement in Carbondale's poorest neighborhoods.[61] Significantly, no mention was made of the war. But the issue could not be avoided for long, especially because by that time U.S. policies in Vietnam had an immediate and tangible symbol on campus. In the spring of 1969, President Morris and the board of trustees approved the creation of the Center for Vietnamese Studies and Programs. Widely believed to be a CIA front, the Center was financed by the

59. Dan Van Atta, "300 Coeds Stage 'Walkout' in Protest of Women's Hours," *Daily Egyptian,* April 16, 1969, p. 2. One female observer wrote that "the boys only made fools of themselves" (Bandit [pseud.], "'Hour Power!' . . . and 'Pants,'" *Big Muddy Gazette,* April 26, 2969, p. 12).

60. Quoted in Bob Carr, "Slaves No More," *Daily Egyptian,* February 27, 1970, p. 4. It is likely that Campbell was alluding to Jerry Farber's classic 1965 New Left essay "The Student as Nigger," which was widely reprinted after its first appearance in the *Los Angeles Free Press.*

61. Norris Jones, "Dwight Campbell's Idea—'Unity Is Strength,'" *Daily Egyptian,* April 11, 1969, p. 12.

Agency for International Development and had a five-year contract to study ways to reconstruct Vietnam after the war. Wesley Fishel, who had been part of a similar program at Michigan State—which was well known because of antiwar activist Robert Scheer's 1966 expose of its CIA connections in *Ramparts* magazine—was appointed as the Center's distinguished visiting professor.[62]

Even before the contract was signed, SDS denounced the Vietnamese Studies Center in the local underground paper *Big Muddy Gazette* as an example of American imperialism. A front-page drawing of a nude Delyte Morris appeared beside text calling the Center's work a "program to administer the colony after a Pentagon victory" and one of the "insane acts of a dying class." University officials immediately withdrew the permit allowing the *Gazette* to be sold on campus. This in turn caused an uproar as many people, even some who did not agree with the paper's politics, spoke out in defense of its free speech rights. As a result, university administrators were on the defensive in regard to the Center.[63]

In late January 1970, violence broke out in anti-Center demonstrations over two days that ended with fifteen arrests. Richard Wallace denounced "the pig power structure" and suggested that "the brutal and reprehensible tactics used by police may be the beginning of a total police state at SIU." Students created a coalition to "Off Viet Studies," and protesters entered a board of trustees meeting in February to demand the Center's removal from campus. Echoing Malcolm X, Wallace told the board, "If we're beaten again, we'll have to resort to self-defense in any form necessary." That night, demonstrators engaged police in a series of disturbances that

62. Harper, *University that Shouldn't Have Happened*, 256–59, 279–86; *Center for Vietnamese Studies and Programs Newsletter*, September 15, 1969, Tom Busch Papers, box 3, Special Collections, Morris Library, Southern Illinois University. For a history of the development of an opposition movement at SIU focusing on the Vietnamese Studies Center, see Douglas Allen, "Universities and the Vietnam War: A Case Study of a Successful Struggle," *Bulletin of Concerned Asian Scholars* 8:4 (October–December 1976), 2–16. On the Michigan State program, see Robert Scheer, "The University on the Make," *Ramparts,* April 1966, pp. 11–22; Stanley K. Sheinbaum, "The Michigan State–CIA Experience in Vietnam," *Bulletin of Concerned Asian Scholars* 3:1 (Spring 1971), 71–75.

63. Dan Van Atta, "Big Muddy Gazette Loses Permit to Sell on Campus," *Daily Egyptian,* April 11, 1969, p. 1. The *Daily Egyptian* criticized the *Gazette* in a cartoon, while running an editorial in its defense on the same page (*Daily Egyptian,* April 16, 1969, p. 4).

resulted in two arrests and $1,500 worth of damage to university buildings and Carbondale stores.[64] Four days later, Campbell and Wallace were suspended for their participation in the protest over dorm hours.

Despite the fact that Vietnam resonated personally with so many students, were it not for the Center for Vietnamese Studies the war might have remained a peripheral issue at SIU, at least until May 1970. On May 1, the day after President Nixon's announcement of the U.S. invasion of Cambodia, a small crowd gathered just off campus and started a fire in the street. The police arrested eight people. That night, someone threw a firebomb into the Vietnam Studies Center.[65]

Carbondale's "Seven Days in May," as the events following the May 4 killings at Kent State came to be known, began the night of the 4th when the student government held an emergency meeting and voted unanimously to join a national student strike. Over the next several days, two to three thousand people attended rallies in front of the library, crowds marched across campus and through the downtown area, and a group of students occupied Wheeler Hall, where the Air Force ROTC offices were located, breaking windows and sitting in until they were forcibly removed by the police. The sheriff called in the National Guard; the 650 troops who were in Carbondale by May 6 would grow to 1,200 over the next several days.[66]

On May 7 two thousand people rallied in front of the library, then marched into town and sat down at the major intersection, Main and Illinois. City and university officials told the "low-key, somewhat festive but benign" crowd that it could remain. When some seventy-five people attempted to block the nearby railroad tracks,

64. "Campus Melee Evokes Varying Reactions," *Daily Egyptian*, January 31, 1970, p. 9.

65. "Eight Demonstrators Arrested," *Daily Egyptian*, May 5, 1970, p. 1.

66. Koplowitz, *Carbondale after Dark*, 52–63, and Harper, *University that Shouldn't Have Happened*, 290–96. Descriptions of the events of May 1970 include a detailed account of the student strike and riots, "Chronology of Events Related to Closing of Southern Illinois University," prepared by Max Turner, Government Department, for the President's Office, with comments by Roy Miller, Government Department (Busch Papers, box 2). For a brief account by a participant, see Alex Paull, "The Nights of Spring: 1970 Remembered," *Carbondale Southern Observer*, May 14, 1982, pp. 5–6.

National Guardsmen and state police decided to move the entire crowd and began firing tear gas into the area. As police forcibly removed people, panic ensued, and many protesters responded by throwing bricks and smashing windows. By the end of the night, there were seventy-nine arrests and fifty-nine injuries, and $100,000 worth of damage had been done to seventy-eight businesses. The mayor declared a state of civil emergency and a sundown-to-sunrise curfew. Violent confrontations continued for several days and the university was finally shut down, a decision supported by a referendum in which students voted decisively in favor of closing the school.[67]

Many of the participants recall these events as being highly spontaneous. Jim Hanson, who was president of the graduate student council that year and one of the speakers at the May 6 rally, says, "Not to say we weren't happy to jump in front of a crowd [and] tell them what we wanted them to hear, but it was all very short-term planning, like hours prior to organizing something." Douglas Allen, a philosophy professor who was later denied tenure at SIU because of his leadership in the movement opposing the Vietnamese Studies Center, says he was "right in the middle of things" and was also struck by the spontaneity of events, explaining that "things really escalated and it got to the point that it couldn't be controlled."[68]

While the crucible of events culminating in the student strike brought together various strains of the student New Left, the decision to close the university revealed the movement's rifts. Of note in the oral histories that follow is the difference between Ray Lenzi's and Larry Vaughn's pride in shutting down the university and Larry Bennett's dismay at the turn of events, which destroyed the opportunity to continue organizing. Douglas Allen echoes Bennett's disappointment: "There was a lot of potential, we were even

67. Koplowitz, *Carbondale after Dark,* 57–63. The vote was 8,224 to 3,675, with another 608 students voting for "free choice." The faculty voted 603 to 341 to keep the university open, with 62 voting for free choice. The staff vote was 1,131 to 447 to remain open and 49 for free choice ("Chronology of Events Related to Closing").

68. Jim Hanson's remarks were made at the panel discussion "I'm on the Pavement, Thinkin' about the Government: Vietnam, Carbondale, and the May 1970 Riot," SIU–Carbondale, April 16, 1997; David Cochran, telephone interview with Douglas Allen, April 26, 1999.

talking about educational things, priorities, and what kind of university did we want this to be. It was exciting, sitting all day in rap sessions, exploring different things like nonviolent resistance. . . . Normally, you'd have a small group of people, but here [was] a huge number of people. There was a sense of excitement building up [and then] the whole thing toppled."[69]

In later years, the somewhat random and spontaneous nature of the events of May 1970 was repeated. For instance, in 1972, when Nixon announced the mining of Haiphong Harbor, Carbondale again erupted, as more than a thousand people participated in several days of both violent and nonviolent protests.[70]

In his address at the May 6 rally in front of the library, Dwight Campbell drew an explicit comparison between Kent State and SIU. Referring to a January confrontation between students and campus security forces outside the Vietnamese Studies Center at Woody Hall, Campbell said, "The only difference between what happened here at Woody Hall and what happened at Kent State is a matter of degree." In conclusion, he urged people to honor the dead by continuing the movement against the war: "Them cats don't want flowers. They want you to carry on the struggle where they left off. Don't just have a memorial service—have a struggle service."[71] With an echo of Wobbly martyr Joe Hill's last words, "Don't mourn, organize," Campbell's speech placed recent events at SIU in the context of the long-term history of the American Left, the national mass movement against the war in Vietnam, and the escalating tensions between SIU students and administrators over local issues. At the same time, his words were somewhat prophetic. While many young people dropped out of the student New Left after Kent State, as the stakes seemed too high at that point, they did not simply mourn— nor did they all flock to careers on Wall Street. Instead, as these oral histories point up, many of them struggled in new and different ways to live out the values of the movement that they had helped shape and that had touched their lives so deeply.

69. Allen interview.
70. Koplowitz, *Carbondale after Dark,* 26–28.
71. "Kent State, Vietnam Protest Draws 3,000," *Daily Egyptian,* May 7, 1970, p. 10.

ORAL HISTORIES II

Local Leaders

RORY ELLINGER

Rory Ellinger was born June 13, 1941, in St. Louis, Missouri. He grad-uated from the University of Kansas City in 1963, then worked in the peace and civil rights movements for three years. He went back to school in 1966 at the University of Missouri–Columbia, where he received a mas-ter's degree in history and did some doctoral work. He is currently an at-torney in the St. Louis area, and serves as president of the school board of University City. He was recently appointed by the governor to oversee the Missouri Foundation of Health, the largest not-for-profit foundation in the state of Missouri. Ellinger continues to be involved in Democratic Party politics. Ellinger was interviewed in St. Louis on July 20, 1997.

Probably liberal Roman Catholicism would have been the most important factor in my becoming a student activist. I grew up and was in high school when John XXIII became pope, and I became very active. I went to a pretty ordinary Catholic high school called Bishop Dvorak. It was pretty mellow.

Another influence I had was my uncle and aunt were very in-volved with the Left in the thirties and forties, and while that was *that* side of the family, my mom and dad were Republicans. They looked down on the books and literature, and the music and the art. My Aunt Eunice and the interesting friends she had definitely had some influence on me. At least she exposed me to another way of life than what existed in Webster Groves. We go back four genera-tions in Webster Groves. It was one of the first suburbs in America.

When I went away to college the civil rights movement was re-ally starting. When I was away at Kansas City University (which was a private school at the time) I was very influenced by the civil rights workers, the heroism of some of those kids. I remember when a civil rights worker was killed in the South, a CORE worker, my history professor, Ted Brown, went and stood at a demonstration. When I went by, we had the classic Thoreau exchange: I said, "What are you doing here?" And he said, "Why aren't you here?" I thought about it, and then I saw some demonstrations in Country Club Plaza where I was working as a checker at a Kroger store. There were some NAACP kids, all dressed like they were going to church, demonstrating out in front of the Woolworths because they wouldn't allow blacks to be served. This was 1959.

Then I met some young people involved in an organization called the Young Christian Student Movement through my activities in the Newman Clubs of America. I became national vice president of the Newman Clubs, and I met some people who helped found SDS and SNCC. In particular, Mary Varela[1] would be the primary influence. I was really taken by the lifestyle of the young Catholic radicals at the time. They saw me as a liberal influence in this very conservative Catholic student movement, the Newman Clubs, and so we got to know each other. They lived communally with the SDS founders: Rennie Davis, [Tom] Hayden, all those people in Chicago. So that was pretty heady stuff for a midwestern kid. I'd go through Chicago a lot because of these trips I made for the Newman Clubs.

When I graduated from college, which was in '63, I went off and worked full-time with the Young Christian Student Movement. I was an organizer in Boston, and I organized these Catholic student groups based on the Young Catholic Worker Movement that grew up in France after World War II when all the youth were going into the Communist Party. This priest organized cells based on the Communist system, but it was Catholic, with the social justice thesis very strong. I did that for three years. I was very involved with that. I went to Selma. I was a bodyguard for Dr. King for six days when he came to Boston. We were all deputized, like twenty of us. That was really exciting. The cops would joke that they wanted him dead, but not in their town.

There was a big student movement in Boston. I helped to organize one of the first demonstrations against the war in Vietnam in 1965 on the Boston Commons with some kids from Harvard, the May 2nd Movement, which turned out to be pretty Left. I don't know

1. A Catholic student activist from Boston who was a founder of SDS and went South to work with SNCC in the early sixties.

if it was Communist. There were all these student movements in Boston and Chicago at the time. The Trotskyite movement was very important; the Young People's Socialist League had all these different branches.

I won a fellowship to go back to the University of Missouri in 1965–'66, so I went back. There were eight people in SDS at that time. Back then I lived on campus. I had come out of all this activity in the civil rights movement—I wasn't in the South with the real heroes that were in Mississippi Freedom Summer or something, but I raised a lot of money and I was involved with a lot of things peripherally and worked at it full-time for three years. I went back to the University of Missouri with this NDEA [National Defense Education Act] fellowship to study Latin American history, and I looked for guys with beards, because back then it was clearly an indication that [you were a radical]. You weren't a bricklayer or carpenter as it is today. Look at all the people who have beards today. But back then it was sort of a radical stance. There was one guy in particular named Gordon Burnside and a history professor named Bill Allen. (Bill Allen later wrote *The Nazi Seizure of Power*. He was secretary of the Socialist Party of America in the seventies.) We formed an SDS chapter. I was involved with SDS on the campus for three or four years. They threw us off at one point, so we changed our name to the Committee of Concerned Students. I was getting older then, too, twenty-five, twenty-six, twenty-seven. I went off at different times. I went to work at Tom Eagleton's office when he ran for the Senate. I went off to Wisconsin for Eugene McCarthy.[2] I had always admired FDR. We had some real radical kids we had to control. They wanted to burn things down and we were always nonviolent.

One thing that was different in Columbia [Missouri]—except for one or two young people, we were really segregated. There was a black movement and it stayed to itself. Jimmy Rollins was the exception to that. The black power movement was pretty small, but it was there. All the white students were in SDS, and sometimes we'd

2. Eagleton and McCarthy were liberal Democratic senators. McCarthy vied for the presidential nomination as a peace candidate in 1968. Eagleton was chosen as the vice presidential candidate to run with George McGovern in 1972, but he was dropped from the ticket when it was revealed that he had once been hospitalized for mental problems.

have one hundred people at a meeting. For things like Gentle Tuesday there were one thousand kids who were on the grass with their little babies. The engineering students picketed us, and this is sort of ludicrous, but they had the National Guard activated and they had a patrol call, and we were out there throwing Frisbees. It was against the law to walk on the grass—you'd get a ticket. So we put an end to that.

I remember one time Jimmy Rollins had taken over the bullhorn to take over Jesse Hall [the administration building]. We wouldn't let him. We said, "No, this is a peaceful demonstration. You're not going to do that." I had left the Church. I wasn't religious at that point, I just stayed active. I'd go back and forth between liberal politics and what we'd call radical for us—it wasn't that radical, but [it was] student activism. I'd go back and forth, and I felt very comfortable doing that. One year I went to Wisconsin. [In] '66 I was leading marches, '68 I was assistant press secretary for Tom Eagleton, who was the lieutenant governor, and then I'd go back. I left Eagleton's office and came back to campus and was involved with some other activities. I ran for the legislature in '72, and I was almost elected in Columbia.

When I got to Columbia, the war was an issue, but it was a very small following. We were much more involved with student rights issues. Women had to be in the dorms at 10 p.m., couldn't go out Sunday night. I mean all these kind of strange in loco [parentis] rules. A lot of us were older. I had spent three years out of college. . . . We also had speakers who came, Bobby Kennedy and Gene McCarthy, all these people who were very prominent on the national scene. Civil rights was still an issue in a very conservative town like Columbia, Missouri, with a lot of people who had been around forever. Then these student upstarts and their young liberal professors . . .

Student rights had a lot of influence. They would prevent us from having an antiwar meeting on the campus. The police would close our meetings down. That would become a student rights issue. The ACLU [American Civil Liberties Union] would get involved, not so much in the war effort but [defending] our right to have a meeting place in the student union. So then we would have these big demonstrations. They arrested four kids in 1966 for writing antiwar slogans with chalk in front of the Commons. We had a big demonstration. Professor Allen and I spoke.

There were probably ten of us who got the *Berkeley Barb* or *New Left Notes*.[3] I think I was probably one of ten people who was actually a paid member of SDS. A lot of people were local members; very few actually paid dues on the national level. As time went on it was more and more focused on the war. The biggest demonstrations, though, had to do with free speech. The biggest demonstration before the Cambodian thing was when we tried to publish a [cartoon in a student] newspaper. It showed the Statue of Liberty and Dame Justice being raped, fairly graphically, by what is clearly the Berkeley Police Department. It was a cartoon that we reprinted. I was the publisher, and we put that right on the front of our underground newspaper [the *Free Press*]. I was selling the newspaper in front of the student union, and I gave my change purse to Barbara Papish [the editor]. I went to class, and as I was coming out, Bert Spector, who was from University City, said, "They arrested Barbara and three of the kids." We all converged on the student union and that led to the most giant demonstration in the history of the campus, where we spoke in front of Jesse Hall. That was free speech. Even Young Americans for Freedom joined us. They were carrying a sign saying "For Free Speech, Not SDS."

Things died down finally. I went off to work for Clyde Wilson[4] and his campaign for Congress full-time. He ran in '70. I was out-of-state coordinator, and I came back and ran for state representative. I got nominated by twenty-five votes. That was a big deal: Former head of SDS nominated for the Missouri legislature by the Democratic Party. It was pretty neat. Eagleton supported me. I really admired his ability to do that. It was courageous on his part; he didn't have to do that.

Those of us who were hard-core politicos, we might experiment with drugs and we had a lot of girlfriends or boyfriends, but when it came to politics we were serious, I'd say religiously serious about that. Especially the war. None of us were going to be drafted. I think one of the great myths is that the reason there were demonstrations was because people were going to be drafted. No women were drafted and half the demonstrations were made up of women. There

3. The *Barb* was a leading underground paper; *New Left Notes* was SDS's paper.
4. A liberal democrat from Columbia, Missouri.

were a lot of returned Vietnam vets on the campus. They became the center of our antiwar demonstrations. We always had them up front for obvious, good reasons.

We took our music seriously, too. I remember I wrote a whole column in the *Maneater* [the student newspaper] where I took lyrics from Dylan and weaved them into a theme. I remember the Buffalo Springfield. We really took all those words to heart: "Paranoia strikes deep." . . . There was a lot of marijuana, a lot of playing around. I didn't go to a lot of concerts—I was too serious—but my good friend Ted said you never had to have marijuana, you'd just go into the concert and everybody would be smoking, everybody would be high. That's as hard as it got. There was never heroin. There was LSD—I never did any of it, but I met lots of people who did. They're fine today. They're doctors, lawyers. . . . Some did get messed up. Jimmy Rollins went to the penitentiary. It can mess up your life. My own brother got into deep trouble. There was that thin line between living this sort of free lifestyle that was connected to the politics, long hair, the open sexuality, the light drugs [and flirting with danger]. Nowadays you can't say that, especially because I'm on the school board, but [these people were not criminals].

We were from conservative Midwest families, and they were always trying to fire us. I was fired once. I remember Eagleton helping once as state senator when they tried to purge the campus. The campus was constantly in an uproar because we'd always be signing petitions, going on strike. I don't know the sequence, but I was a full-time activist for three or four years on that campus. We just lived and breathed the movement and we were totally involved. We went to Washington, all the different mobilizations and all the organizing. We organized a lot of buses, a lot of kids; hundreds of us went up there from Columbia. And then every two years, four years, there would be a Democratic convention. It was McCarthy, then two years later there was a midterm convention.

We all seized control of that. We took over the precincts in town from the Democratic Party. We were constantly agitating, primarily around the war. Student rights and civil rights took a back seat by then. Blacks could go into places, although there were very few [blacks] on campus and we weren't very attuned to institutional racism. Still, we noticed a lot of racism. There were people in the law school who would openly use the "N" word. It was in my lifetime that the first blacks graduated since the Gaines case [see p. 99].

Our relationship to national SDS was really nothing. We were off on our own. In fact, we'd be very suspicious of people [from outside]; we'd think they were agents provocateurs. There was this one guy in particular who had come back from the Marine Corps. I was always suspicious of him because he was so highly radicalized. Barbara Papish and I went to an SDS conference in Washington, D.C., I don't remember the year. I was hearing all this discussion among the national leadership; it was really amazing. But I didn't have a word to say. I just sat there. I went to one other convention, but as I got off the bus two policemen were there. I thought they were going to arrest us, and I was picked up. The SDS leaders naturally had a lot of paranoia about it. It turns out they were there, these two young cops, to tell me my father had died, so that was the end of my national experience.

Nobody ever came through. We never had any [SDS] national leader or even Mobilization[5] leader. This was all local. We read some of the stuff . . . I got *New Left Notes*, which had really amusing cartoons. Wonderful art and cartoons. Funny things, like they showed a zillion little kids running, scattering, and they showed the police with nets trying to catch them and put them back in the cages. Really, that was about it. We'd get a packet from Chicago, where the national SDS headquarters was, but we had no contact, no phone calls, nothing.

We felt very uncomfortable with the disintegration of [national] SDS. By then I was already out of that; I was most active in SDS from 1965 to 1967. You still had people like [Carl] Davidson, Rennie Davis, these sort of really intellectual-oriented national leaders.

We always flirted with becoming violent. We always wondered if we weren't just being cowardly, afraid to give up our lifestyle. But we had all these alliances with the university professors' wives— there weren't very many women professors—that would be a total turnoff to any violence. This was a middle-class, primarily white antiwar movement, and we did all these things. We sat in the streets,

5. The National Mobilization Committee against the War was a broad coalition that worked to end the war in Vietnam. The Student Mobilization Committee—discussed by Dan Viets—was an offshoot of the national "Mobe."

we took over the student union. I remember when we accidentally broke a window; "Oh my God, oh my God." And I remember the dean, "That's okay. I knew it was an accident." They didn't come in with the billy clubs. The closest we ever came was when we took over the student union, and they put their gas masks on and we thought we were gone. I mean, we thought they were going to weigh in. They had a bunch of us singled out, and we stood there, linked arms and sang "We Shall Not Be Moved." And they left. We called their bluff and they left, and then at ten or eleven o'clock at night we started drifting away, and by the next morning we were all gone. So somebody was wise enough to say, "We don't want this thing to turn into Columbia [University] or Berkeley."

Every time they'd do something stupid, like arrest the four kids, we had this massive demonstration. When they arrested Barbara Papish and the other kids for selling the *Free Press*, we had this march on the state capitol; it was in the *New York Times*. So somebody was smart enough to say, "Don't wade in there with billy clubs and gas." First of all, you have all these young seventeen- and eighteen-year-old girls, just young girls right out of high school. And then you'd have guys like me, twenty-five, twenty-six, twenty-seven, and people who had been in Vietnam. There was that mixture and there would be a lot of innocent people who would be hurt.

We went to Warrensburg [Missouri] once because at Warrensburg there was a big ABM missile. Bill Wickersham[6] organized that. We went there in buses, and they welcomed us. That was it as far as links with other schools. That was [one] weekend; that was it. It was a big demonstration, a lot of publicity in the *Kansas City Star* and the *[St. Louis] Post-Dispatch*. It was ABM silos. I remember I gave a speech: "Don't condemn these people, because they need jobs and these provide lots of jobs. We need alternatives to bombs."

Wickersham got chased by two guys in pickup trucks with shotguns trying to kill him. There were occasionally things like that. We got grabbed; a lot of us were paranoid. Had this been our house in Columbia, Missouri, we would have put the bookcase in front of the window. We were afraid of bombs. I got jumped once and beat up a little bit. Gordon Burnside had a lot of violence directed at him. I remember one of the black leaders had a pistol pulled on him in

6. A local peace activist who was a professor at MU.

the middle of a football game. He was waving a black power flag and this deputy sheriff came over to him (I wasn't there) and he said, "Put that flag down." The guy said, "You can blow my fuckin' head off," and the deputy put his gun away.

During the '68 Democratic convention I was in [Senator] Eagleton's office. I was Mr. Young Liberal and I remember we just all watched it together; we weren't allowed to go. In '68 I was back in the system; I wrote press releases and speeches for Eagleton.

It was a horrible time. King died—several months later [Robert F.] Kennedy was killed. We had a lot of faith in the political system when we started out, particularly those of us who came out of the civil rights movement. Things had really changed, but the war never ended. It just seemed to go on and on and on no matter what you did. It just went on and on and on, and that got very discouraging. So it almost became a relief that someone like Eagleton would run for office because it gave you a moral avenue to do something against the war that wasn't planting bombs, which was sort of the other alternative. You had to either go through liberal politics or you had to . . . I had intellectual sympathy for some of these young men and women who went off the deep end and unfortunately killed people and messed up their lives permanently. I turned my draft card in, and then I was going to be arrested. So I got a good lawyer, but the other guy didn't. He wouldn't take his draft card back and he went to the penitentiary. So I kept up my antiwar activity, but I would make compromises.

We read a lot. Catholics, Protestants, Jews, all the students, we were all reading the same things, across the country: Robert Theobald on industrialization, and Camus, Marcuse, Debray, *Revolution in the Revolution?* Che Guevara was a very inspirational figure to all of us.[7]

We were pretty hard-core. We would meet down by the draft board in Columbia, people with armbands looking out not so much for the police but [for] rednecks. Guys in pickup trucks went outside there and would run us down. Barbara Papish was one of the

7. Albert Camus, a French existentialist, wrote several novels on the theme of alienation. The French war in Algeria also moved him to write an antiwar tract. Herbert Marcuse was a Marxist scholar, part of the Frankfurt School, who also wrote on several basic New Left themes from alienated labor to revolution. Che Guevara, the Latin American revolutionary, was captured and killed in 1967.

first women leaders; she'd be in her sixties today. She was way ahead of her time in being a feminist. The idea of Gentle Tuesday [in Columbia] came from her. She said, "Let's have some fun." "People are dying in Vietnam, Barbara," would be our attitude back at her, right? But she convinced us to do this and it was just a really neat, gentle day. It really was a gentle Tuesday. People felt confident enough to bring their babies and picnics and their Frisbees, and there was a rabbit. I remember all these straitlaced guys with their slide rules sitting on the steps chanting, "Down with SDS. Support our boys in Vietnam." I helped do the leaflets. It was just a very nice day. We know that Jesse Hall was filled with state police and they kept out of sight. They thought there would be a student takeover. A lot of people dropped acid—I was with a young woman who did—and [there was] a lot of pot-smoking openly. A lot of young ladies without brassieres on, no nakedness or anything. A lot of long hair.

I was surprised by the turnout. I was one of the naysayers. I thought this would not work, and I was very severe. I carried a bullhorn around the whole time. I was waiting for bad stuff to happen. I remember there was a general call: "Enough of this. We're going to take over Jesse Hall. People are dying." I had my bullhorn. We had this little debate—I won—and these guys went home. I was a little worried about the police coming because they were pretty heavy-handed. People [sometimes] got shot. If you called in a panty raid, you could get shot. Guns were drawn. Omar Bradley—I remember the name vividly because General Omar Bradley is from this area— Omar Bradley was a cop at the library, and he carried a .44; someone is going to steal a book, you're going to shoot them on sight. They had this mentality that the students were enemies. . . . We got the FBI files and they were spying on us. There were taps on our phones, they were going through taking names . . .

We were just local, we were all midwestern. I've never been to the West Coast. I went to the East Coast once when I was in the Boy Scouts. I don't think any of us came from the East. A few people came from Chicago and they were more sophisticated than the rest of us.

We were always involved in Democratic Party politics. We were never radical enough that we wouldn't participate. We were registered to vote and we would try and take over the party, while I'm sure on the East and West Coasts you had the May 2nd Movement, which was Chinese Communist. You had the Trotskyites, you had the Young Communist League, you had all these people, plus SDS, which kept its ties to the Democratic Party. We know that Senator Humphrey was very much in contact with Tom Hayden throughout this whole time, just like I was in contact with liberal state legislators, Eagleton and people like that. We were liberals. We didn't burn buildings, but we broke the law. They said, "You can't step on the grass"—we did. They said, "Women can't stay out past ten"—we'd have mass sleeping on the mall. Women stayed out breaking the dorm rules. They'd tell us to disperse—we wouldn't. Kids got arrested for trespassing.

When I left, there was a student on every major committee. Student power really did make a difference. By then kids could vote, and that made a big difference. They had to treat us with respect now, because [we] could vote [them] out of office. Me and Harriet Holmes would bring students up to vote and get turned away, turned away, turned away. We took it to court, and before it ever got to court, they changed. They let us vote. This was long before the eighteen-year-old vote. Students weren't allowed to vote in Columbia, Missouri. We just kept going to the registrar. I remember accompanying people up there. This one young woman would turn them down. She'd say, "Where do you live?" And they'd say, "3945 Stafford Hall." "No, really, where do you really live? Where are you from?" "I'm from Cleveland," or "I'm from St. Louis." "Well, I'm sorry, I won't register you to vote, then. You can register at home." And [she] would turn them away. We changed that; a lot of people did. A lot of students got elected, too, right out of college. They would get elected regularly to the Columbia City Council. I ran and lost. Al Tacker was the first to get elected.

In the long run, I think the student movement had a lot of very positive aspects, both in Columbia and the nation as a whole. The fact that eighteen-year-olds can vote . . . whether or not they exercise that right, you have to treat them with respect or they'll get mad, and then they can exert that power. They have a right to power. I think American foreign policy is very different, too. Now the president has to fight to get agreement to send troops abroad. Interesting how a lot of antiwar people want to send troops abroad [to Bosnia]. Certainly civil rights has proved incredible. Women's rights grew out of that. It all kind of came out of that whole fermentation. There were some bad things. A lot of kids went to the drug culture. That was a bad thing to come out of that period.

The sixties affected my life in many ways. It's twenty years later and people are still calling me. I was just a local leader. Other than that I've been dedicated all my life. I like politics. I've been on the school board here for six years. Racial issues are more important to me than anything else. Our school district is largely African American. A lot of poverty. I'm very involved in these kinds of issues. I got involved because I have a history of activism. We chose to live in University City knowing it would have a liberal atmosphere and a history of activism, and we knew all the politicians from here.

I ran for the legislature and got nominated in '72. I lost the general election and I went to work for the Missouri Association for Social Welfare. I was the lobbyist at the state capitol. I did a lot of that kind of stuff. I went to law school, but not until I was thirty-seven or thirty-eight. Started law school pretty late. Linda and I didn't get married until I was forty. She had been very involved. She had been in the Peace Corps, Catholic background like me, women's movement. She was the state's ERA [Equal Rights Amendment] chair. That's how we met.

We really did see ourselves as part of a tradition [of the American Left]. It's so egotistical to see ourselves as part of a historically important movement, but we did, absolutely. We would save things. A lot of us saved leaflets; I still have leaflets from that period of time. I'm a pretty small leader, but I anticipated, believe it or not, that this would be important in history. . . . Because I knew a little bit about labor history, primarily, I knew what we were doing was important. I still think so. I think it's a really important part of our lives. I don't know that I ever would see myself as Che Guevara or the Reuther brothers [organizers of the United Automobile Workers], but I did see myself as part of a tradition. I thought the student movement was really important, and I particularly always revered those people who were in the Mississippi Freedom Summer.

BILL EBERT

William F. Ebert III was born in Kansas City, Missouri, in 1949. He served as student body president of the University of Kansas during the 1970–1971 academic year, graduating with highest distinction that spring. He received his J.D., with honors, from Southwestern University in 1983. He currently practices law in Topeka, Kansas, where his specialty is domestic relations and mediation. He is an adjunct professor of law at Washburn University School of Law, in addition to being a certified mediator and trainer. Ebert was interviewed in Topeka, Kansas, on April 19, 2002.

I distinctly recall one spring when there were a whole lot of people down around the ROTC building, and Governor [Robert B.] Docking, who was a Democrat, was poised with the Guard to come over and basically set up shop. [KU Chancellor] Chalmers prevailed on the powers that be somehow to see if he could handle the situation internally. He and I went down there, and there were people standing around with Molotov cocktails in their hands. He mixed it right up and defused the whole situation. There were a number of us that were saying, "There's a way to do it, but this isn't it." That was as volatile a situation as I'd seen in a while.

That might have been the night of the Kent State shootings. I was sitting in Chalmers's office when he got the call from the chancellor at Kent State, and I just saw the color drain right out of him. He went pale as a ghost. Bringing the Guard to Lawrence would have been the biggest mistake they could have made. It would have been a terrible scene. There were people with connections to the Weathermen that were there. I think there were a number of undercover FBI. One guy in particular I remember, who said his name was Jack Pratt. He said he just read what was happening, saw what was happening in Lawrence on TV [in San Francisco], and so he came. He couldn't name any of his connections in San Francisco or anything else, so I'm pretty sure he was undercover.

There was a curfew imposed in Lawrence for a relatively short period of time. . . . Just east of the campus, streets like Tennessee, Kentucky, Ohio—that was referred to as Hippie Haven. The first night of the curfew a number of people got together and put all their stereos out on the roofs or the front porch, and put a Jefferson Airplane record on: "Got a revolution." At the same time, they turned them all on. You'd see the National Guard trucks driving up and down the street with all this stuff going on in the neighborhood. . . . Those images stick in your mind and don't leave very soon.

I was born in Kansas City, Missouri, in 1949. I think I was in the first grade when my dad, who had been a pharmacist, took a job as a pharmaceuticals representative for a company that was later swallowed up by Dow, and we moved to the west side of Topeka. I went to school in the Topeka public school system, attended Topeka West [High School], and desperately wanted to go to either Harvard or Yale or Princeton. Those were the only three schools to which I applied. I was not accepted at any of those, and I had a little bit of difficulty trying to figure out what went on. I subsequently discovered that my high school guidance counselor had decided that KU would be a better place for me to go, so she hadn't sent my test scores in. It's actually a blessing in disguise, because I had four really wonderful years at KU and I don't think I could have matched them anyplace else.

I started at KU in 1967, ran for freshman class president and was elected, and that was the beginning of my involvement in university governance issues. I first got interested in school-type politics when I was in high school. In junior high I was a homeroom rep, or some such thing, but it didn't really get to be very organized until high school. Then we had a student senate and a house [of representatives]. We had three at-large senators from each class, and I think I was one of those for a couple years. My senior year I was the parliamentarian for the student senate. I went to Boys State, ran for attorney general there and was elected, and then got to go to Boys Nation, which was really kind of neat.[1] It was an interesting time to

1. Boys State is a program sponsored by the American Legion to teach participants how government works. Boys Nation simulates policies and practices of the federal government.

be in D.C., because the nation was pretty well polarized about that time. I remember the fellow that I went with, a guy by the name of Larry Wohlford, he's from Hutchinson (I think he's a veterinarian now, but I've kind of lost track). We of course got the red carpet treatment from Senator [Frank] Carlson and Senator [James B.] Pearson, who were there at the time. In each instance when we were introduced to them and walked into their office, the very first thing they said was, "Would either one of you boys like an appointment to West Point or Annapolis or the Air Force Academy?" And of course we're both not unaware of what's going on in Southeast Asia, and so neither of us were takers. But that was an interesting experience that probably did influence my interest in what was going on in the world and what was going on in Washington, D.C., in particular.

My folks were not particularly politically involved. My mom was a homemaker until my brother and I got old enough that she didn't need to stay home and watch us. Then she got a part-time job. My parents both worked very hard to guarantee that my brother and I would be able to go to college. I'm very grateful for that. I didn't have to work when I was in college. I did [work], probably the last part of my junior year. My senior year I worked a little bit, but that was the year I was student body president and things were really crazy.

I was pretty involved in my church—Christian church, Disciples of Christ—up until the time that I went to college. And then, when I went to college, the First United Methodist Church in Lawrence had a minister whose name was Ron Sunbye. We used to call it "The Sunbye Show," and we'd go. . . . He was perfect for a college town ministry because he was always relating scripture back to current events. It was kind of like a supplemental class in current events with a religious twist and the Lord's Prayer thrown in. I never joined the Methodist Church or anything else, but that was my childhood spiritual upbringing. I was involved in Boy Scouts; I became an Eagle Scout. On the Eagle team, we'd go around on Sunday afternoons and present the Eagle award to other Scouts.

As a kid I was consumed with sports, and some of it was at a pretty competitive level, so you get used to winning and you don't like losing. I didn't really have the size to participate in athletics much after the junior high school level, so I shifted to debate in high school. One topic had to do with compulsory arbitration in labor-management disputes in major U.S. industries, and one had to do with proliferation of nuclear weapons, and one had to do, I think, with whether or not China ought to come into the United Nations. So it seemed like I was constantly involved with controversial subjects, really digging into them and looking at them deeply. I'm sure some of that rubbed off, because after you've looked at enough problems pretty soon you start thinking about how you can be part of the solution.

In '67, by all outward appearances the KU campus was still probably much like it looked in 1957. The sororities and fraternities were kind of dominant on campus. There had not been a real obvious convergence to the left or to the West Coast lifestyle that was in full bloom in Berkeley and San Francisco in particular. But that changed graphically and dramatically within about eighteen months or two years. By 1969 the campus was politicized. There were a lot of people in Lawrence that were activists who were not students, and most of them ended up being down there in that area that was called Hippie Haven. And there were a lot of people who had been left-leaning in their political analysis way before I even got there.

The country as a whole was undergoing a metamorphosis of sorts at the time, and Lawrence always reacted the same way as Berkeley did, that Madison did, or Boulder. Sometimes it wasn't always exactly at the same time, but there were always people coming through Lawrence that were from Madison or Boulder or San Francisco. It was a mecca for the Midwest as far as radicalism was concerned, and as far as activity was concerned, too. I remember one time I was talking to a friend of mine from Topeka, and he was involved in student government at Washburn [University]. They were having a faculty appreciation demonstration the same day that we [KU students] were having some kind of a big demonstration down on Jayhawk Boulevard against the war. So there was a big, big difference in the levels of development on the campuses. Same with K State [Kansas State University]. K State never developed any kind of a political profile other than pretty much standard Kansas G.O.P. conservatism. Even to this day, Lawrence is the garden spot of the state.

Being freshman class president was more status than clout. There was a slate of freshman class officers that conducted some business; most of it was probably social. But the university governance at KU underwent a pretty big change in 1967 or '68 when the university senate was created. That had a student senate component and a faculty senate component, and it had representatives from both. And then it had an executive committee that was the real nuts and bolts of it on day-to-day business. That was called the SenEx. I was on that for two or three years. A lot of university policy got formulated in that body. Charlie Oldfather from the law school was on that committee; one other law professor, Dean [William M.] Balfour, who was dean of students; and the chancellor and a couple of others. We spent more hours than I can even stand to think about meeting up at the chancellor's office on various things. Of course those people, and rightly so, were all very image-conscious about the wording of any press release or anything else, so we would just labor over these public statements that were going to be made. I found it to be quite tedious at times, myself, but then I was a twenty-year-old kid and there were a lot of other things that I would have rather been doing. But I stayed with it.

The war in Vietnam was a major crisis of conscience for a lot of people in those days, [myself] included. I had friends that were serving there, I had friends that died there. I didn't know if I should or should not go. I still to this day feel somewhat guilty that other people that were my peers went and sacrificed their lives, and here I [was] in the Midwest going to college and doing what college kids do. There was one [time] that the guilt got to the point where I actually went to enlist in the Rangers, but couldn't really bring myself to do it. So I was concerned about the war. . . .

Race relations in Lawrence, Kansas, were deplorable in the late sixties and early seventies, and had been for quite some while before that. I had an interest in seeing to it that, at least as far as we could influence the campus life, we did a better job of learning how to peacefully coexist with one another and stop the conflict and the tension that existed. Shortly before I took office as student body president, that summer, two students were actually killed. Nick Rice was shot, right across the street from the Union. There used to be a tavern there called the Gaslight, and I think he was in there having a beer and heard some commotion outside and walked outside and stepped right in front of a bullet. No one was ever prosecuted for that as far as I know. Then there was another fatality—a guy by the name of Rick Dowdell. I think the Dowdell name was fairly well known [by] the Lawrence Police Department at the time. About all that anybody ever really knew for sure was that he, allegedly in an effort to escape two officers, was shot in an alley someplace east of Massachusetts Street. I felt a certain amount of responsibility as the student figurehead to try to bring some voice of reason or some calming influence, but I didn't have any illusions. The problem was way bigger than me.

I thought that the whole idea of involving students more in the policy-making decisions of the university was a good thing. I realize that there are limits to that, but I also thought we hadn't gotten close to the limit yet. That was a worthwhile endeavor. There was always a conflict between the students who thought that it should be the purpose of the student leaders and student governing bodies to address the issues—worldwide, nationwide, whatever—and [the] group of people who said, "Well, wait a minute, we're not really here to complain about the war in Vietnam, we're here to get the parking fees reduced and to get the student activity ticket expanded or price reduced," and that sort of thing. So there was always a debate back and forth about what was the proper investment of time and energy on the part of the student senate. I felt like, the way the climate was in Lawrence, it would have been an abdication of responsibility for us to be silent on the issues that everybody in the country was struggling with at the time. So my personal opinion was we should speak out on anything [about which] we feel like we have something constructive to say. [This is] not to diminish the importance of the other, more practical things that students had a right to be concerned about.

I remember one big flap that came up over the price of the student activity fee because the athletic director at the time wanted to do something which severely restricted the use of the activity fee. A big fuss came up over that, and the student senate took a stand directly in opposition to him and he did not like that. He wasn't used to it. His name was Wade Stinson, and Wade was an ex-Marine who played football and was used to running that show. When the student senate got in his way, he was not happy. That kind of incident was just indicative of the climate of change that was happening, where the students were willing to take on what had been a traditional authoritarian figure and say, "Wait a minute, this isn't right, we're gonna do something about it."

There were always people that had their single-issue causes, just like there are today. That was the time when the Gay Liberation Front, the GLF, was in its infancy, and they were always interested in trying to attract as much attention as possible. We dealt with some issues about where the student senate budget money was going to go, and for what kinds of purposes. But we, the student senate, didn't have a heck of a lot of money to throw around. The people who did that were primarily SUA, Student Union Activities, and they could bring in speakers or bring in concerts and things that we just didn't have the economic firepower to do.

As student body president, it would have been impossible to guide the student body in any particular direction. With the extent of strong feeling and divergence of opinion . . . I thought that if we could make it through the school year without losing any more buildings or any more lives, that would be quite a success. I do remember, shortly after the Kent State tragedy occurred, we had a university convocation. It was hard to decide what to do under those circumstances. There were people that wanted the university to be closed down. There were people that wanted the university to continue. The people who didn't want that were committed to shutting it down and they would have taken action to do that. Fortunately, [Chancellor] Chalmers was attuned enough to be very well aware of that, even though he had some serious detractors who did want him to give the appearance of caving in to any wild screaming Maoist revolutionary drug-crazed hippies. So we hatched this plan that we would convene the student body and submit the whole thing to the democratic process and take a vote. Those of us that knew anything at all [knew that when] you ask a bunch of college kids if they want to stay and take their finals or if they want to dismiss school, it's not a very close question. I spoke on behalf of the executive committee to recommend that that option be exercised, and I still think that was the right thing to do.

That was an interesting day—an awfully high percentage of the student body showed up for that. I don't remember the statistical count, but there were a lot of people there. At the conclusion of what I had to say, the Black Student Union rose en masse and marched [up] and basically took over the microphone. It was me and Chalmers standing out there, and there was no percentage in not letting them have it. Besides that, everybody was focused on what had happened at Kent State and they [the black students] felt as if,

"Well, now, wait a second, we've been striving to have our cause heard now for all this time," and I think they really truly did feel as if they were being slighted and their concerns and issues were not being properly addressed. So they engaged in a little self-help. There wasn't any violence that day, but there easily could have been if there'd have been the Guard there or something like that. To the extent that I guided or influenced anything or anybody, that was the one event [where I think I had an impact]. I don't know that there was a lot that anybody could have said that would have changed the outcome, but at least we managed to get through that period of time without any serious violence. Not that what happened wasn't serious, but it could have been worse and it wasn't.

Then that summer a couple of other students and I went to D.C. to talk to the Scranton Commission on University Violence and Unrest [the President's Commission on Campus Unrest], because we wanted them to come to Lawrence. We were that concerned about the climate there. They heard us out, and I think they were tempted. They sent a front team out, to check it out themselves, I guess. I don't know what ultimately led to them deciding not to do that—it might have even been some incident. . . . I don't know if that was when they mined Haiphong Harbor or what, but the Scranton Commission issued its report without coming to Lawrence.

It was just a couple of weeks after I got elected student body president, I remember walking out of my house and seeing the student union burning and thinking to myself, "This could have the potential of being a real long year." I don't think that my "administration," my group of people, successfully carried out any real agenda. You have to understand, it was really impossible to do very much of anything in an organized way when the school and the country at large were in such a polarized state. Everything was polarized in those days, and there was so very little in between. Just keeping the peace was probably as much of an accomplishment as one could reasonably expect, given the limited authority that student activists had. There were a lot of people that were far more left in their politics than I was, but under the circumstances that existed at that time, it probably was a good thing that at least some moderate voices could be heard. Plus when you're in a position like that, you can't really take the chance of publicly espousing a point of view that is openly supportive of violence—I didn't believe in it and I didn't see it ever accomplishing anything constructive, and fortunately we made it through the year without taking on any more major heat.

The Student Mobilization Committee operated pretty much independently, did pretty much whatever they damn well pleased. Not that the student senate was ever at odds with them—it wasn't that—it was just that they kind of had their own agenda and did their own thing and didn't depend on any formalized hierarchy that existed within the university governance system. One of the things I remember best about the year is that we even had trouble getting a quorum at many of our student senate meetings. I remember thinking, "We're hamstrung here 'cause we can't even get enough of the representatives here. They've gotta show up to do any business." We'd send out notices, send out letters, publicize it in the *University Daily Kansan*, do whatever we could. I remember at least three or four, maybe even five times out of the year—and we'd try to meet once monthly—where we just couldn't muster up a quorum.

A lot of it was discouraging to me, frankly. Discouraging because the issues that we were struggling with at the time seemed so huge, and our limited ability as single human beings to begin to grapple with them seemed so minimal. Sooner or later, I think, the radicalism of the late sixties merged into more of a self-critique in the early seventies, where people started to realize they'd better start changing themselves before they try to worry about changing the world. I certainly observed that to some extent in Lawrence. It quieted down. After about '71 or '72, the outward, visible political activism diminished about as rapidly as it had appeared. It was really kind of a 1968–'69 through '71–'72 phenomena; it was pretty well restricted to those years. Not that the climate in Lawrence changed. It's just that the active political demonstrations and that kind of thing diminished quite a bit. Lawrence still has a very cosmopolitan feel to it and always has—that didn't change—but the conspicuous political activity kind of went by the wayside.

I went to Berkeley, sat right there in Sproul Plaza one day, and there were a group of people that we used to affectionately refer to as "Jesus freaks" that were kind of off on one side, and then there were a group of people that were sitting on that little bench there around the fountain and they were playing their guitars, and they were playing the refrain to that Rolling Stones song "Sympathy for the Devil." And there right in front of us ensued this huge fight, where the Jesus people were grabbing the guitars and smashing them and splinters were going into the fountain. So that's when I decided to go back to Kansas.

When a group of students disrupted the ROTC review in 1969, the whole point was should state universities be training officers—in other words, state sponsorship of people that are going off to fight a war that many people felt was illegal or immoral or both. My feeling on it then is the same as my feeling about it now, that there's no way that a few ragtag, loosely assembled, left-leaning people are going to stop the ultimate operation of ROTC, on our campus or anyplace else. But as an expression of protest it was probably pretty effective. It got a lot of attention. Most people in Kansas were not used to seeing that kind of thing. Most people in Kansas, of course, had no idea what the climate and the culture of Lawrence, Kansas, was like, not a clue. I wasn't there that day. I didn't participate in that, [but] a lot of people that I knew well did. Some of them ended up going to jail. I just didn't think it was worth going to jail for, personally. I thought there were, for me individually, more effective ways to try to [publicize] the underlying message that was trying to be conveyed. I certainly wouldn't criticize the people that did it. They got their message across, that's what they intended to do, and it worked real well.

There was a lot of connection between the counterculture, life-style differences, and [politics]. You'd see kids that started at KU coming over from Johnson County as freshmen in 1967 with their chinos and button-down oxford cloth shirts, and within a year they were walking around in bell-bottoms with hair down to the middle of their back and a bunch of beads, smoking dope. There was a tremendous shift in people that—probably the most outrageous thing that they did [previously] was go to the Hawk or the Wheel and drink beer on Friday afternoons—were suddenly potheads. It was not uncommon for the air on Jayhawk Boulevard to smell like marijuana, not at all uncommon. And if you go down to Potter's Lake, it's a certainty. It influenced the political process, if you will, the same way it influenced the way of life in Lawrence generally. It just . . . came along like a big tidal wave, and a lot of people got swept up in it and it affected a lot of the things that they did.

There were a lot of people that represented counterculture ideals and interests that were involved in student government, there were a lot of them that weren't, and there were probably some that were operating in a completely clandestine fashion because a lot of the things they had in mind were illegal. I know that the Weathermen went through Lawrence once in the late sixties, and they were financing their trip by selling heroin, which was a complete and utter contradiction. It was as much of an "anything goes" time as I remember seeing in my lifetime, and it was then when I started to feel like, "Well, here I am, I'm twenty-one years old and I'm not sure that anything could happen today that is gonna surprise me." That was pretty naive, but that's what I remember thinking. It seemed like every day was a completely new adventure, and experience of the world and new things was an exponential-change process rather than an incremental one. I think other people that were there during that period of time probably would have to agree that there was an awful lot going on in a very short period of time in that community. It was pretty fascinating, really.

My dad and I had some pretty deep philosophical differences. Some of that's pretty normal—kids and parents think about things differently. I don't think I ever did anything that would have embarrassed my parents. They were excellent parents. I never had problems with them as far as rebellious-type behaviors. They were wonderful parents, set good examples. I remember the day that my dad dropped me off, he pulls up to the fraternity house that I was going to live in as a freshman. I wasn't even eighteen yet, I was still seventeen years old, and he unloads all my stuff on the curb and he looks up at these guys that are up there on two-story ladders drinking beer and washing windows, and he goes, "Well, don't let the books get in the way of your education," and turned around and drove away. So they were always important influences. I can't say that I gauged my behavior by whether or not they would approve, but I don't believe that I ever did anything that caused them to be disappointed or embarrassed. The clothing that was the counter-culture uniform was really kind of a source of disdain for my dad in particular. He just didn't care much for it, and didn't mind saying so. That's one thing . . . but it's pretty mundane in the overall scheme of things. To the extent that they would know about my involvement through anything that might be reported in the media, I think probably the one thing that might have bothered my mom a little was when [Governor] Docking summoned all of the student body presidents out to Cedar Crest [the governor's residence] one night—that would be from Wichita State, from Emporia, from Washburn, KU, K State. I had suspicions that he was going to use this as a photo shoot, a publicity stunt to make it look like he was for the young people and all this stuff. I remember making some comment to which he responded rather gruffly, and I just said, "Well, on behalf of the University of Kansas, I am leaving this meeting," and I got up and left. That hit the papers. I don't think there was much else. I think they probably interviewed me after the Union burned. I know the FBI paid me a little visit.

There was also—I can't remember how this started—it was called a police-community relations program. This was back in the days when everybody was really getting into the sensitivity training stuff. Lawrence somehow got a grant and put together this program whereby police officers, people from the city council, people from university government, representatives from all these different interest groups—I think we even referred to one interest group in the city as "street people"—got together to try to talk about the things that were troubling Lawrence and the university community and to see if we could come up with some ideas. Toward the end of one of these meetings, some of the police officers started drinking a little beer. I started getting real attentive to what they were saying, and one of them came up to me and said, "I just want you to know that I've seen a dossier on you," and I said, "Where did it come from?" He said, "Straight from army intelligence." I said, "I guess they're at liberty to do what they want. I'm never gonna see it." He just said, "Yeah, I thought you ought to know." There were a lot of people that were being watched back in those days. We'll never know the extent of that. I don't know that I ever really thought of myself as posing any kind of a risk that would justify the investment of taxpayers' money to quite that extent, but there were a lot of paranoid people back in those days.

My parents and I did talk about the Vietnam War. I think that they were pretty much middle-of-the-road Americans. My dad had not been in the service. He had volunteered in World War II, but was not able to serve due to a medical condition. So he didn't come from a military background, and that generation of Americans' concept of war was a lot different than what was going on in Vietnam.

World War I, World War II, Korean War—those were not guerrilla conflicts. I think they started out like most Americans thinking that this was a minor irritation down in some little place in Southeast Asia that none of us had ever heard of before, and that we'd take care of business and bring our boys home by Christmas. And I think that like a lot of people they continued to be supportive because that was the patriotic thing to do. But when the kid that played left field on my baseball team got shot and killed the first day he got off the plane, I think my dad started thinking, because that brought it home pretty closely. It could have been me, it could have been any number of people that he knew of my friends. He thought Nixon was the biggest lying SOB that ever walked the face of the earth—he might be close to being right—so I think that by the time that war was over he just breathed a big sigh of relief and said, "I'm grateful that neither one of my boys got killed." Because by the time the war was over, if you couldn't see that that was the most bungled-up mess of a war effort that we have ever tried, then you're blind. He gradually changed over time to the point that I think he saw that we were not willing to make the commitment that we needed to make to win it and we were sending people over there and getting them killed for no damn good reason. And then the minute we leave, it falls to the North. So . . . a lot of disillusionment, generally speaking. But my parents were not active antiwar or pro-Vietnam in any sense. They were intelligent, astute people who paid attention to current affairs, but had a lot of faith in the government, that the government was going to do the right thing.

That was the crisis of conscience around the Vietnam era. . . . People in masses began to realize, "People have to be the watchdogs." That was something brand new for a lot of folks. The fifties were flaccid—"I like Ike." I could watch that very process go on with my own parents, who were middle-class working folks in probably one of the most Republican states in the nation. And that was pretty interesting from my perspective, because pretty soon my dad would start asking *me* questions. Instead of challenging what I may have said or done about something, he would actually inquire. He's the kind of guy that wouldn't have done that if he didn't truly want to know or respect what I would have to say.

The arguments that I had with my parents had more to do with race relations and with lifestyle choices. "You shouldn't be living in a house that has unmarried members of the opposite sex in it," and of course everybody did. That kind of thing. In terms of describing their values, the term "old-fashioned" would not be inappropriate: family and church and marriage, and those kinds of things were pretty high on the totem pole of priorities for them. And a lot of that stuff was being wholesale challenged. I think they were like everybody else, not totally comfortable with change.

The women's liberation movement was in full fling, and it was certainly very much alive and well in Lawrence. There wasn't anything that you had to be more conscious of, really, than being careful about any old clichés or assumptions or generalizations that might have existed before, because there were a lot of pretty radicalized feminists that lived in Lawrence and they were not afraid to speak up if someone said or did something that was clearly not appropriate. You saw a lot of that. The year that I was student body president, I think that the student senate was comprised of almost half women. It was right about that time that professional schools, especially law schools, started seeing their female enrollment increasing dramatically. KU was maybe not at the head of the pack, but certainly not far behind in terms of progressive thought on that particular subject.

My vice president, Greg Thomas, was black. I'm not going to say that was a conscious thing as much as it was a recognition of the need for a broad-based slate of student leaders. The name of the political party that we formed was the Alliance. It really was aimed at giving credibility to the process by virtue of having representative people. The process at one point didn't have much credibility because it was all the same cookie-cutter, stereotypical sort of people. We had people that were in SDS that were in there, and we had people that were in the Young Republicans. We were definitely a left-leaning organization—the whole campus was left-leaning then, so you take a cross-section of kids and you're going to be left of center, even in Kansas.

There was definitely a very real sense of brotherhood and sisterhood that existed in those days, and it was largely measured by the length of one's hair, if you were male. That was one of those telltale signs, like "I'm hip"; you might as well be wearing a sign. There was no universal signal like that for women. There was a sense in Lawrence that we were all part of a thing that was going on everywhere, and we just happened to find ourselves in this particular place at this particular time. There were a lot of people that moved in and out of Lawrence from the East Coast [and] from Madison and Aspen and Boulder—Boulder was really like that, too. I'm not proud to broadcast this particularly, but there was also a lot of illicit drug trade that went through Lawrence at the time. A lot of that had to do with the now famous organization called the Kaw Valley Hemp Pickers, who were a bold and outlandish group. There was an annual event called the Big Eat, and the Kaw Valley Hemp Pickers were the gracious hosts of that activity. They would typically ship their harvest to Chicago, primarily, as I understand it. Really big business at the time. Drug use was open and blatant and substantially widespread.

The time that Abbie Hoffman came to Lawrence . . . We were down at Potter's Lake, and Abbie's down there, and George Kimball. Abbie Hoffman is standing with his feet apart and George Kimball pulls out his .357 and puts a couple shots right between his legs. It tended to get even more degenerate and crazy than that. George, as I understand it, is now a sportswriter for the *Boston Herald*. He was a pretty interesting character. The craziest thing that he did was somehow getting snuck in on the Democratic platform for sheriff. And he won. And the party was just appalled. George was a large guy, and typically had on some kind of a vest. His hair was always long and kind of scraggly, and he had one glass eye—just a character. Obviously very intelligent. He might have come to KU to be a student. I don't know. He might have just been passing through and stopped. I think that's the story I heard, that he was just passing through and he liked it and stopped and stayed. But he was one of the colorful characters around that time.

I think that the student movement in the country as a whole, in which Lawrence was certainly a notable and visible part, did succeed to the extent that political consciousness was raised generally throughout the population, with the recognition that our country was capable of doing some things that were pretty clearly wrong. I think that the war in Vietnam ended sooner because of the student movement. It certainly had an impact on LBJ. . . . But ultimately, what did we accomplish? I'd have to say from my perspective today, not a great deal in a global sense but a whole lot on an individual basis. You can't go through that period without having it mold you and affect the way that you think about things for the rest of your life. The magnitude of all of the collective, individual changes is probably pretty huge, pretty staggering. But in terms of what the student movement accomplished: we shut down a few universities for a few days at the end of the school year, we forced administrations to spend a little bit more time hearing what the students truly had to say, probably made colleges and universities more politically sensitive generally, and added a dimension to our collective conscience about what we can and cannot do with impunity in this life. [We] caused people to think about more than football and drinking beer—nothing wrong with those things, I'm not saying that, that's the way KU was in the mid-sixties. Based on my experiences going over there to see my daughter when she was going to KU, it's a little more like that now than it was in 1969 or 1970, but everything goes in cycles. History has a way of doing that.

One effect that period had on me was that it pretty effectively burned me out on politics. I became so disastrously disgusted with being misquoted in the newspaper. I hated that. I hated feeling as if I had to make some kind of correction so that what I really said could be known. One of the things I concluded was that if you want to be in the limelight like that, then there's a pretty good-sized price to pay, and I had enough of a dose of it that I was not interested. I wanted to be a private person and live my life without having what seemed like at times an albatross responsibility to speak for this group or that group or try to represent myself as being an accurate reflection of some cross-section of people. I did not want to worry about that anymore. And the political process was not satisfying for me in the sense that the other elected representatives upon whom I had to rely didn't seem to give enough of a damn to make it to the meetings. I don't think we functioned effectively, and why waste your time struggling with something that you know is not going to function effectively?

There was another event that occurred in my life that was pretty significant that had a lot to do with it, too. My best friend all the way through high school, he and I both had wanted to go to Ivy League schools, and it didn't happen. We both ended up at KU, and we spent some time living in the same place; we rented a little farmhouse out on the edge of town. I didn't know what I wanted to do after I graduated, but we both graduated "with highest distinction"

[as] they call it at KU, which is either the top 1 or 2 percent. I remember we were sitting there at the stadium, at the convocation when we were graduating, and we knew that we were going separate ways because he got accepted at Harvard Law and I got a fellowship to go to the Pacific School of Religion. Larry went on to Harvard Law, and I really didn't have very much of an idea what I wanted to do. I went out to take up the fellowship, and I realized that I was not invested in that program and communicated with the people that had offered the fellowship [saying] that they really should give it to someone who was more committed than I. So I came back to Lawrence and just kind of hung out for a while. I decided to go visit my friend right around Thanksgiving, so I did. He seemed to be doing okay but was rather moody, and the next spring I got a call that he committed suicide. His father asked me to do the eulogy, which was probably the hardest thing I ever did. The impact that that had on me was . . . I just didn't want to think about politics, I didn't want to think about very much of anything. I just kind of wanted to try to sort out what all of this means. So I took off for Alaska and spent a couple years up there, which was really a lot of fun. But I got completely off any kind of political mainstream. I never did get actively involved in party politics, didn't ever really want to. By the time I came back from that and was thinking about getting married and having a family, I had other more pressing personal concerns. I just didn't have time. But I lost my taste for it at KU.

I always knew I was going to law school. I got married and I had a child, and I was working in the construction business here in Topeka and doing all right. It was really hard work and long hours; the construction business is a tough industry to make a living [in]. Finally, one day my wife said, "If we don't make a change and get you to law school, you're never gonna make it." So I looked around for the best night program that I could find, because I knew that I had a family and had to work. I attended Southwestern University School of Law in Los Angeles, and spent about eight years out there going to law school and then fiddling around with real estate, and then finally decided to come back to Topeka. Law school was an interesting experience, much different from my enjoyable days on the beautiful KU campus. I was in kind of a skyscraper-type law school building in the Miracle Mile district of Wilshire down by La Brea.

My class consisted of two police officers, three physicians, a couple of IRS field auditors, a bunch of real estate developers, people that already had something going on and they were looking for a change; they were movers. I think it made it a lot more stimulating. It's a lot different going to criminal procedure class when you've got a police officer who just came off a shift; I mean, you hear it firsthand. Then I just practiced here in Topeka once we finally got relocated. I do almost exclusively domestic relations and mediation. I teach the mediation skills class over at the Washburn Law School, usually once a year. Students in law school are learning how to be adversaries, and then they come into my class and I have them reading *Getting to Yes* and all these other books on how to negotiate effective agreements, etc. For the first half of the semester, it's as if I'm not speaking the same language as they are, but eventually they come around. The mediation that I do is generally with couples that are divorcing or have divorced and have differences of opinion over how they're going to manage their time or residential arrangements with their children. One thing about this business is that it's never boring.

Especially in retrospect, Chalmers never did get the public recognition he deserved for the wise hand that he had in leading the university. For whatever criticisms could be leveled against him, I know that he, through his own astute judgment, prevented a lot of destruction and violence that could have taken property and life, for which I doubt that he ever will receive credit outside of a handful of people who happen to know firsthand. And I think that's too bad. You talk about being in a thankless job—that had "no win" written all over it from the very start. Giving credit where it's due as well to university officials, it's hard to imagine a more student-friendly dean of students than Balfour—kind of a student of human nature. Instead of reacting to what was going on around him, he seemed to be fascinated by it even though he was in the latter stages of his career. I think he really looked at it as an opportunity to learn more. I had occasion to spend quite a bit of time with him and developed a tremendous sense of respect for his abilities.

RAY LENZI

Raymond C. Lenzi was born November 19, 1946, in Farmington, Illinois, where his high school mascot was the Farmington Farmer. He received three degrees from SIU: a BA in political science and economics (1968), an MS in community development (1977), and a Ph.D. in geography (1985). He is currently associate chancellor for economic development at SIU. He loves the outdoors, practices yoga and meditation on a daily basis, and, he says, has "deep roots and love for Southern Illinois, its people, and the hills and forests of the region." Lenzi was interviewed in Carbondale, Illinois, on July 15, 1997.

When I think about what politicized and what radicalized me during that period, there are a couple of things that stand out. One is a date: April 12, 1945. That was the day that a Japanese kamikaze plane hit the deck of a battleship my biological father was on during World War II and killed about a hundred men immediately. My biological father was on that battleship over three years. He came home from the war a hero. I grew up with all these pictures of him in his Marine uniform. But at the same time that he was a hero, he was really very damaged and he was crazy. My mother would [later] tell me the stories of what happened. He came home from the war, he had nightmares every night, and when I was eleven months old he killed himself. I never knew him. I know that he was an exceptionally bright man, first-generation Italian immigrant. . . .

Everybody's story is a little different and I don't know exactly what role that had—maybe I would have been a protester anyway—but in some ways I was brought up as an all-American kid to worship this father I never knew who was a military hero, and at the same time my mother was whispering in my ear, as she showed me the photos and read from his diary, that my father said that war

161

was hell and the only way he'd ever go back into the military was in a pine box. Looking back on the stands I took, I think my mother's stories of what happened had an influence, because I knew firsthand that war could not only kill people but that it could destroy them mentally. That probably had a lot to do with my own hesitation about supporting the [Vietnam] war.

There was also the context of the times. When I first came to SIU in 1964, women had to be in dormitories at ten on weeknights and midnight on weekends. Men had no hours. When I was a freshman in college we were still having protests to desegregate hiring practices in Carbondale. The civil rights movement was just culminating in the passage of federal laws that guaranteed equal employment, voting rights, all the things in a democracy which at this point we take for granted. I really see what happened in 1970 as a culmination of a whole period of history where people were kind of throwing off the shackles of what had existed. There was a whole revolt against the status quo that was for women's rights, gay rights, and black minority rights, and against the war. The war was probably the single most crystallizing element of that movement, but all those other things were going on at the same time so it was very easy for people to really question the system and the existing authorities.

In the spring of 1965, my freshman year, there was a protest in front of Morris Library. It was called the Rational Action Movement. It was sort of SIU's answer to the Free Speech Movement at Berkeley, which had been the previous fall. There was a big stage set up, a folksinger singing the Bob Dylan song, which I had never heard before, "The Times They Are A-Changin'," and I sat there on the grass listening to this and got fascinated with this whole thing and decided to see how I could get involved. They offered me a chance to run for student government. I ran for the student senate that spring and I was elected.

There was a lot going on being in student government. In the summer of 1966, the National Student Association, a collection of all the student governments from all over the country, had their annual conference at Champaign-Urbana. There was a great debate between David Harris (who later married Joan Baez), who was a pacifist and student body president at Stanford, and Allard Lowenstein, who later became a congressman. These two guys debated Vietnam policy. The debate wasn't about whether you should support or not support the Vietnam War; it was about what to do about it. David Harris's position, which was very radical, was that the only moral response to the war in Vietnam was to turn in your draft card or burn it. Actually, he subscribed to turning it in so that you became a direct opponent of the war. Allard Lowenstein argued for going through channels and so forth.

This debate took place in a lobby, as a rump session of this conference, in a room full of three or four hundred college students. [Harris and Lowenstein] were both highly charismatic, intelligent, and it had a big influence on me. That same NSA conference had a resolution before it to oppose the Vietnam War and oppose the draft. It came down to the fact that the SIU delegation was the swing delegation in whether this resolution would pass at the national level or not. The SIU delegation was split, and I actually became the deciding vote on that resolution. It was the first time on a national level that students had taken a position to oppose the war, and so it really did become at that point a national conspiracy, so to speak.

I was student body president for a year. The standard thing was first of all they [the SIU administration] sent you to a national training laboratory in Maine, right on the Maine–New Hampshire border near the White Mountains, the prettiest peaks in the Northeast. All the student leaders, the activists, kind of had mixed feelings about this. It was a nice vacation in the mountains but we regarded it as an attempt to brainwash us, basically curb our assertiveness and activism. That was our suspicion because the administration scheduled it and paid for it. It wasn't something student government leaders identified as something they wanted.

Administrators went with us. We drove out there with administrators and went through all of this together. It was a pleasant week really, and afterwards we went to the World's Fair in Montreal. For a poor kid from Farmington it was probably the nicest vacation I had up to that point. We kind of enjoyed it, but at the same time it was like, "What are you up to?"

By this time [1967] some of the more conservative schools from the Southeast and Texas had dropped out of the NSA because the year before it had taken a position against the war in Vietnam and the draft. But overall the conference was bigger and more lively than ever. David Harris was there again, but there were different people there this time, too. Summer '67—it had become like there was no longer a debate about the war. That issue had been settled, even though it was fifty-fifty the year before. This year the issue wasn't being against the war, it was how to mobilize the campuses and the citizens in general against the war, and what methods do we use and what should we be doing?

That year there were more radical speakers, people who had been in Vietnam and actually experienced the bombings by American planes and seen people who had been killed and maimed. I remember one guy in particular who had been to North Vietnam and he told stories about how the Americans were purposefully, according to him, bombing the hospitals. That the hospitals would go out of their way to paint giant red crosses which covered the whole roof of the building. Major hospitals in Hanoi had these crosses in order to say "this is a hospital" to the bombers, and they were being bombed directly. At the time we believed it, whether it was accurate or not. These were Americans telling this story and they were people our age, and this was the most direct information any of us had about what was happening there. So the moral outrage was just growing.

The other thing was that it was the beginning of the hippie period and the NSA also had entertainment—where did you divide the line between speakers and entertainment in those days? Two things I remember from a NSA conference at College Park, Maryland. One was a band called the Fugs. They told the story that they were from Texas and that they weren't too sophisticated in Texas.[1] What they did was go up to a girl and say, "Excuse me, I like apples, you like apples, let's fuck." They really got off on offending people's sensibilities. One girl from SIU who was in our delegation was just . . . she couldn't handle it, got up and left. Most of us thought it was very funny.

The other thing they had was Timothy Leary, and he came out with this guy who was sort of his running mate or whatever, a big black guy, and Timothy Leary and this guy both sat in these giant pillows with sitar music playing in the background. Timothy Leary's speech was "Tune In, Turn On, and Drop Out"—and that was his whole speech. It wasn't about activism; his speech was about getting into drugs and dropping out of society. I mean, he was very di-

1. The group was actually from New York City.

rect about that. Society was sick and the more you protest the more you are just feeding the machine. So that was something really different that I hadn't been exposed to. I had not yet tried marijuana, I don't think, by then. . . . I was pretty much purely a political activist up 'til that point.

At SIU there was never a serious split [between political activists and counterculture types]. Especially from '68 to '70 everyone was pretty much brought together in protesting the war. Some of the hard-core Trotskyites would make their comments, and they would never even smoke a joint. I was kind of in both camps, so I could never really understand the intolerance of either group.

In 1967 the SIU Student Senate and the student government had not really taken an official position against the war. Once the student senate was back in session for the fall, I introduced motions to oppose the war, to oppose the draft, oppose military recruiters on campus, the whole ball of wax. One of the things I discovered was up until this point I had been a political animal but my politics were always a little murky. Yeah, I was questioning the war in Vietnam, but I didn't really run on a campaign to oppose the war, and I was still a fraternity guy when I was running that Spring '67. All my fraternity brothers really supported me. They really were the political machine that put me in office—they gave me money, they helped campaign for me. Other people supported me too, but I was part of something called the Action Party. It was founded in the spring of '65 with those first Rational Action Movement protests and it was always kind of a coalition built around student rights. The Rational Action Movement was actually a coalition of people who were Republicans, civil libertarians, and Democratic liberal activists, and the war brought out those differences. I mean, I ran with a guy who was a Young Republican. I actually chose him as my vice presidential candidate. I didn't really see that as a big negative or a big problem. We had agreed on most issues up to that point. We had agreed on student rights issues and he was probably as adamantly for student rights as I was. But when the war came to the forefront, when I started having student senators that were my allies introduce resolutions against the war, Richard Karr, my vice president, was just really incensed that I was taking these positions. Now, he was identified with this administration that was increasingly going in the exact opposite direction, because even though he was a civil libertarian and agreed with me on student rights issues, he was really a strong anti-Communist. There was no middle ground for us on this issue. So student government became somewhat divided because he was always trying to stop what I was trying to do and I was always trying to do these things, but I had the majority on the student senate because that's where things were going.

We introduced resolutions, we had protests, but in some ways it was like history; it was bigger then anything anyone was doing. The media and the whole generation was shifting its opinion. Something was happening—several songs said that sort of thing. We thought we were influencing it, and in some small way we probably were—I mean, the Beatles were getting stoned and their hair was growing long and Martin Luther King was turning against the war, Muhammad Ali was turning against the war, Walter Cronkite was starting to question the war very openly in his broadcasts. Certain senators, Fulbright[2] and others, were starting to say, "What's going on? Maybe we need to look at this," and so the whole public opinion that year was shifting. As far as students on campus, there was a growing protest by the summer of '68 and by the beginning of that next fall the majority opinion had clearly turned against the war.

The other thing that was happening, which is very hard to measure, was everybody was getting turned on. I mean, it's the other side of Timothy Leary's talk. They weren't necessarily dropping out, but they were smoking pot, they were dropping acid. As more and more kids got turned on, that increased their sense of negativity toward the government: "What do you mean they put you in jail for doing this?" That was just another reason to assume there was something evil about the authorities and the government system.

The civil rights movement had turned into the black power movement and was getting more and more radical, and it was just like the whole American system was on trial and you had a whole new generation examining it from the point of view of its theoretical promises in terms of constitutional rights, in terms of the goodness of America. Suddenly all these things that the largest generation in history had been told and taught and believed for the most part were brought into question. All the hypocrisy and shortcomings of

2. Sen. J. William Fulbright held nationally televised hearings on the war in 1966 that helped legitimize dissent.

the American democratic experiment were clearly laid open for examination. At that time you're just getting through segregation, there's massive prejudice on a scale that today we can't really comprehend. There was also a counterculture where rock music was maybe shaping things as much as the TV media in general, a whole industry of music that is protesting the war, promoting drug use, protesting racial injustice . . .

"Universal Soldier" was one song I would listen to over and over. People would just listen to those songs over and over. Country Joe and the Fish: "One, two, three, what are we fighting for?" So there were a lot of songs that just hammered away. . . . As far as the drug use side, there was Jefferson Airplane. And the Beatles, of course. Their whole message at that point was antiwar; they were clearly taking a whole generation with them. Once the pattern started, it was like an avalanche. Within a year or two, it was just like the attitudes of a whole generation had shifted.

By this time you could hardly listen to popular music without hearing these themes, and people would say, "Let's smoke a joint, you've got to smoke a joint and listen to this album." And that was part of what you did, turned on not only to drugs but to this music and this message or that book.

There were several local groups that were sort of the local banner bearers for some of this music. The music lived not only in the stereo but through the local bands that would do this music. That was just a big part of how people's outlook was shaped, either getting together to listen to music indoors or going to concerts.

Coming back from the NSA convention, part of the tactics were to introduce the resolutions, get the word in the newspaper. The *Daily Egyptian* [the student newspaper] covered all those things [that were] controversial at the time. The *Southern Illinoisan* [the regional newspaper] covered it. I even went on TV in St. Louis once and responded to an editorial they had done about student protests at SIU. So media was one of the tactics—newspapers, TV, radio—and we tried to get on as much as we could wherever we were allowed to talk about these issues. Even though we weren't that sophisticated, we understood then that the media was the way to reach a lot of people at once. We came back with a commitment not only to introduce resolutions and to talk about it to the media but to have a local protest.

The other thing was to get involved in the national protest movement. That fall of '67 was the first really big antiwar protest in Washington. We scheduled a bus, I believe student government paid for
it, and we scheduled a bus to go to Washington. That was an eye-
opener. I have a friend who still teases me about this trip. Here we
were going to this antiwar protest in Washington to protest the war
in Vietnam and some of these people are already hippies, I'm not a
hippie yet, I'm still just the clean-cut guy who thinks the war in Vietnam might be wrong, and me and this other guy from my hometown, Farmington, Illinois, we're a couple of Italian kids . . . we're
on this bus but we bring along the football because every time the
bus stops we get out and run patterns. We'd play catch with the football, but these guys were hippies and they were sort of antisports:
"Look at these guys there. We're going to an antiwar protest and
they're playing football."

But this trip was interesting because we took off one day and we'd
drive all night. The bus stopped somewhere, it must have been eastern Kentucky or Maryland or Pennsylvania or someplace out there
as we're starting to get closer to Washington, and it's still the middle of the night, it's like four in the morning. And we stop at this
truck stop and there are like hundreds of buses with kids in them
from all over the country. It was an eye-opener, because up to this
point you've been to some student government conferences, you've
been to some small protests with a couple of hundred people in
Carbondale where you had people heckling you, and suddenly you
are in this truck stop and there's nothing but antiwar people.
There's a few truckers sitting around looking like "What in the hell
is going on?" but there are literally in this truck stop thousands of
antiwar protesters and nothing but buses of people and you start to
get a sense of what's happening. You go on to Washington, you get
there at sunup, you arrive and you see not thousands of people, but
thousands of buses and hundreds of thousands of people. And you
look and as far as you can see in any direction are people with
protest signs, kids with hair that's getting longer, and banners, and
it's like you just have a sense of solidarity. People on the right in
those days talked about a conspiracy and there was probably a little
of that, but it was more of an informal sense that there was a large
national movement that you were connected to in a real way—not
in an organizational sense, but you had a sense of national solidar-

ity, a national movement. That was the first time I ever really had a sense of a mass movement, that day. Up to that point I knew there was a smattering of groups, but suddenly you fill the streets.

When you were part of the movement you started to see what the tactics were, you got an education firsthand. You make signs, you make banners, you put where you're from [on the banners]. At the national demonstration you saw people from all different states, then you mimicked those things at the local level. You have your own protest, bring up signs representing organizations or other universities, whatever, but you learned the tactics of an organizer, how to make the biggest impression with whatever you've got. You start to say, "Oh, that's how you do it"; you start to see what gets the press's attention. Going to the national protest was really good.

That year the student government formally sponsored teach-ins. So you bring together professors and students that know about [the Vietnam War], you have talks and you show movies, pass out books and tell people that they should read these books, and start arranging to have antiwar speakers through student organizations and student programming council sponsorship. We went through some battles on that, but we did bring a couple of antiwar speakers to campus. One of them in particular was not only antiwar but civil rights/black power: Dick Gregory.[3] We brought him the spring I was student body president. He gave a talk in the women's gym, and he was great because he not only supported our positions but he was funny.

I don't think we were doing too much door-to-door organizing around Carbondale. Students were still pretty afraid of the community. In '68 we were still pretty shy of the community and probably we were a little unsure of ourselves in terms of standing up to adults on these issues. We were more comfortable among ourselves, at least that's how I felt.

One of the first alternative institutions we created was the Free School. The Free School was first of all about teaching things which were not being taught in the normal educational system at that time. One of the foremost of these things was why the war in Vietnam was wrong. We had those classes and we had yoga classes with

3. A comedian and an antiwar and civil rights activist who had become a national figure, Gregory was an SIU graduate.

meditation, tai chi, organic gardening, all those things. The Free School was big. By 1967–'68 we had a full foldout in the *DE* [*Daily Egyptian*] with forty or fifty classes. That was one of the first places that you had methodical teaching about the war in Vietnam and Vietnam's history. People learned about Dien Bien Phu, the French and Eisenhower and how we got into it. The fact that it was a civil war and why Ho Chi Minh was great and all those things.

The attitude out in the general community once you got away from the campus was still very hostile, although . . . my stepdad was a coal miner and the truth is I probably got my radical analysis of society more from him than from anybody else. He didn't trust the system, he didn't think it was fair, and he taught me that at the kitchen table every night. He was a blue-collar worker and he was still pretty patriotic when the war started, but he never really said "don't do it" or "you're wrong." He would debate it with me a little bit, but he never said, "I think you should go." So I think there were people out there who were hostile, but others were more afraid of being rejected.

We certainly had more acceptance among kids our own age, our own peer group there in Carbondale around campus, so we stuck to that. We had a great base. The campuses became the base for the national network of antiwar protest.

When we closed down SIU in the spring of '70 it sent a big message. We got a lot of media coverage throughout the whole state of Illinois, and it shocked the legislature and it shocked the governor and the people in power. That was happening nationwide—we could carry on that protest and target the university. In a way it was unfair to the university because the university hadn't started the war. They were a good target because we controlled the numbers in that geographic territory and we could create the crowds. We could put them on the defensive, make them the target, whether it was over the Vietnamese Studies Center or recruiting on campus or the ROTC program. But I always felt that most of the protesters understood that the university wasn't the enemy; they were just the most immediate representation of the government establishment and one we could actually deal with most effectively. First of all, they were the least inclined to really strike back violently and they were going to treat us with the greatest amount of tolerance. So we used them, and it was a hard time for the universities for that reason, because they were caught in the middle. They weren't the enemy really, but they became the enemy because they were handy.

Now as a person who works for the administration I feel kind of strange about it all because I realize the really awful position some university administrators were put in, where they had to defend policies they didn't necessarily believe in. But things were getting out of hand and they were supposed to do something about it. After Kent State the dean of students was reading the rules about disrupting classes and [a local character known as] Anteater slugged him and knocked him down. The poor guy. What a position to be in, because he just happened to be dean of students in 1970—that was his crime.

As the year 1967–'68 progressed, I became increasingly more radical. I also probably realized my stage was running out, so I became more obsessive about what I could do to stir things up. Look, here's a person who was student government president, who was getting stoned and who was also about to graduate college, which means his student deferment is up. So a lot of things are coming together here rather quickly. It's all easy to see in retrospect, but at the time you just have a very agitated young man who is increasingly nervous about getting this thing called the war over with, not only because of his personal convictions but because subliminally he realizes something is staring him in the face here—the theoretical arguments about burning your draft card, going to Canada, going in the army, or doing something else are quickly coming on the horizon. So I just became more and more agitated and started getting involved more actively, not only in protest about the war.

In a controversy in the spring of '68 I openly said that women should simply ignore the student hours—they still hadn't changed the hours policy and we were totally outraged on that issue. So we passed a resolution saying that women should simply ignore the hours and then we also passed a general amnesty for all political protesters, which meant a lot. Anybody involved in protesting women's hours, the war in Vietnam, or whatever other issues we put in the resolution was hereby absolved. We were declaring what was legal, and this totally outraged the administration. I mean you can't do this, declare a general amnesty. You don't have the power to do that and you're leading students on. You're going to get them in trouble, which was true—we were encouraging people to break the law. So that became a big controversy in the spring of '68, that we were openly, flagrantly encouraging people to break university rules. The administration took me into a private meeting, I guess the dean of students or vice president told me if I didn't stop making statements encouraging this that they were going to kick me out of school. I basically just ignored them.

Then another weird thing happened that spring. I discovered that my advisor had made a mistake and that I was actually three hours short from graduating that spring, graduating on schedule in four years. This was very upsetting to me personally because my mom and dad were looking forward to it. . . . So this is how my radical political year is going to end. I don't get to graduate. It shows how straight I really was that I worried about that. It really worried me horribly. But one of the hippie professors said I should go see Tom Davis. Tom Davis was an English professor, had a beard. He was involved in our protests, and Tom Davis arranged for me to take a proficiency exam for some English course where I had to write an essay. I did actually write a legitimate essay on a book I had already read. It was a well-written essay and they gave me credit, but I was worried that the administration was going to find out that I had passed this proficiency exam and somehow question it. But that didn't happen. Anyway it was a very nervous spring for me because I'm getting ready to graduate, I had that problem getting graduated, and I'm being threatened with expulsion, and . . . the protests are getting more and more loud, more antagonistic, particularly over women's hours. That's the one getting kids in trouble. But then I graduated. It seems like all of a sudden it was over for me. It seemed strange not to be student body president anymore. Before, I had a stage, a phone, an office. Suddenly I am out of school.

I went to substitute teacher training in Chicago that summer, so I was kind of out of the political loop. But what was happening the summer of '68 while I was in Chicago for substitute teacher training? The Democratic convention, so I was down there every day.

I was at the protest every day playing chase with the cops. It was pretty neat being there, but actually the night the shit really hit the fan, the night they nominated Humphrey,[4] I had just left that after-

4. The nomination of Hubert Humphrey, Lyndon Johnson's vice president, was perceived by the antiwar forces as a defeat.

noon. Not because I wanted to avoid it; I didn't know. I had a plan to go to Arkansas trout fishing with these two guys and we were supposed to leave that day. We were debating whether to stick around. We had been involved with three or four days of protesting, but it didn't seem like anything was really going to come of it. So we took off to Arkansas, drove all night. The next morning we were crossing on the Norfork Lake ferry just as the sun was coming up, and the radio was on and it was telling about what happened the night before in Chicago. Then we were kicking ourselves because we didn't stay for that evening.

I met Jerry Rubin there. I don't remember if I saw Abbie Hoffman or not. Bobby Seale,[5] all the guys who went on trial later, Dave Dellinger . . . These guys were giving speeches, hippies and antiwar protesters were riding the horse on Grant's statue, cops were trying to chase kids off of statues. It was just a running battle the whole week with that kind of hit-and-run tactics. It all just came to a culmination that night, but it was fun, it was exciting. I just remember that there were ongoing protests, but because they wouldn't let us get to the convention it just seemed like nothing was going to come of it. The night that brought the big confrontation when they tried to march to the convention and the cops attacked them—that was going on all week. It really wasn't different except it was just bigger that night and it really came to a head.

I was in Chicago up 'til probably sometime in October or November, and then this guy Bill Strackany, who had been to California a couple of times—he was more of a hippie than an antiwar person—wanted me to go to California with him. It was significant that he wanted me to go because he didn't have a car and I did. So one night he gets me stoned and we go to see this movie called *Revolution*, and what it's really about is the hippie communes of northern California. Pictures of naked people running around on this farm and having a great time and smoking pot and planting gardens and living the good life, and he convinces me we should leave the next day for California. So after I got out of the draft, we loaded up the car and headed for California. We stopped in Carbondale and picked up some girl whose father ran the fish hatchery outside of town, and

5. A leader of the Black Panther Party who was originally slated to be tried as one of the Chicago Eight. He ended up being tried separately.

the three of us took off cross-country to Colorado, Utah. It was great, a little escape.

I remember stopping in Farmington, Illinois, on our way to Carbondale and talking to my mom and telling her I had quit my job and I was moving to California. The morning we left, she looked at me and she said, "Now we don't care if you go to California, we want you to be happy, we want you to do what you want to do, but," she says, "the only thing your dad said was he hopes you're not going to go out there and get mixed up with those hippies." And I'm thinking, "Oh God, Mom, that's exactly what we have in mind. I won't tell you that." So I go, "Okay, Mom, all right." And where are we headed for? We're headed for Haight-Ashbury, precisely, exactly. We've got friends who live there.

California was the hotbed of protest at that time, but really the hippies had kind of peaked out in Haight-Ashbury, we found. Still, there was a lot going on. I was in Berkeley, sold the *Berkeley Barb*. That's what I did for money. That was also the fall that the San Francisco State [University] student strike was taking place and so I went out there a lot, participated in that protest, saw Mr. Hayakawa, who was president of the university and later became a senator.[6] I went over to Berkeley on the eve of the election of '68. Jerry Rubin and Eldridge Cleaver[7] both spoke and everybody was smoking joints in the auditorium listening to these guys. The next night when Nixon beat Humphrey I had a feeling like I should have registered. I'm really convinced that's how Humphrey got beat in that election—a lot of young people who were against the war wouldn't vote for either candidate who would have otherwise voted Democratic, and that's what put Nixon in office, plus the split away of the South because Wallace[8] took it from the Democrats. In any case I had a lot of good political experiences that influenced my thinking in California. I ran out of money. California was too much for me and I was getting a little bit burned out and I wanted to go home.

In 1970, I was living out in the country down by Cobden [fifteen miles south of Carbondale] on a farm. I was definitely already start-

6. S. I. Hayakawa was known for, among other things, his harsh treatment of student protesters.

7. Black Panther Party leader.

8. George Wallace ran as the candidate of the American Independent Party on a "law and order" platform.

ing to retreat a little bit from the center of the trouble, but I had not retreated from political activism in any way. I was still at all the protests. In fact more outrageously, really, because I was more radicalized and alienated. I still maintained [that] the positions we took on issues were right, but I was also confused and not very happy at that point in time. When Kent State happened (I was married and in graduate school by that time) there had been protests all winter, increasingly confrontational, with [military] recruiters on campus. I remember locking arms and circling recruiters, being grabbed by the collar and threatened by former fraternity friends who were on the football team. Things were just getting increasingly antagonistic, and that was happening all over the country, so Kent State was not an aberration; neither was Jackson State. Things were getting more physical and more violent because people were frustrated. The war wasn't ending—in fact it was still intensifying at that point in time—and the protests were escalating. When Kent State happened, my wife came to me in tears. She says, "I've got these books, I've been to the travel agency, we've got to move to Australia or New Zealand." She was dead serious. She wanted to move right then. It was just how she reacted to the situation, and so she wasn't real happy that my response was to get involved with the Student Strike Committee.

The song that came out a few weeks afterward, "four dead in Ohio"—that feeling was reverberating through all the campuses in the country. I think it was the night of May 4th that we had the first Student Strike Committee meeting in the basement of the Lutheran Center. There were about ten of us there and we made the plans for the rally that took place on May 6. We had the protest on the steps of Morris Library. Notice that we now have a "free speech area" on campus in front of Anthony Hall. In 1970 you could have free speech anywhere on this campus. There could be a rally anywhere you wanted to have it. The free speech area was set up in the wake of the seventies basically to proscribe and limit the areas where there could be free speech on campus. The whole campus was a free speech area before 1970.

I remember being on the stage of the protest holding [a] coffin. The last speaker was a young woman. We had agreed that the last thing that would happen at this rally was that she would announce that there was a student strike, and she would start chanting over the microphone, "On strike, shut it down." I could see that she was hesitating so I stepped up and whispered in her ear, "Start chanting, 'On strike, shut it down.' "

These events have been publicized and commemorated as the "1970 riots." I would be the first to admit that there were riotous activities, but my own characterization of it would be "the successful 1970 SIU strike against the war in Vietnam," because it was a very conscious planned activity that was organized. The goal was to shut down the university as a statement to the state and the nation against the war in Vietnam. Even though definitely things got out of hand and got a little disorganized at times, there were leaders with a conscious strategy who wanted to shut SIU down, not so much because SIU was evil—although there was the issue of the Vietnamese Studies Center—but because it was a statement to society that the war had to be ended. From that perspective the student strike was successful.

The protest to close the university created conditions that virtually made it inevitable, because what happened was students started to cut classes, faculty members stopped holding classes, and by this point things were becoming so unraveled that completely apart from the fear that some people in responsible places had about people getting killed, which was a very real concern, was what was happening with the students. I remember these conversations: "We've got to close this place down now or we're going to flunk out of school." Because you've missed two weeks of classes and you were probably distracted before that—it had been a whole running string of protests and people were behind on papers, they had missed tests, they had not been to class, and it became an issue. There were a lot of issues, but that was one real issue—your academic career was in jeopardy if you didn't close the university down. Then the teargassing of the students, especially of the more conservative fraternity/dormitory-type students by the police; they got radicalized. It all just got compressed. It was sort of like John Reed's *Ten Days That Shook the World*[9] on a little smaller scale. Up to this point you had tried every tactic, the media, protests, blah, blah, blah. But Kent State was the teach-in; it instantly created credibility. Then when the police and National Guard came in and tried to control things, beat

9. An account of the 1917 Russian Revolution.

people up and teargassed them, it was confirmation of everything the protesters were saying. Or at least that's how young people perceived it, that's how we perceived it. It went from a hard core of students who were very strongly antiwar, who had maybe been involved in some protests up 'til that point, to the whole campus, maybe with the exception of two or three thousand really conservative kids who just completely steered clear of everything. But virtually all the students were brought into it. People had been killed, some friend of theirs had been teargassed, somebody else had been beaten up, and it just . . . but I also remember it all came to an end very quickly. "The university's closed? They really closed the university? They did, didn't they?"

[President Delyte W.] Morris came back and had his referendum and then it was really final, then it was really closed, so you went home, you left early. I was married and such, but I always went home at the end of the quarter to see my parents. I was still pretty connected to them and I can remember my dad was really agitated. It wasn't that he thought the war was right. He had already given in on that point. He thought that my life was in danger. He said, "What's going to happen? I'll tell you what's going to happen. It's going to be a revolution and we're all going to get killed." This is from somebody who as a young boy saw people shoot at each other during the coal mining union organizing. He saw people who were shot, and he felt it was getting to that point and was very upset. I can still remember that moment at the kitchen table with my dad and how I felt, because something inside of me said—and I think it happened to a lot of people at that point in time after Kent State— that you somehow have to back off, be a little cooler about things because otherwise a lot of people are going to get killed.

That was the spring where it really came to a head about what do we mean by revolution? Up to that point everybody from the Black Panthers and the Socialist Workers Party and the *Berkeley Barb* [had been] publishing things like how to make bombs and Mao's quotes about all power coming out of the barrel of a gun . . . everybody was asking that question: are we going to have a physical revolution? I think as much as the spring of '70 was a success [in] closing down lots of universities and sending a huge message to society, it was also the moment of reckoning for a lot of people who saw violence close at hand. . . . I mean, there was a guy whose leg was blown off here in Carbondale. There were lots of people who got lacerations from bricks, there were cars that were wrecked, police cars, and a lot of people asked themselves, "Could I pick up a gun?" And you had already answered that question in regard to going to Vietnam, and you realized you couldn't. Whatever you did you were going to do it peacefully, and that was the path you were going to take. As much as there was going to be this radical talk of revolution, it probably was going to be a gradual process of changing opinions and so forth, because unless you wanted to go to an all-out physical confrontation with guns against the U.S. government, then there was no other alternative but to continue to educate, protest, and mobilize.

So I think that moment after the spring of '70, that conversation with my dad at the kitchen table, was sort of the start of really grow-ing up. Okay, it's fine to say what's wrong, but what are you going to be responsible for? It was realizing that we had pushed this thing as far as we can push it for now.

DAN VIETS

Dan Viets started at the University of Missouri in 1969, where he double-majored in philosophy and psychology. He received his BA in 1983 and his law degree, also from the University of Missouri, in 1985. He was senior class president of his high school, student body president at Missouri in 1972–1973, and president of the Graduate and Professional Council while he was a law student. He is currently a criminal defense attorney in Columbia, Missouri, where he mainly represents people charged with nonviolent victimless crimes. Viets was interviewed in Columbia, Missouri, on March 18, 2002.

I was actually born over in Falls City, Nebraska, but I always lived in Missouri. The hospital across the river was the closest one. But I lived and went to school in the small town of Craig, Missouri, up in northwest Missouri along I-29. I was born on November 26 in 1951. My father was a farmer and my mom taught school. My mom was a little bit active with the Republican Party up there; I remember going to county committee meetings with her. In fact, when I came down here as a freshman I had a job waiting for me because she'd been active with the Republican Party in Holt County. Our high school superintendent was active enough with the party that he offered me a job down here if I wanted it, working for the USDA. It was a good job. It paid more than minimum wage, I could pick my own hours, and the work was not disagreeable and certainly convenient to campus. I had that job until March of my sophomore year. In March of '71, the [*Columbia*] *Missourian* carried a story that simply said that I was involved in the planning of an antiwar event in which no civil disobedience, law violation, or any sort of unseemly conduct was anticipated, but merely being involved in that lawful and peaceful antiwar event got me fired. The next day when I came in, the Republican appointees who ran that office, who I had never met before, called me in to ask me how I thought I could criticize President Nixon at the same time I was working for him. It hadn't occurred to me that I was working for him, and it certainly hadn't occurred to me that I had sacrificed my First Amendment rights by taking that job, but that's the way they saw it and I was fired. So I went to the ACLU. But the office here had, for my own good, disguised this as a layoff rather than a firing, and tried by doing that to insulate themselves from any legal action. So I left that job.

In fact, that's when I walked up the street here [in downtown Columbia, Missouri] to the poster place, and I thought, "Well, these guys won't give me trouble for antiwar activity." And they didn't, and they needed somebody, and I was so glad, I went to work there.

My dad had grown up with the Lutheran Church, Missouri Synod, and my mom joined the church when she married him. It took up a lot of our time, interrupted a lot of other things I'd rather have been doing. My dad was a faithful churchgoer, and certainly wanted us to be as well. When I was a senior in high school, a cousin of mine who was several years older than I, as part of the church youth group, wanted to stage a debate about the Vietnam War. I don't think I had done anything up to that point to indicate that I was opposed to the war. But she asked me if I would be willing to study up on it and try to articulate the antiwar position. And *that* really was influential. After I started reading, and I can't even remember what it was that I read at that time, but I pretty quickly became persuaded that was actually the correct view. So by the time I got to school here just a few months later, I was looking for a chance to get active in antiwar activities.

Almost getting drafted affected me, too. I came really close to getting drafted my freshman year. Under the lottery system, your birth date determined your likelihood of getting drafted. I believe I was 51, which was certainly plenty low enough to get called, and I was called for my physical. I remember getting on a bus here at the Greyhound station on Tenth Street and riding into St. Louis for the physical. And it was right out of "Alice's Restaurant," it really was.[1] It was a great big impersonal federal facility, and I remember going

---

1. Arlo Guthrie's song (and the movie that followed) portray in humorous detail his experience at an induction center.

through it. . . . I had consciously tried to lose weight. At that time I was skinny enough that I thought I might be able to fast down to a subdraftable weight, but that didn't pan out, so I relied on my lack of hearing. I've always had, since I was a little kid, some hearing impairment. So we're going through the process, and I did the hearing test, and they said, "Okay. You're all right. Go on to the next . . ." And I said, "Wait a minute! I really can't hear." I insisted a little bit, and they said, "All right. Here's a note. Come back in two weeks. Go see this guy." So I went back to a doctor's office on the Washington University campus, and I remember going in, it was me and this big, husky farm boy from somewhere else in the state. And the two of us go over in a cab ride, and we're each assigned to a different technician there, to go into a sound booth and do a really serious hearing test. I remember that my doctor reminded me very much of Albert Schweitzer, just physically and in his demeanor, and the nurse that handled the other guy was right out of *Cuckoo's Nest*—it was Nurse Ratched.[2] So they give us our test, and they give us each an envelope to go back to the army induction center. It was a sealed envelope, and of course we're both real anxious to know what's in that envelope. We go back in and we sit outside the sergeant's office. He calls in the other guy, who comes back out and says, "Well, they say I have to wear cotton in my ears around the heavy artillery," and I'm thinking, "Man, I don't have a chance." I go in and talk to the same man. He opens my envelope and looks at it and says, "Well, have you had a lot of hearing problems in your family?" And I say, "Oh, yeah. Very bad ones." And he says, "Well, son, I'm afraid you're not gonna be able to serve in the military," as if he expected me to be very disappointed, and I'm sure I tried to be. But that was a close brush with military service. It's probably not the most honorable way of escaping it, but it's the way I got out of it anyway. When my country called, I just couldn't quite hear.

One of the biggest influences after I got down here to MU was the Vietnam Veterans Against the War. Now those guys, I thought, they had the insight and the experiences, and if *they* thought the war was a bad thing, how could anybody else say otherwise? I remember Dale Kindred. . . . He was one of the very early active Vietnam veterans

2. The controlling, sadistic nurse in Ken Kesey's novel *One Flew over the Cuckoo's Nest*.

against the war. I was also influenced by Jay Magner, who's a doctor in St. Louis now. He had been a medical assistant in the war and had seen a lot of ugliness. He was just one of those people who seem kind of like a saint, and he could articulate why the war was a bad thing, again with the moral high ground of having been there. Those guys had a big influence on me, and . . . it seemed to me if they agreed that the war was wrong then we were all correct. I think they gave me the courage of my convictions. I don't know that there was anything in particular that they said or did, but it was just the fact that they were there and they were with us. I felt like that made it clear, removed any doubts I had.

I started school here in the fall of '69. My perspective came from a tiny little town in rural Missouri, not even near any sizable towns, and with a high school class of fifteen people. We had been warned all through our high school years that "Those of you who think you're gonna go to college better be ready for a tough experience. You're just gonna be a number down there. You better buckle down now 'cause you'll never have a chance if you don't." None of that was true. I just really loved it as soon as I got here. I loved Columbia. Just being in a city was a change for me, a small city at that. But I loved the campus, and I felt right at home. I just loved being part of the university from the beginning.

The earliest demonstrations that I was involved in were not about the war. My second semester here I got involved in demonstrations about intervisitation, that is, about the ability to have other-gendered visitors in the dorm. That was really student government, and I had been student body president in high school and I immediately got involved with MSA [the Missouri Student Association] and student government to whatever extent I could. I wasn't immediately an MSA senator, but I became one at the first opportunity. That certainly was what led to my involvement with the intervisitation demonstrations. The year before I got here, there had been a long, patient effort by student government leaders to get the university to compromise just a little bit and to allow very limited visitation by members of the opposite sex in the dormitories, and the fraternities for that matter. I was in a fraternity. I was in the Lutheran fraternity here, which I think my parents encouraged, hoping it would be a wholesome environment—it wasn't. I lived in this fraternity my first year and a half. At any rate, the student body, even the most conservative of its leaders—Jim Heeter was our student body president at that time—and even Heeter, even the right-wing students, had to admit they were betrayed when the university, the board of curators actually, just without hesitation slapped down the whole idea.

So these demonstrations came about that were actually called by student government. In February 1970 the student senate declared, "There will be intervisitation this Friday night." And I think it went on for several Friday nights in a row. A couple hundred of us, men and women, marched through the women's dorms, marched through the men's dorms, with very little incident at that time. And then, kind of itching for a fight, probably, we went over and camped at the lounge area of the student union, the old Bengal Lair, and when closing time came we just decided we weren't going anywhere, we were going to hold the Bengal Lair. And the dean of students, Jack Matthews, "Black Jack" Matthews, came over and pointedly read us our warning and told us we were going to be evicted, and we were. The university police came over and herded us out. I remember standing there just kind of passively resisting along with many of the others who were present as they kind of pushed this big crowd of people out, and we started bleating like sheep as we were herded out of there. And then I'm standing under the arch at the student union, a place that's never been closed in history. I'm just standing there, and these university cops, I'm sure feeling some frustration, one of them comes up and pushes me off the steps. I really was tempted to overreact but I didn't—but damn it, that just always has stuck with me, the idea of being pushed around for no reason, just unnecessary. That left an impression on me.

Another thing that stuck with me was in May of that year, [the] Kent State and Cambodia demonstrations, and I can remember coming down from my room, getting ready to go to class, and I walked by the breakfast table and saw the *Missourian* laying there and the headline something like "Four Students Killed at Kent State Antiwar Demonstrations." I remember thinking specifically that this is getting pretty serious now, that they're killing us. I identified as one of them. These weren't just [some people] off somewhere else; this was one of us. This was one of us who was fighting against this war, and if that was the response the government was making, it was going to get grim pretty quick.

There were great demonstrations here in May of '70, the best I've ever seen. That's probably true across the country. In the wake of the Kent State killings and the Cambodia bombings, we had the biggest demonstrations, I think, in the history of the campus. It came about almost spontaneously, at least it seemed to me. It was a gathering of thousands of students on the side of Jesse Hall, between Jesse and the Columns. Thousands of students stayed there for days at a time. A lot of students stayed overnight, and lots of other students who left for the night came back the next day. It was just a presence there. And [John W.] Schwada, the chancellor of the campus at that time, seemed to feel that he had to make a strong response, and I'm sure there were pressures from the legislators and others around the state to make a strong showing. A lot of professors declared they weren't going to hold classes, or they weren't going to hold finals, and in each case these professors were disciplined for that. There was a letter that went out that summer to all of our parents warning us that we weren't in school to cause trouble—just thinly veiled threats.

There were three days of intense demonstrations. I remember the climax of the event, it seemed to me, was when university police came on the scene in riot gear, with Plexiglas helmets and I think with batons drawn, and started herding students. Initially it was those who were on the steps of Jesse Hall. I'm sure they issued some token trespassing warning and then said, "Anyone who doesn't leave the steps now is gonna be subject to arrest." And then they start arresting students, and they filled up a school bus with students from the steps of Jesse, and the rest of us are sitting there thinking, "Well, I guess we're next." But I think most of us were saying, "We sure as hell aren't gonna run just 'cause they arrest a few people." So we sat there waiting for the next busload to be taken away. And by golly—they haven't learned this lesson yet; at least they hadn't up until fifteen years ago [during the antiapartheid demonstrations]—they didn't check with the jail. They don't have a lot of spare space in the jail. So they turned that bus right around, brought those students right back to the quadrangle, and they all came back, and boy, that was a big positive rush, to see all of our comrades just being turned loose again, coming right back where they came from.

Much later, back in the mid-eighties when we were demonstrating against apartheid and university support for it, I was involved again as a student with a lot of those activities. We didn't see it as civil disobedience, but some students had built shanties on the quad as a form of protest, and university administrators at one point decided they were going to arrest a bunch of us, and they arrested forty-two students. I wasn't arrested, for whatever reason, but they took forty-two students away from the quadrangle down to the jail, and sure enough . . . I remember I followed them to the jail that day. It was the old Boone County Jail, which was just a little dungeon behind the courthouse. They let me in there, as if I were a lawyer—at that point I think I had graduated and was studying for the bar exam. They let me in there to talk with the students because they realized in short order they did not have room for forty-two people just to be dumped on the jail. That was a really interesting dynamic, because we perceived immediately that the university had screwed up again here.

SDS had been totally evicted and disbanded by the time I came here. I guess Rory [Ellinger] had graduated by the time I came here, so he was just a name, a legend, but not anybody I really came to know until later years. What a great guy. It seemed to me in those days that I had just missed out on the really great demonstrations, like I just missed out on Rory and the SDS. I felt like that must have been really great, to have been here back then, and never realized at the time that these [days] are really just as good. Anyway, the following year [1970–1971] I came back and got involved with a group that called itself Student Mobilization Committee. We had no idea of the philosophical underpinnings or affiliations of these groups. It was just the one that seemed to be there and available at the time. Later on I understood that they were just one subgroup of antiwar activists and I think they were characterized as Trotskyites and the other group thought that they were Stalinists. I didn't know the first thing about any of that. We went under the name Student Mobilization Committee because that seemed to be a coordinating group for national, especially Washington, D.C.–based, demonstrations.

A friend of mine named Paul Blackman was a year ahead of me in school, and we both became very active in the Arts and Sciences divisional student government. He was president and I was vice president, and we used that as a platform for antiwar activity. And we both got active with SMC. The climax of that year, in May, we did

one of the things that I know Paul is very proud of still today: we re-
named McAlester Park. It had never officially been named anything. I'm not sure if we dug that up or university administrators
dug that up, the ones who were kind of sympathetic and kind of
wanted to act like they were on our side and kind of wanted to me-
diate between us and the hard-liners at the top. So it developed that
it had never been named anything officially. It had just been called
McAlester in recent memory because [McAlester Hall] was next to
it. So it didn't take a lot of caving in by the university for them to
just say, "Okay, we won't argue. If you want to call it Peace Park,
you can call it Peace Park." The university didn't care much one
way or the other what they called it. Anyway, we had a big march
on a Saturday in May of '71. We marched from the downtown over
to the park, and Paul gave a speech, and the memorial to the Kent
State and Jackson State students that were killed was first put in
place that day. We declared this would be Peace Park from then on.
What was interesting to me was to watch the evolution over the
next several years in the *Maneater*, but also in the [*Columbia Daily*]
Tribune and the *Missourian*, how any news story that talked about
the park would initially say McAlester, but then in parentheses,
Peace Park. And then at some point it switched, and it became
Peace, and in parentheses, McAlester Park. And then eventually the
McAlester was dropped and it's been Peace Park ever since. That's
kind of cool.

Another little change in the landscape that I had a role in is the
flying of the UN flag on Jesse Hall. That's something that came
about through student government, and I was very vocal in pushing for it. That might have been when I was MSA president or a
year or so later. It had been three flags up until that time and somebody had the good idea that, since we have so many international
students, we surely ought to acknowledge our "internationalness"
on this world-class campus and put the UN flag up there. There was
certainly resistance, but we prevailed. It was another one of these
little bones the university could throw us without losing a lot of
face. So it was put up there, and it's still there. But every few years,
right up until the present, some right-winger gets pissed off about
that and we have to fight and kind of push to keep it up there. But
it's nice that it's still there.

I led the SMC after Paul graduated and stayed active in student government at the same time. In '72, if I remember right, I ran for MSA president and one of the reasons, I'm sure, that I got elected was because I had been so identified with antiwar activities. Certainly not the whole student body agreed with that, but enough of them did and the ones that cared to vote in that election did. But then the irony was after I got elected to that position and I felt that was my primary responsibility, I became less active in the antiwar activities. I never felt like I dropped out or disowned those groups at all, but I remember that I was far less active and felt bad about that. Antiwar activities were diminishing, certainly, but also I just felt like my priority had to be doing that job. At the same time, I felt kind of bad that I wasn't more active and I always tried to be supportive when I could in that position. I'm pretty sure we saw that those groups got more money than they had before.

When I ran for MSA president, I was actually approached by a group of folks that were not close friends of mine, a man who'd been the head of the Residence Hall Association and the man who'd been the head of the black students—it's still called the Legion of Black Collegians [LBC]—on campus. They both came to me, and I think there were only three people being elected at that point, so we were a three-man ticket. They had come to me first and asked if I'd run for vice president with them, and I said, "Well, no, I don't think I will, 'cause the guy that's running for president is a friend and I respect him, and I'm not gonna do that." Then they came back to me later on and said, "Look, how 'bout if we run for vice president and you run for president," and probably appealed to my vanity, and I said, "All right, all right, I'll do that." It really was the kind of thing where I wouldn't have done it if they hadn't come to me and asked me to, and those guys worked pretty hard, the residence-halls guy especially.

The man I ran against and beat in that election is still a good friend of mine—he's a lawyer down in south Missouri, a very nice guy. These guys were "the establishment" in terms of student government, but they weren't sellouts and they weren't right-wingers by any stretch of the imagination. They were very dedicated and serious student activists who were concerned about student governance of the university. They weren't antiwar activists for the most part, but they weren't unsympathetic to the antiwar activists. It's just that their issue was getting the students a serious role in decision-making around the campus, and that seemed important to me, too.

The conflict I got into was over funding of student groups. It seemed to me that Gerald Boyd, who had been the head of the LBC, really expected a big payoff for the LBC, expected them to get a big budget boost. If I recall right, we certainly gave them an increased budget, but not enough to satisfy him. I don't remember what other issues there were, but he wound up resigning as vice president before his term was up because he was pissed at me, I don't remember what for. Later on I saw Gerald . . . late one night I'm nodding off at home, I'm watching Letterman or something, and the news comes on after that. It's a Ronald Reagan press conference, and there, in the press conference, big as life, is Gerald Boyd, *New York Times*, questioning Reagan about something. And Reagan called him by his first name, you know, like he's an old buddy. So Gerald's done well.

The University YMCA was a hotbed of radical activity—it seemed like, anyway. It always struck me as ironic that they would be branded radicals. But the university police actually—we thought of it as "broke into" [but] I want to choose my words carefully, they probably had a key—but they got into the Y's offices after hours. They took the typewriter ribbons out of the typewriters and transcribed what was on the typewriter ribbons. That's the level of paranoia and invasion of privacy that was going on because they were worried about us "radicals" on campus. It was years after that, but I know that both Rory and I were honored to be among the people who were revealed to have a file at the university police department. All of us who had files were contacted—it was like the Nixon enemy list[3] of MU—and we were invited to come over and view our files before they would be destroyed. Of course, when you went over to look at the file, it was all clippings. Anything else had been sanitized out of those files. Of course I can't prove that there were other things in there, but why bother just to keep a clipping file? The university does that. After they gave us a chance to look at the files, they told us they were going to be burned. I don't think they ever apologized, but at least symbolically they kind of disowned that practice.

3. President Nixon kept a list of "enemies" and, with his staff at the White House, devised ways to punish them.

The cultural and political activists were in many cases the same people. There was certainly a counterculture, and many of us thought we were part of it. It extended through the community, and for many, many years thereafter certainly was very visible. I always felt a major part of it was Everyday People, the social service agency, in its early days. It was an independent group—I served on their board for several years, after they moved up here [downtown] and became more of a community than a campus entity. What happened on campus, it seemed to us, was that its very important function became a function of the university, as it should have been. What always impressed me the most about Everyday People was they would publish these lists about the good and the bad dope in town, "good" in the sense that it wouldn't hurt you and "bad" in the sense that it might hurt you or that it was at least a rip-off. There were these great little counterculture tabloids that were being published in those days. Everyday People published one, and then their reports were republished in other independent campus papers.

Their original house was on Ninth Street between the business school and the religious school. There was a big old wood-framed house, privately owned, and that became the Everyday People house. You could go there if you overdosed; you could go there if you needed to be talked down; you could go over there if you just wanted to hang out or crash. Unfortunately, even in those days I think it became a place for a lot of nonstudent hangers-on to congregate—"outside agitators," as the university would characterize them, but in this case ones that were down on their luck. It was a very important part of the counterculture, in those days especially.

There was a lot of overlap between the counterculture and just the mainstream culture, especially on campus. I remember one day I was out in front of the student union—I think I was MSA president then—and I was with Pat Barrow, who had run for MSA office with me, and we're both out there having a good-natured conversation, and a foreign student came up and very sincerely asked us, "Are there any hippies around here? I would like to see some hippies. Are you guys hippies?" And we both said that we didn't really consider ourselves hippies. We wouldn't be insulted if we were called hippies, but we thought that real hippies, first off, didn't go to college probably, and we were far too mainstream.

Another thing I remember about the counterculture was Osmosis, a coffeehouse near here. It was a fairly sizable nightclub, a really cool joint. You could go in there, just a bunch of couches and chairs and kind of folksy performers. It was a neat place. And of course the Chez [Coffee House] started out in those days, over here in the Presbyterian Church. There's an entity that's still functioning, much as it did then. But in those days, that was a free forum, a place for countercultural expression. I always thought of it more as artistic expression than just political.

Of course, I became part of the counterculture. It must have been the spring of '71, after I got fired [at the USDA], I went up to the poster place to apply for work and was just lucky enough they were looking for somebody. It became my part-time student job. I didn't know what marijuana looked like at that point. I had never smoked marijuana. But part of the business was pipes that were not intended for necessarily but were often used for marijuana-smoking. So I remember learning a lot about the counterculture down there. The *Missourian* wrote a clever feature about the man who owned that store, Dan Neenan: "Man behind the Counterculture Counter." I remember thinking, "Well, yeah, I guess we're part of the counterculture here in one sense or another." At least as far as it was commercialized, I was certainly part of the counterculture. We had a whole room full of black-light posters and a lot of them were political themes. A lot of them were certainly cultural themes. A lot of that stuff we sold back then would be worth a lot of money now. . . . That was fun. I enjoyed working there, and enjoyed the people I met there. I wound up working there until '75.

After I had gotten out of school—I hadn't actually graduated technically, but quit going to school near my graduation time—it turned out that Dan was looking to sell that business, and I managed to buy it. I borrowed a few thousand bucks from my mother and got a bank loan; Neenan must have cosigned on it, because they wouldn't have loaned me money otherwise. He must have cosigned the loan knowing that if I screwed it up he could come back in and take it over. I'm sure that's how the bank looked at it. But I wound up being able to keep the business going and had it for sixteen years. I still had the business through law school and for at least a few years after that.

I did worry about how all my activities would affect my future. My parents warned me. I remember my father warning me, "Now you know"—I don't think he said the word "Communist," but—"you know who's behind all that antiwar stuff." Then again, I think they pretty quickly realized that wasn't true. They knew I wasn't a Communist and so maybe that was overblown, maybe that wasn't really true. I worried about consequences with my relationships with my parents. They were very tolerant people, as I look back on it, extremely tolerant for rural folks. But I worried also about consequences in terms of—here's one of the ironies—I worried about introducing any sort of, say, resolution in the student senate about marijuana laws, even though I was persuaded they were a horrible injustice, because I was afraid it would damage my credibility as an antiwar activist. That may strike people as a pretty weird attitude now, but at the time that was a concern. Because all the antiwar activists were characterized as dopers anyway, just like any progressive activists still are to some degree, but I recall being concerned about that. I also recall being a little concerned about whether it might make it hard to get a job later, but I was never really very job-oriented. After I got really active with MSA, I changed my goal from going to journalism school to going to law school. I wasn't obsessed with going to law school, but I had all these friends who were going, and it just seemed like that was the natural thing to do. If I was so into going to meetings and things of that nature, then law school would be a natural way to go. And it was, and I'm so glad I went to law school. I was so lucky that I got in, because my grades were not great, and they stayed not great after I got into law school. Actually, I got very active with the antiapartheid groups at that time, and so I just never tried very hard. I viewed law school as well as undergraduate [classes] as a pass-fail proposition, and I passed. That was fine with me, and I just enjoyed the culture of the campus. It's tempting still to go back.

I should have graduated in the spring of '72. The class that always tripped me up was sophomore English. I just hated writing papers, and I especially hated writing papers on things I didn't care about. It was like pulling teeth, writer's block—I just couldn't make myself do it. Finally I got into a summer class with a relatively young professor or grad student who let me write about what I wanted to write about, and I enjoyed that a lot and he was happy with it. So I finally aced a course I had failed two or three times in a row just for not doing it. I remember I proudly showed my parents my diploma. The only reason I bothered to go back was to go to law school. I decided I wanted to get serious about that. Frankly, part of my motivation was the fact that a lot of people who were in the nontraditional-smoking-accessories business were getting prosecuted. That never happened to me, but it seemed to me the handwriting was on the wall and it might be good to look around for another line of work, and that one appealed to me even more as a potential defendant. So it was a good kick in the pants to get back to school and get into law school. It is kind of funny how things come around. One thing leads to another, and what seems like a big setback turns out to be something you're glad happened.

I had a little bit of a sense that midwestern activists were different. One time that came out was when I went to a National Student Association convention that was out in Fort Collins, Colorado. It was really a consciousness-raiser in the sense of understanding that other people active in antiwar groups had another agenda, an agenda that went *way* beyond fighting the war. It was when I was MSA president or just about to become MSA president, and we had this little junket down to Fort Collins. And that was a fun time. The National Student Association was a real hotbed of radicalism back then, and even if I didn't seriously subscribe to everything I sure enjoyed being around people that did and listening to them and hearing these issues debated. I remember the plenary sessions of that convention with hundreds of people and [people] going to the microphone, and so much of the debate was cast in terms of the Trotskyites versus the Stalinists, and I know I didn't identify with either group and I was pretty sure most of the other hundreds of midwestern, and for that matter national, students there didn't have the least idea what that was about. But there were sure some people there who did. The people who thought they were going to lead the student revolution saw this as a place to be and to try to bring it about. I felt like I learned so much about feminism at that conference, and I don't remember exactly why. It just happened to be the first time that I really heard anybody with a coherent feminist philosophy articulate those ideas. And I just picked up literature from dozens and dozens of groups around the country. That was the first time when it really started to sink in to me that feminism was an important issue and what it meant.

I was active, and remain to a degree active, on behalf of gay rights

back from the very first time I came to this campus. I don't know
why exactly, but I've always cared about that issue. As far as I know,
I never knew a gay person until I came to MU. But I remember as a
freshman, one of my roommates—who's still a good friend—he
was just freaked out that I would go to a meeting of gay rights activists. He was, I think, seriously worried that I was going to be con-
verted or something. This [meeting] was just at a private home over
near Paquin and Wall Streets; that was the center of the counterculture then. For some reason I've just always identified with people
who were underdogs, and it just seemed to me that, damn, these
guys weren't bothering anybody, what the hell do people want to
give them so much trouble for? It was never one of my major issues,
but I was always very sympathetic. I was very proud that I introduced and argued for the motion to recognize the gay students organization on this campus when I was one of the leaders of the
student senate and I was head of the committee that considered student organizations for recognition. That saga went all the way to
the U.S. Supreme Court, and that became literally a textbook case.
When I was in law school, I studied that case. It was in my constitutional law textbook. So I was *really* proud, then, that I had a small
role in that.

I'm also proud of the fact that I encouraged the local ACLU chapter to pass a resolution encouraging our city council to pass a sexual
orientation amendment to our human rights ordinance. Actually,
some of the gay rights groups here in town were debating it too
much and just needed to move, and I kind of wound up giving
them a boost that not everybody there was happy about. But, in
fact, the ACLU persuaded Matt Harline—a student activist who became a city council member when he was a graduate student—we
managed to persuade him to introduce the amendment and managed to get a majority of the council to pass it. We had some good
people on the council at that moment, so it passed, but it wouldn't
have come up, frankly, if I hadn't pushed it. I didn't do the bulk of
the work, but I kind of forced that issue, and it turned out that was
the right moment to do it because we had a majority on the council
and it passed. So I'm proud of that, too.

Not long after I got out of school, the city council appointed me to
six different citizen advisory boards and commissions. One of them
was the Human Rights Commission, and I managed to get elected

to chair of that group, and I was proud of that. Not long after I'd been MSA president, I was the chair of the city Human Rights Commission, and that seemed to me like an important role. I thought being on all these boards and commissions gave me a springboard of legitimacy to run for city council, and I ran for mayor in, I believe it was '77. I'm sure most people in town who had ever heard of me still identified me as the antiwar student body president. But I ran for mayor of Columbia that year. Partly I ran that year because if I didn't run, it was going to be a one-person race. Les Proctor was not an evil person, but goddamn it, he was just too much of an establishment guy. He was a member of the City Council, for one thing, which certainly gives you a leg up in that race. He had been chairman of the Planning and Zoning Commission, the most significant city commission. He was a bank vice president, and he came from a very old and very wealthy Columbia family. I just couldn't *stand* it that this guy was going to be mayor just for asking for it. So we gave him a run for his money, partly because of Chris Kelly's help. He had come to Boone County, and was then the head of the Human Development Corporation. I remember him walking into the shop— here I am in my twenties, a head shop owner, known troublemaker . . . Chris walks into the shop one day and introduces himself and says, "Hey, do you have a campaign manager?" And I said, "Well, no." And he said, "I'll do that for you if you want." He didn't know me, either, except from the papers, but of course he turned out to be a very effective campaign manager. He and Nanette—his wife, who is now a federal judge, and Chris is now a local judge—they were living near the Ribacks. Riback Road was kind of a little counter-culture in itself, and they had all these rental properties and it seemed like all the people that rented them were left-wingers. Hazel Riback and her family were old and strong Democrats, and so Hazel held a little fund-raiser for me at her home and just the fact that she did that probably made me more acceptable, to Democrats at least. And we wound up getting over 40 percent in that race. We thought 10 percent would have been likely at the beginning of it, and 41 or 42 percent seemed pretty respectable. In fact, Les Proctor was quoted on election night saying, "Well, we thought we'd do a little better than that." That made us feel good.

Later I ran for council in the sixth ward, which I had carried for mayor, and it was a dirty race. Not only was my opponent kind of a dirty player, but someone at the *Missourian* must have decided that it was a matter of importance to the community that I not be elected. I remember to this day, . . . Judy Gibbs, who was a J School student who was covering me for that campaign, wrote this big feature on the Sunday before the Tuesday election. . . . In the middle of Judy's article, in parentheses, under her byline but in boldface type, somebody had inserted in her story the statement that we sold heroin paraphernalia at my shop. It just pissed me off. To him it probably didn't seem to matter if it was pot or smack, but to me that was a pretty significant difference. I lost that race by, like, twenty-two votes. The other reason that I seized upon was the fact that the election was immediately after spring break, not during it, but right afterwards, when everybody comes back on a Sunday and they don't know there's an election on Tuesday. So I didn't get elected to the City Council.

My family was proud of my being student body president at MU. Frankly, I think that my parents were much more concerned that I just seemed to spend more time down here and less time up there as the years went by. I don't know that they really cared one way or the other about my politics. My mom even came around to the point of view that the drug laws really are a bad thing, not that anybody ought to use drugs, but that prohibition's just really not a good idea. I don't know if she adopted those views because I did. . . . I hope I didn't embarrass them too much up there in the old community, and I'm glad that I got to go to law school and graduate before she died. So I hope she was proud of that.

For the past couple of years, I've been doing a weekly hour on KOPN [the community radio station], and I'm not so sure I'm giving to the community there as much as I'm getting from the community. I think it's a real privilege to be able to spend an hour on the radio pontificating and spouting off about whatever's pissed me off lately, and bringing on guests that are people I really want to talk to. Usually I do a half-hour interview, most often over the phone, with somebody from anywhere in the country. I call the show "Sex, Drugs, and Civil Liberties," and it's mostly drug policy because that's what I know a little more about. I have people on from around the country that are experts in drug policy and [discuss] issues that are in the news related to drug policy, especially the medical marijuana issue. I enjoy doing that. We're really lucky to have an institution like KOPN in this community, and I was really lucky that they asked me to do a show and let me continue to do it. I always clip the newspapers, for no particular reason. I just see something I care about and I clip it. Finally, with this radio show I have something to do with my clippings. I gather them up each week and take them in there, and tell people what I think. This might be embarrassing, but I actually do think of myself as a Limbaugh on the left. I figure if he can get away with just being totally opinionated and obnoxious, I can too. It's just as legitimate. In one sense, at least, it's kind of a model. As despicable as he is, he's successful and kind of set an example. He's occasionally amusing, and I listen to him when there's nothing else of a public-affairs nature on, because there is, at least between the lines, some information to be gleaned from his show.

We play a little jazz; lately I play all Louis Armstrong. I point out that, "Here's the guy that Ken Burns and a lot of other serious historians think is the greatest musician of the twentieth century, not just jazz or blues but the greatest musician of the twentieth century, a man who smoked marijuana every day of his adult life and his creativity and productivity and work ethic didn't seem to suffer in the least." Carl Sagan is another of my favorite examples. . . .

I have, in the past fifteen years in particular since I got out of law school, focused and put in a lot of time with NORML [National Organization for the Reform of Marijuana Laws]. For most of the past ten years, I chaired NORML's national board, and I really do believe that it's a horrible scandal that we have hundreds of thousands of people in prison for nonviolent victimless crimes. I don't feel the least defensive about working on that issue as opposed to some others that a lot of people would think are more worthy, I guess. But gosh damn, I work with people who are the victims of these laws almost every day, and so it really does keep me motivated on that issue. So I give a lot of time and a lot of money to that cause. Especially with this medical marijuana issue, the morality of working to repeal that prohibition on medical use, there is no more important issue, I think. Maybe there are, I don't know. Hunger, nuclear war. But goddamn, helping people who are suffering from cancer and AIDS, glaucoma and MS, to live a little bit more tolerable life, I think that's pretty important. People say, "Oh, you guys are only interested in that issue because you think it will help you to get marijuana legalized in general." And that's not true, that's not the only reason. But we're the only people that are sticking our necks out on that issue, and if we don't do it nobody else apparently is going to. I don't feel terribly shy about that. . . .

It would have been very easy for this campus to have been another Kent State. We're just lucky the National Guard wasn't called in here. For that matter, the university could have shot us. They took some hard-line positions, Schwada in particular. . . . Chip Casteel was MSA president the year before me, and he was right there in Schwada's face every step of the way. He wound up going to work for Kit Bond[4] as soon as he got out of school. In those days . . . the Republicans were viewed as the reformers, and [Gov. Warren E.] Hearnes and the Democrats who had been in office for so long had such a grip on the politics of the state, there weren't really any progressive reforms being done. Chip wasn't the only one of my activist friends who worked for Bond. But he was right there standing up to Schwada and the university administration on a whole bunch of issues, to me a really inspiring guy. His predecessor was a guy named Paul Peters from over in Washington, Missouri. The same thing. To me it seemed like these guys—they were only a year or so older than I was—were so mature and so wise and had such a well-thought-out and coherent philosophy of what this university ought to be and what it ought to be doing. I was always really happy to be able to come behind guys who had broken a lot of new ground.

We built a lot of things in those days, and they're still with us. Not just the symbolic stuff. There's also a group called the Associated Students of the University of Missouri that is specifically a lobbying group for students. They're not as activist or radical as we'd like them to be, but they're still there and still doing good things, for the most part. We actually started a student store back in those days. We opened up a shop that ran for years that sold records and school supplies and books, mainly, at a discount. It's hard to make a business go, so it didn't survive, but it ran for several years.

When I was MSA president, there was continuity. That was one of the things we were proud of and that I'm still convinced was extremely important to getting the university to take us seriously. There were at least three years of pretty darn serious continuity of

4. Christopher S. "Kit" Bond is a Republican who became governor of and later U.S. senator from Missouri.

purpose and policy. Otherwise the university administrators would just wait you out for a year and get a new student leader in who didn't care about your platform. By God, at least for those three years there we had MSA presidents who advocated exactly the same policies, and the university administrators learned that they couldn't outlive us. In fact, *they* were leaving before we were. One of the things that Chip had kind of started and I fought for as hard as I could was to get the university to allow us to allocate student fee money to off-campus independent enterprises. One of them was Everyday People. One of them was our MSA student store. I can't remember the third one, but they were all enterprises that were independent of the university. The university argued, "We can't use state funds to pay some nongovernment entity." And we said, "Oh, so we need a contract for services. Just like you pay hundreds of nongovernment entities every day of the week to render services, we're gonna do a contract for services with Everyday People. They'll keep track of how many students they serve. Likewise the student store is clearly serving students, but we'll make a contract with them. We'll say, 'If you do this, we'll pay you.' " But the university really fought that. We actually had a little money set aside that was MSA's money, but the university administrators just couldn't handle the notion that student government would have a little bit of money that we could spend without their okay. But we spent some of that money on Everyday People, and we spent some of that money on the student store. They froze our accounts. What they said at one point was, "We're going to essentially ignore any allocations or recommendations made by the student senate for spending student fee money until you guys agree that you won't spend money that we can't veto anymore." We stood up to them on that. Of course the allocations [that were] already made went on. There was a period of a few months when it was questionable whether our allocation of student fee money for new projects was going to be honored or not. Eventually, we just spent the money out of the account, let it expire, and they never really stopped us from spending student fee money. But it was a confrontation that we had to fight the year I was in office.

There was one year when students lay down in front of the ROTC marchers. There was, and there may still be today, an annual ROTC march on the quadrangle. Some of our activists lay down in front of those marchers, and they just walked over them, and it seemed to me that everyone was accommodated. It wasn't especially ROTC that was a focus. I don't know that there was a focus of antiwar activism other than that we wanted the university to go on record opposing the war. That was basically what our demand was. Very similar to the apartheid situation. We just wanted them to make a moral statement. I think I can say for a lot of us, we wanted to be proud of the university. We saw ourselves as being loyal and true to the institution, as much as anyone could be. And we saw ourselves as having a legitimate right to help determine what this institution's policies were going to be, and that when it came to an issue like support for the war, then we wanted to be part of an institution we could be proud of. That was true with the apartheid issue, too. We won that argument hands down, ultimately. They just gave up and did exactly what we wanted them to do. And they were glad they did, a few years later. That was so much fun. I mean, in retrospect, it's fun. At the time it was kind of tense.

ORAL HISTORIES III

Grassroots Activists

LARRY VAUGHN

Larry Vaughn grew up in a small town in Southern Illinois. He came to SIU in 1968, where he became interested in New Left issues via participation in the counterculture. He found a community centered mainly around lifestyle issues, including drugs, communal living, and, later, gay liberation, but which also took an interest in resisting in loco parentis, avoiding the draft, opposing university relations with the military, and living more in harmony with the natural environment. Vaughn still lives in Southern Illinois, and in the nineties he created and ran a country retreat for gay couples. These remarks were made at the panel discussion "I'm on the Pavement, Thinkin' about the Government: Vietnam, Carbondale, and the May 1970 Riot" at SIU–Carbondale, April 16, 1997.

I grew up in a small town in the Midwest in the 1950s. I guess that was the Ozzie and Harriet period,[1] but in reality that wasn't true. There were a lot of social and political influences that I experienced as a child. My grandfather was in Kentucky when they were organizing the unions. They were trying to organize the miners down there—there were a lot of Eastern European immigrants that had moved to the United States and worked in the coal mines around here—so I had known a lot about this sense of protest from an early age. My brother actually was involved with the SDS when I was in my mid-teens and I had several takes on this period of time. The confluence of the technology and social environments was the critical thing bringing us through to the point that it did in the seventies, late sixties. The Beatles, all the early music was really changing the way young people perceived themselves. *Life* magazine did a lot for me with all the coverage of the hippies and Berkeley, California,

---

1. The television show *The Adventures of Ozzie and Harriet* epitomized the happy American nuclear family in the supposedly complacent fifties.

and also the stuff that was happening on the East Coast: Peter Paul and Mary, Bob Dylan. So I was becoming aware of this change that seemed to be imminent, and I can remember listening to *Sgt. Pepper's Lonely Hearts Club Band* one day and finishing that crescendo or that note [they] held for so long and I called up a friend of mine right after that and said, "This isn't an album, this is a life." And I really felt that, so I was primed, I was really primed, by the time I got to Carbondale.

When I first got here, I hung out in West Frankfort with beer-drinking, fast-car-driving kids, so I started hanging out with the same type in Carbondale in the dorms. Over Christmas I went home for the holidays and a friend of mine had gone to Stanford University, and he brought some pot home. So we got in the car and drove out into the country. Instead of drinking we started smoking pot, and by the time the holidays were over it was like my whole perspective on how to have a good time had changed. So I came back to the dorms and I started hanging out with an entirely different crowd of people. A lot of these people were from Chicago and a lot of the social movements and political movements had been going on up there a lot longer than they had around here. So these people were already fairly radicalized socially and politically, and that kind of accelerated my development and my attitude.

One of the things happening at the time was the in loco parentis issue. I remember the first protest I ever went to was a march over to the girls' dormitory at Neeley. We stood outside, and at curfew time all the women walked out of the dorms and they refused to go back in. At the same time, a sense of power was developing within me that I could actually change something. I don't think it was such a direct political action, it was just a product of all the social forces that were acting on me that I would just no longer accept what I was told. So we started doing acid, which was a big change. That really seemed to, at the time, open up our experience, make us see the world in a totally different way. So we would spend a lot of time talking and interacting on that level. I was not directly involved with the political student body or any of the other organizations. I was reading the *Big Muddy Gazette,* I was reading the *DE,* I was listening to what was going on in the streets—that was my conduit of information and inspiration.

The war in Vietnam affected me directly from high school. I actually had older friends, brothers of friends, sons of my parents' friends who had already died in Vietnam. For me it was a real thing. That was one of the most important aspects, that we knew that we could die, that we could be killed. It wasn't just a joke, it wasn't something on TV. So we began to think about the motivations for the war and this was the first time, I think, that a whole generation was starting to criticize what the government was doing. When you removed one layer of complicity and duplicity, you began to see all these other layers. And you began to realize that you really couldn't trust the government, that the government's motivations and rationale were not in your best interests. And that was the big questioning that began to take place.

There was a lot of political naïveté at the time. I think a lot of us were involved in things that perhaps if we were to look at them now we would say that we were in some ways being manipulated by the leftists, but at the same time I think it was a very healthy dose of reality and I think that it led to so many other things that came later on. A lot of the movements, like the women's movement, began to grow during that time. Of course it had been around for decades, but I think this mass alienation of the youth really fueled social movements like never before, because we saw that governments lied to us, that our cultural norms were not necessarily universal, that the things that we had always been told weren't true.

My experiences in the seventies were varied. It was a lot of fun, it was like the time of your life, every day was a party. We had this thing called Pot 101—every day at one o'clock we would meet over in Thompson Woods [on the SIU campus] and get high and talk. There was an equality amongst men and women which began in high school, probably around my sophomore year, where men and women no longer segregated themselves. I can remember in early high school and grade school a guy could date a girl and they would hang out together but you wouldn't just go out and pal around with a woman, and that began to happen and continued on through college.

Things that everyone takes for granted these days, there were a lot of social freedoms that we actually pioneered during that era, so there was a tension that began to develop in everybody. I mean, everyone kind of knew something was going to happen in the fall before the spring riots. It was just like all anybody could talk about at every party; every gathering, that's what people were talking about. The social scene back then was very, very different. Cigars weren't part of it at all. As a matter of fact, you were looked down upon if you drank. People got together in their houses, and that's where things took place. They had big parties, and also there were several business establishments in Carbondale that were centers for hippie activity. It would be equivalent to the coffeehouses now. There was a place called the Purple Mousetrap, which was a pizza joint. Then there was Poppa C's, which was famous for this great strawberry pie that you could get there late at night when you had the munchies. And there was Spudnuts, where you could actually study occasionally. You were always running into people who were constantly moving between these places. That whole alcohol thing wasn't happening, and so the whole social milieu was different.

I guess after Christmas break things were getting pretty intense. I can't remember the chronology exactly, so I'm just going to give you an impressionistic view of what was happening. It got to the point where people were just forgetting about classes because we were so pissed off and the war just had to end, and the momentum was building and building and building and that's all people would talk about. "We got to end the war, we got to start the revolution." "The movement"—that was another term people used—and there was all kinds of literature coming out, all kinds of books by Abbie Hoffman and Dave Dellinger and different people about what was going on. Then there was the *Whole Earth Catalogue*, which I think is a pivotal publication because it began to sow the seeds for some of the things that would happen in the seventies, which to me were equally as important.

People were beginning to get information through music about how . . . the hippies were leaving the cities on the East and West Coasts. They wanted to get away from all the crime, they wanted to get away from all the corruption, from the pigs. One of the songs was you wanted to go someplace where all the pigs have tails, and you wanted to get out to the country where it's real life, where you can really experience things in a different way and try to act upon some of the ideals we'd all been thinking about. That was happening kind of simultaneously with this antiwar movement.

The antiwar movement really came to a head in the spring [of 1970]. I remember the first time we stepped into the streets it was actually like the beginning of the Halloween Party.[2] It became this thing, that if you could get all these people together you could take the streets. I can remember that sense of exhilaration and power as, one by one, people got up enough nerve to step into the streets, because the cops were there. And it just became all of a sudden this wave of people running into the streets and then this whole exhilaration that we had ... power, we could do something. When it came to a head it was very, very intense. The police were vicious. They looked at us as all these spoiled brats, these college kids doing this. I saw people get beaten so badly that you wouldn't believe it. I saw a guy with buckshot wounds hiding in a shed over by the pizza place, Italian Village. I ran into it myself, and there was this guy in there who had been shot by the police. So there was a lot that went on that wasn't reported by the media.

What we did is we divided up into groups, and we would roam around the streets and we would take bricks and we would pound police cars with all these bricks. The police cars looked like junk cars on wheels, completely torn up. It became so polarized that we didn't think of them as people anymore. We were just out there doing what we thought we had to do. I remember being at the dorms, and we had surrounded what was the campus police building at the time, and we basically had them held hostage in their own police station. Over by Brush Towers [high-rise dorms] we turned a car over and set it on fire. These are scenes that are hard to imagine ever took place. Then the National Guard came in, and I can remember being in the Towers and it became evening and they surrounded the entire complex around there with fixed bayonets. It was such a strange thing to look out your window and see your whole living quarters surrounded by soldiers with fixed bayonets. We went down there and I actually ran into a friend of mine from high school who was in the National Guard. He's standing there with his fixed bayonet, and I'm talking to him and he's trying his best just to ignore me. From then on everything just went crazy. I mean it was just a pitched battle and the destruction on Main Street was ... People had no way to vent their frustrations. You have

2. Carbondale has had a big street party on Halloween for decades. Vaughn is referring to the origins of this event, which in more recent years has occasionally turned violent and ugly, helping to explain why the community still distrusts students.

stones, they have guns, you don't have a strategy, you don't have a military. You pick up a rock and you throw it. It's just human nature. It's such a basic instinct to fight back on whatever level you can.

Everything ended abruptly. Suddenly the school was closed. We had a huge party; people were running through the streets naked. People were standing on the tops of cars and driving up and down the streets, and all of a sudden it was over. Everyone was supposed to go to Boulder, Colorado, for the summer, from all over the world. So we went out and got our VW bus. We went to Boulder, Colorado. There were literally people from all over the world in Boulder, camping all through the mountainsides. There was also this circuit that was going down to New Mexico and the mountains down there, where all the hot springs are. You had people from everywhere getting together around the campfires, at bars, all kinds of places, talking about what their experience had been. I talked to people from Los Angeles, New York, Ohio, Europe. It was just an amazing event, and it really galvanized this perspective.

One of the big things during that summer was [the belief that] we got to get back to the land, that's the only place we're going to be able to do this. We had this ridiculous illusion that by getting out of the city we'd somehow get out of the control of the government and set up our own way of living. So I was bound and determined. I had to go back to school, because if I didn't I was going to get drafted. So I came back down here and I got a house outside of town and we started to live this new hippie communal lifestyle that was our thing. Changed our diet, we started eating better foods, we started cooking for ourselves, we started gardening, and the whole political aspect shifted. Our lives became our politics. We were going to live this life and that's how we were going to change everything. So the next year I was actually able to move to a farm outside of Carbondale and we got cows, horses, chickens, ducks, and we let our hair grow real long and we let our beards grow. Music at that time was encouraging everyone to do this, that's what the cool thing was: Get back to the land. There were all these publications coming out telling people how to do this, and that whole period had an immense effect upon my life. It taught me things, and skills, ways to interact with people that I've carried through 'til now.

One of the things I learned in that time period was the idea that you really did have to take care of each other. It was like, your family maybe had thrown you out, they thought you were weird, or you felt you just didn't fit into the rest of society. People really started learning how to take care of one another. Shortly, people started having children, so the whole issue of child-rearing and passing some of this legacy on to your children became a part of our lives too. That's when a lot of the local co-ops sprang up. Neighborhood Co-op, which is now over on Jackson Street, the genesis of that was during this time when all these real-life things started happening—women having babies . . . and people got sick and those sorts of things began to happen. Real-life issues began to happen. We had to develop institutions to take care of ourselves. There were women who began practicing midwifery and learning how to do that, and there were people who got into natural healing, and I got really heavily into macrobiotics, and there were some physicians who did free or very cheap care. So you began to see how people could take care of one another. Now you would actually change institutions.

I am a gay white forty-six-year-old male who is HIV positive, and the big thing for me was this empowerment that came from the sixties. It allowed me to realize my own self-worth and to be part of the gay rights movement, and the gay rights and women's rights movement to a large extent came out of that period. So that's kind of where I have been and where I am now. That's my take on it.

WAYNE SAILOR

Wayne Sailor was born in California on March 7, 1941. He received a BA in psychology from the University of California, Berkeley, and an MA and Ph.D. in psychology from the University of Kansas. He is currently senior scientist at the Beach Center on Disability/Schiefelbusch Institute for Life Span Studies at KU, where he has been a professor in the Department of Special Education since 1992. His professional career has been dedicated to efforts to advance the inclusion of children and adults who have disabilities in mainstream settings, including general education classes in schools. Sailor was interviewed in Lawrence, Kansas, on April 16, 2002.

I was born in L.A., grew up in Santa Monica, went to Santa Monica High. From there went to Cal Berkeley, graduated from Berkeley in '62. Did one year of graduate work there in '63, and then they abolished the program that I was in. So two of us came to Kansas, which had a clinical psychology doctorate that was what we were after. I got my master's and doctorate at KU in clinical psych. I was here from '64 to '69. And then they threw me out of here in '69 because of the ROTC demonstration, which was kind of the seminal event on this campus.

My dad was a businessman. He owned meat and delicatessen components of supermarkets. His claim to fame was he started the first supermarket in Los Angeles, which was then the Hollywood Ranch Market. He did that with a partner, and from there he went on to meat and deli. He lived in Hollywood. My mother and dad divorced when I was young, and my mother was in Santa Monica and my dad was in the Hollywood Hills. So I wound up spending time in both places, which for a kid was about as good as you can do— from the beach to the observatory. It was fun.

My dad was an L.A. Republican. He didn't see anything wrong with Mayor [Sam] Yorty, who I was appalled by even in high school. He was a Shriner and a Mason. The politics of L.A. businesspeople were pretty much moderate Republican by today's standards. My mother's parents are from Kansas—Council Grove, Kansas, which is a little town in the middle—and they had a Democratic tradition, more liberal. So my mother always voted Democratic and had more of a sense of compassion, toward the liberal end of things.

My mom didn't see any problem with my political activity. Her advice was always, "Try not to get killed or put in jail." My dad's thing was, "The less you tell me about it, the happier I'll be." We had a good relationship, actually. My brother visited once, spent the night at Reconstruction House—the commune in Lawrence where I lived for a time—and he used to talk about it at Thanksgiving dinner, so I had to put up with a lot of humiliation and joking about that.

I was pretty apolitical throughout high school. I was mainly into drinking and having fun. But when I got to Berkeley, I got radicalized in a hurry. I took a class in introductory sociology, and I wrote several papers, and received an F on each one. (They were conservative perspectives on things.) Then the House Un-American Activities Committee was holding hearings in San Francisco, and the T.A. [teaching assistant] for the class politely suggested that I might "learn" something, as he put it, if I went over and tried to find out what was going on in the HUAC meetings. So I did. I trotted over there with my little ring binder and my pencil. Then I got hosed off the stairs of the city hall by the fire department, and that hurt. It made me mad. I never did learn much about the House Un-American Activities Committee, but I learned what it was like to be in a peaceful protest and be attacked by the established order. So I wrote a paper after that in which I basically attacked the whole premise of what was going on, and I got an A-plus on that and a note from the T.A. saying, "You're finally starting to learn something."

From then on I was involved in numerous civil disobedience activities, nothing big time. . . . When I left Berkeley to come to KU it was the year that they started the Free Speech Movement at Berkeley, Mario Savio and all of that, so I felt like I had left burning villages behind me. KU was a very interesting place. I expected it to be a bunch of country hicks and nobody even knowing how to spell "politics." Instead, it was a pretty restive community organized primarily around civil rights and having had some pretty serious confrontations with police and other officials in trying to desegregate parts of this town, even in the sixties, particularly housing. And also black students at the university were starting to find their voice and coming together, confronting issues on the campus. So I started going to meetings of SDS, Students for a Democratic Society, and affiliated with the campus black power movement a little bit as a white "also-ran" type. I got more involved with campus politics, and then the Vietnam War stuff started to surface here in a big way. Efforts to have a peace movement got nasty responses from the university, the state, and the community, and then it became a more violent, organized activity which culminated for me in the ROTC demonstration. It went on to even more heavy action here, but again I left; I went to University of Toronto for my first job. It was like leaving another burning village behind. It seemed like every time I went somewhere else, the place I had been really erupted. But I was very much involved in the activities that led up to those events.

I felt kind of guilty leaving Berkeley because there were some things going on there when I left that I felt I should have committed to and remained involved with, but the opportunity to continue to pursue graduate training was too good to pass up. I got funding and everything, so I left [Berkeley]. But I was pretty determined that I was going to stay politically active and involved.

The Vietnam War, the assassination of Kennedy, the subsequent assassination of his brother, the assassination of King . . . it began to cumulatively feel like anybody who cared about people was going to get gunned down. The timing may be off on this, but I was also reading Ronald Laing,[1] for example, who struck me as somebody who really understood how people and systems engage. His idea was that mental illness is basically a construct that benefits the existing order. Now we would call that postmodern thinking, but then it was a renegade psychiatrist's ideas. I was captured by that, and some of the writings of Alan Watts, Marcuse. I had a burning desire

1. Better known as R. D. Laing, his argument that madness is a creative response to an insane environment was popular at the time.

to try and be a part of the problem instead of a part of their solution. So I was ready to get involved in Kansas.

There was already a big SDS chapter here. The first meeting I went to of SDS was in an auditorium in the student union and it was pretty close to full, which surprised me. It was a very radical organization, and there was a large number there. Sometimes the jocks would come with their white T-shirts, and they would stand in the back and punch at their muscles with their fists and look at us like "if you try to leave we'll pound you." But we never had much trouble with them. There were a number of us who were pretty good-sized who would rumble with them if that's what they wanted to do, but it never came to that.

When I started in SDS, we were trying to get involved in organized white support for the black power movement. There was a guy on campus named Leonard Harrison, a brilliant theoretician of the black power movement, and he taught a course called Black Power, but [it was] not recognized by the university. We had what we called an alternative university—that's where feminism got its start on this campus, with women teaching other women about some of the history and issues of feminism. That was all done through the alternative university. But anyway, Leonard or his wife at some point introduced me to Pete O'Neal in Kansas City, who was the head of the Black Panther Party there. So we would have these meetings between some of us identified with SDS and the black power group to ask what those of us in the white community could do to support that effort. Out of that came the underground paper that we started, called *Reconstruction. Reconstruction* was originally an effort to communicate black power issues to the university community and communicate to the black power movement the white concern with the war. It was like if we can get these two sets of issues integrated in some way, then we can advance our agenda a little bit. And our agenda was trying to get a more pluralistic, egalitarian system in place.

Harrison's wife had trumped-up charges against her. If she had been convicted she would have had to do jail time. The Harrisons fled to Africa. The same thing happened to Pete O'Neal. In the 1980s there was a move on to pardon Harrison and invite him to come back, but it wasn't completed before we got our current governor.[2]

2. A reference to Bill Graves, governor of Kansas from 1995 to 2003.

Harrison was a major resource, a true black intellectual. It was really a shame to have him get run out like that.

I used to deliver *Reconstruction*. I had an old green convertible Buick, and I would drive down to Kansas City [Missouri] to a poor African American area, and I would take the bundles of papers and give them to O'Neal. We'd sit inside and smoke a joint and talk about stuff, then I'd get back in the car. As soon as I pulled away from the curb a plainclothes police car would pull right in behind me and follow me all the way to the Kansas line and watch me as I disappeared into Kansas. It really gave you the feeling that there's not much that went on that they weren't on top of.

We used to kid about . . . the radicals and the hippies. The radicals like to get out there and get stuff done, and the hippies thought we were masochists, [that] we just want to have people club us and gas us. The hippies mainly had fun with music concerts, lots and lots of drugs, lots of sex. So sometimes we would feel like, "Gosh, we should quit doing this stuff and do what they do." And we would for a time. We'd disappear into the rock concerts and go to the parties, smoke the dope, but then, at least in my case, I'd start thinking, "I'm coppin' out. There are people who need us to do what we're doing, particularly people in Vietnam who are getting killed for no good reason, and maimed," and so on. So then we'd shuttle back out of that and back into the world of demonstrations and planning the newspaper. So we bumped up against each other, the counterculture and the radical movement. It was an easy detente, I'd say. We made common cause in the sense that we were both outlaws as far as the white establishment was concerned. But only we had a true affiliation with the black community. Hippies didn't see the point in that. It was a hopelessly white counterculture; there were no Latinos in it, no blacks. It just seemed to be a lot of people having fun, sort of self-centered. But that may be a little unfair because our paper was roughly fifty-fifty, after it evolved from the first few issues. The artwork and the movie reviews all were done by people who identified with the counterculture. We had this big old Victorian house on Tennessee Street, 615 Tennessee, called Reconstruction House because that was where the paper was put out. I lived there, and my roommate there was Dick Langsdorf, who was very much in both camps but probably more in the counterculture camp. The two coexisted, but were somewhat different.

When I got here, the antiwar movement was already under way. There were people like Gus diZerega, who as I recall had a very theoretical slant on it. He described himself as an anarcho-syndicalist, and I couldn't even converse on the subject, so I went off to read about it so I wouldn't feel silly. But after reading two or three books I decided I'd rather be perceived as silly than try to master this stuff. It had to do with Emma Goldman and Trotsky, and I just couldn't keep my eyes open with that stuff. Then some of the students, the typical middle-class ordinary KU students, would be really upset by what they would read in the paper and see on television about the war. So they would come around and talk to us at meetings, and they would join the demonstrations. People would throw things and yell and call us Commies, and we just had police presence all over us and following us. Some students were getting trapped in alleys and beaten by the police—that happened on a fairly regular basis. Particularly the blacks, they were seriously harassed by the police, physically—they were brutalized by them. So these kids, when they would experience that, it made them mad, and then they would get more involved. When we would have a meeting to have a demonstration or a human be-in or something, there would be lots of them. Each time, it would grow and get bigger and bigger. When I first got here, it was right on the border of moving from a primary orientation with civil rights issues to antiwar issues. The blacks on campus affiliated with the antiwar movement to some extent. As one of them pointed out to me at one of Leonard Harrison's class meetings: "You white guys get out there and you don't pay a big price. We get out there and we go to the hospital if we're lucky." And he was right. I saw that a number of times. When a crowd was charged by the police with sticks, they went after the blacks, they didn't go after us. So I kind of understood why there were these two really separate sets of issues.

The presence of ROTC was one big issue. But we would seize [on] other campus issues. One I remember well because it was kind of funny. The university had one of its little budget crises that it has now and then—like it's having now, for that matter—and the administration announced that because it was so strapped for money it was going to have to close the library on Sundays: "Effective immediately the library will no longer be open on Sundays and it won't be open after 10 p.m. on other days," or something like that.

So we thought, this is ridiculous. Part of it was that it affected us directly because we were so busy doing all of this extracurricular stuff during the day that the only time we could hit the library and get what we needed was late at night and on Sunday. So we decided to organize a protest, and we went to the campus paper and they ran an article, and we said: "There's going to be a massive demonstration to keep the library open. Don't let the pigs close the library." And the university was smart enough to see the potential national headlines on that one, so they quickly [acted]. . . . The next morning there was an article from the vice chancellor saying, "We found the money, the library will remain open, everybody can relax." And I thought, "Yes!" A minor victory. But what it did was show the students that these lefties, who were being portrayed as Communists and evil people, when they got involved in something that mattered to *them* could make a difference. So in a sense it bought us some credibility and increased the ranks.

We did a lot of planning. We would have these meetings; our focus was, "We have to generate the maximum amount of public attention that we can get." So everything that we would do as an organized event was calculated to generate headlines, get radio and television coverage. Because we figured that's the only way; otherwise it's just a tempest in a little teapot. And also we were all reading Liberation News Service and pretty well understanding some of the issues that Berkeley and Wisconsin and other places were involved in. So we would pay attention to that. One [issue] I remember is that the university would host a police academy on the campus, and cops would come from all over Kansas and . . . learn new police tactics and all that stuff. We picked that one and decided we shouldn't allow the pigs to create a sty here at the university. "We'll make trouble for them," which we did. We invaded their meeting, and went around and took their sticks and banged them on the desks in front of them, just taunted them. In retrospect it seems suicidal; I'm amazed we got out of there alive. But we intimidated them. To their credit, they sat there, seething. Their captain at the front said, "Don't move. This too shall pass." So after a lot of that, we left. But the press, who we had dragged along with us, took lots of pictures and ran lots of articles, which blew up into the headlines "Hippies Attack Police" or something like that.

This campus was different. The culture of this campus was defi-

nitely different from Berkeley. In Berkeley, people were dead serious; you wouldn't be joking about stuff. On our campus it was
more laid-back. We had this thing called the Kaw Valley Hemp
Pickers syndicate. In a sense that was the culture that dominated.
We had a farm where we all went swimming naked, and there was
a rope hanging from a tree limb. So all of these things that we did,
we did with intensity, but we also did with kind of a laid-back camaraderie about it as well. There was a kind of sense of humor
about the whole thing that I think probably wasn't present at some
of the other universities. When I finally got assimilated into the culture here, which took quite a while, I thought to myself, "This is
very different. This is an interesting place." Kansans are kind of
quiet, bedrock people that really engage you in conversation, but
then when you are about to start getting angry will hand you a joint
or who knows what. It's just a different kind of culture. And I
thought it worked pretty well. In fact, I think the blend of counterculture lifestyle and radical politics could come together here in
ways that probably . . . I know you couldn't do it in Berkeley. In
Berkeley, the radicals just hated the hippies; they were practically at
war with each other, whereas here in Kansas it was much easier
going. We had a clear focus of who the enemy was.

One of the issues was student governance. We really went after
the university as being in loco parentis, making all the decisions for
the students even though we're paying the money to fund their
salaries and all of that stuff. That was another issue that got lots of
the students interested and involved. We had big demonstrations in
front of Strong Hall [the administration building] about student
governance and student participation. The nice thing about universities is that if you confront them, they always cave in. They're not
like the government, where you confront them and get beaten. We
changed university governance—there was a committee that united
the faculty senate together with the student government—the Student Government/Faculty Senate Joint Committee[3]—which the student government kind of ignored because they were fraternity kids
and they didn't care about what the university did, so we filled in the
gap. We got students appointed to all the key committees. Life actually changed quite a bit at the university as a result of that infusion. I

3. This is the SenEx described by Bill Ebert (p. 147).

think it may have cost the chancellor his job, because the regents didn't care too much for KU being infested with student radicals. But from our perspective it made more sense, because the voice of the "consumer" was involved in decisions.

We felt very much connected to a national network, which I would describe as the antiwar movement. In fact, we would travel—I was in Ann Arbor a few times, Madison, Berkeley a lot. We would always hole up in people's houses that were part of our group; it was kind of a national fraternity. In fact, it was an international fraternity because Danny Cohn-Bendit[4] came around a few times. In his thick French accent he would give us a briefing on how the farmers were going to burn down France and it's all going to be wonderful, first France, then the U.S. . . . Actually, France came pretty close. We never came close.

For rank-and-file Kansas kids, the black power issue was a tough one. Kansas kids grow up in communities where there are no black people, and they hear the N word a lot. So for them to embrace something as fierce as the black power movement, with Oakland, Huey Newton, and the guns and all of that, was quite a stretch. There was a fair bit of support on campus for the civil rights issues. When you had a civil rights demonstration for housing or something, a lot of kids would come, white kids. Particularly after they shot one black student—the police shot him dead, and that really galvanized the community. Then when there was a demonstration, you would have trouble finding the blacks because there would be so many whites. But the black power issue, that was a little bit too much. In fact, some of our meetings we had with Harrison and O'Neal and that group were around [the strategy]: "To continue to get more awareness and involvement in this community we've got to downplay Huey Newton, the guns, and the wicker chairs,[5] and the Chicago Seven. We have to mainstream this a little bit more." . . . It was a strategy that I think was effective in bringing more whites into awareness of black issues.

By 1969 the student body president had become radicalized, so . . . the student body president, who's a fraternity boy, is now wearing

4. Daniel Cohn-Bendit was a student leader of the May 1968 protests in France.
5. A famous photograph of Newton, one of the founders of the Black Panther Party, shows him posed in a thronelike wicker chair, holding a spear and a shotgun.

armbands [to protest the war] and saying this campus's support for this war has got to stop. And the place to make it stop is with this military worship, this big ROTC parade, and all of this stuff. We want an end to that. So the student body president handed the chancellor a petition signed by a huge number of students that said we want an end to the presence of ROTC on this campus. We'll begin with an end to the parade; we want the parade canceled. The chancellor basically said: "Oh, no. We're committed. ROTC's here, it's in our bylaws. We always hold an annual review. So, no. In fact, we're going to put up a big fence around the stadium and you better keep your people out of there or there will be trouble." That quote got into the campus paper—"If you come, there will be trouble"—and that was enough to get everybody's attention, including some faculty.

So we showed up at the appointed time and confronted the fence—they did a typically shoddy job of fencing the place, so it was easy to get through it. We went up into the football stadium and first took a big section of the stands, and there we did chanting and "We Shall Overcome" songs until the actual parade started. A guy we knew suddenly appeared with a great big bag of sticks, like batons, the kind the police carry, only not polished mahogany, just big thick sticks. He started handing them out to everybody and said: "We're gonna have our own parade. These are your rifles; put 'em on your shoulder and start marching. Their soldiers are coming this way, and our soldiers are gonna go that way. Let's see who blinks." They also had set up a police barrier and campus marshals and everything to try to keep us in the stands, but we just ran by them and went down on the field with our sticks and started to form a platoon, although half of us were stoned and nobody could figure out which way to face and nobody knew how to do the commands—it was typical silly left-wing stuff. But their parade had started, their band, and all of the dress, and here we were, and somebody yelled "Charge!" So we just broke ranks and charged at them.

The chancellor had decided to bring in force in case something like this happened, so the highway patrol came, I think a company or more, there were a lot of them, and they were under one of the goalposts on the campanile side of the field, and . . . there were two or three rows of them in the front that were kneeling and they had rifles aimed at us with tear gas deals, and they had gas masks on. So it was a formidable-looking sight. Here's all these canisters—we knew they weren't going to shoot bullets at us, but we knew they would shoot these tear gas canisters, and from what I heard they can hurt when they hit you. Then behind them were huge numbers of uniformed police with clubs and shields. So we're out there testing to see how far we can push this thing.

When they yelled "Charge!"—I actually wasn't one of the ones that did this, but a bunch of the radicals charged the ROTC. The ROTC cadets, to my amazement, panicked, and then threw down their guns and ran. They ran back into the football stadium. . . . Everybody cheered, like it was a victory. I think they thought we were actually going to come and beat them with sticks. And I felt sorry for them then, because that was really humiliating. In fact, I actually felt sorry for the whole university—what a fiasco. Then we thought, "Well, now they're gonna definitely unleash the barrage and we're gonna take it big time." The captain of the highway patrol went up to the chancellor and said, "Give me the word," and the chancellor said: "No. We're not gonna do that. I'm canceling this event immediately. Tell your men to hold their fire." That highway patrolman just about died. . . . They wanted so badly to unleash a barrage. But in that case, it got canceled.

We milled around for a while. The university had a lot of people with cameras taking photographs of everybody, and those photographs were later used to identify us. They held a kind of kangaroo court down in the music building. Our job was to get up and make speeches about how righteous we were and how everybody should [protest], and their job was to say you are hereby thrown out of the university. I got off easy because I had already finished my doctorate, my final orals, so they threw me out after I had already earned my degree. They couldn't take it away from me. But they did bar me from coming to the graduation ceremony. They said, "If you show up for that, you'll be arrested." I was in Toronto then, so they mailed me my Ph.D. [diploma] in Canada.

That was the ROTC event. It was in a way staggering because of the magnitude of the victory. I think most of us were convinced that this was the Armageddon, that this was our final stand and we would be seriously annihilated, because all of the rhetoric that the university had put out up to this point was "If you dare disrupt this, you will pay dearly." So we were shaking in our boots down there, thinking, "This is it." Instead we wound up winning the biggest victory, probably for this campus, of the whole [effort]. That set the stage for all of the big events that occurred the year I left. That was when the student union burned, the National Guard came in, there were student riots. But I think it was because the students then felt tremendously empowered, like "We can bring this thing to its knees."

When the student union burned, that really upset everybody. They thought that was going a little too far. I felt really sorry for the guy that ran the student union, because he was a genuinely nice person. He tried to walk this line between the student radicals, the counterculture, and then the ordinary students who used the union. Whenever we'd ask him for space to have an SDS meeting, he'd always say, "Oh, sure." When that burned, it was just devastating to him. It was like a slap in the face, because he took the whole thing personally.

I did my own thing in Canada. We were involved up there with the war resisters group and deserters. We had a house north of Toronto on Lake Ontario, in a community called Fairport Beach, and our house always had houseguests, deserting Americans from the army and navy, and then the draft resisters that would come across the border. What we tried to do was get them into the workforce, help them get landed-immigrant status and get jobs, and when we couldn't get them any kind of immigrant status we would at least get them some paperwork that would help them stay up there and not [return] to the U.S., where they would face prison time. I had a teaching job at the University of Toronto, so I was doing this on the side.

The question is what lived on. There's no doubt in my mind that we brought down Richard Nixon. We did that. We stopped the war in Vietnam. No question about that. We did that. We gave students a sense of participatory ownership in their education, and that lives on today. There are students on committees at this university because that was written right into the bylaws. We did that. Students on this campus are aware of the history of what happened, and they take a kind of pride in it. They were up there on the map with Berkeley and Wisconsin and Michigan [and] Kent State, and in the aftermath, knowing that we were right and they were wrong, it's something that they take some pride in. Also the women's movement lives on at this campus. There is a strong feminist movement here. The KU Queers—that's the gay-lesbian alliance—that's still here.

I've never had to pay the kind of dues that some of my colleagues did. This university hired me. I'm a full professor with tenure. I'm the only one they threw out that they subsequently hired. I taught at the University of Toronto for two years. I got married, and my wife wanted to come here [the United States] to get her Ph.D. I talked her into coming back here because I wanted to get back anyway. So we came back, lived in Lawrence for five more years while she did her Ph.D. During this time I was working as a staff psychologist at the Kansas Neurological Institute and continuing to [work with] the remnants of the counterculture and the radical movement. Things had really scaled down when the war ended. And also, as my friend John Naramore talked about at the reunion,[6] after the events of the National Guard and the burning of the union, people here felt it was time to back off a little bit. Why destroy the university in an attempt to enlighten it?

I came back during that period. It was more of a retreat; there were intellectual discussions. The alternative university was still intact, but there wasn't much of active politics. Then in '75 my wife and I headed out to California. I got a teaching job at San Francisco State and we moved back to Berkeley, lived in the Berkeley Hills. I taught at SF State and later at Berkeley, about fifty-fifty, as part of the joint doctoral program we had in special education. Then in 1991 the California managed-care system eliminated my wife's job, because they wouldn't pay for neonatal follow-up, which was what she was into. We had to go somewhere again where we could both work, and as it turns out, Kansas was looking for somebody to run its university-affiliated program for adult disability. So I applied for that job and Wendy put in an application for Children's Mercy Hospital in Kansas City. Lo and behold, we got both offers and it came together, so we left Berkeley again and came back here. Now we're trying to scheme a way to get back to Berkeley.

My views haven't changed at all. I'll be a leftie right up 'til the end. I just don't see a reasonable future for the country, for children, under John Ashcroft and George W. Bush. These people are about fascism, making war, using brute force, the arrogance of power. . . .

6. A reunion of KU activists in the summer of 2001.

All this stuff is to me unacceptable. So whatever I can do to help them not do that, I'm happy to do. Right now it's just mainly writing checks here and there; there isn't too much you can actively do. My own professional career has been [about] getting kids with severe disabilities included in general education, which is kind of a civil rights effort. At least I view it as another way of advancing pluralism.

TRISH VANDIVER

Trish Vandiver is associate professor and chair of the Psychology Department at the University of St. Thomas in Houston. She has a BA in general studies/peace studies (1976), an MS in child development (1981), and a Ph.D. in psychology (1988), all from the University of Missouri at Columbia. She is actively involved in both the Social Justice Committee and the Service Learning Program at the University of St. Thomas, where she organizes the Social Justice Seminar Series each spring. Her research is about children's conflict. Vandiver was interviewed by telephone on February 27, 2002.

I was born in Bonne Terre, Missouri, in 1945. Bonne Terre is sixty miles south of St. Louis. It's in what used to be called the Lead Belt, because of the mining. Most of the mines have dried up, and there isn't really anything that has replaced it. My dad was a construction worker, a pipe fitter, and my mom worked in the schools. She did a number of things, but ended up working in the school cafeteria. I was raised Southern Baptist and was religious until early in high school. My parents were Democrats; my father was a real believer in unions—but they were not nearly as left-leaning as I became. They supported the war in Vietnam. My brother died there.

What influenced my thinking when I was growing up? Reading! I read a lot of material my parents didn't approve of, including material by black authors and about the civil rights movement. I remember reading *Black Like Me*, partly because my parents didn't want me to read it since it was so controversial. I read some philosophy, Sartre and others. I read a lot of John Steinbeck, a whole variety of things that were very different than what I had been exposed to in school or in my family. I grew up in a town of 3,500 people and was otherwise pretty socially isolated from the ideas I was beginning to form from reading.

I got to the University of Missouri in 1968. I had gone to a junior college first, Mineral Area Junior College, now a four-year college, between Bonne Terre and Flat River. I met two people there who had a major influence on me. One was a guy who had been heavily involved in early political activity at the University of Missouri, things like he wrote the preamble to the Constitution on the courthouse steps. He seemed to have gotten in a lot of trouble for doing that. His parents found out he was involved in political activity at the university and they pulled him out of school there and sent him to a junior college in a small town. We spent a fair amount of time talking about his activities and what they meant. The other person was a white guy who had lived in a poor black area of St. Louis and had also gotten into trouble, a different kind of trouble. He was sort of a punk, I guess, but had a real social conscience about the lives of poor people, and poor black people in particular, from his experience with them. I was in a creative writing class with him and he did a lot of his writing about those kinds of issues. Both of those were real sensitizing experiences for me. I became friends with both of these people, and they really influenced my thinking before I arrived at MU.

I worked on the school newspaper at the junior college, I put together a creative writing section, and I sought out people with different points of view. I didn't go into the junior college scene as much of a radical. I supported the Vietnam War early on while I was at the junior college, but gradually began to think it was a mistake before I arrived at MU. I was already interested in the civil rights movement. These were both major issues for me. I had one history instructor at MU who really opened my eyes to the inequitable treatment of people in South and Central America by the U.S., and I began to become disenchanted with the U.S. government. It was a feeling of personal betrayal, I think, that I could no longer trust what the government said. I attended SDS meetings, but I don't think I ever became a member of a national organization. I was certainly influenced by people at those meetings.

By 1968 I had decided the war was unjust. This was mainly from learning more about it and talking to people. My brother was five years younger than me. He went to Vietnam when he was twenty-one, in the early seventies. My parents always supported the war and he thought he was supposed to do what my parents thought was right, and he also wasn't very happy with what he was doing. I think he saw the war as an obligation.

When I arrived at MU, I was in journalism school and wanted to work for a paper. Someone told me about Barbara Papish and the *Free Press*. I got in touch with her at an SDS meeting and began to work for the paper. Activities at Missouri were pretty mild compared to places on the East and West Coasts, but they still scared the administration at MU to death. We did more talking than anything until the *Free Press* incident, when people, including me, were arrested.

My parents probably didn't think much about my activities until I first got in trouble over the *Free Press*. Then, of course, they were terrified. The FBI found it necessary to investigate my background and interview friends and family in Bonne Terre about my activities at MU. That really caused my parents to be upset and feel terrible about what I was putting them through. There was a period of several months when we barely spoke. My parents were from small towns and from a socioeconomic group where you just didn't do those sorts of things. They were more liberal than some people from that background, but they still didn't like what I was doing. I get along with my parents, but we still don't talk about that period—they prefer to see it as some sort of anomaly.

I lived in a dorm my first year at MU, then got an apartment. They had women's hours in the dorm, but my roommate and I . . . you could check out a key to stay out later, so we used to check out the key every night. So even though there were hours, we could check out this key. Sometimes we came in early and sometimes we came in later. Nobody really policed us. That was really funny. They had dorm hours, and they locked the doors, but they didn't tell us we couldn't stay out late. It was easy to get around the dorm hours.

There was a student hangout at 9th and Elm Streets. The people who were activists hung out there, and I talked to them. That's how I found out about SDS. There were maybe twenty people who came to meetings on a regular basis. John Schuder [a pacifist professor] was the original sponsor, until national SDS became more interested in violence than nonviolence, then he had to step away from that position. When I joined SDS most of what was going on was talking about the problems with the war, talking about the problems with the university administration, and so on. There was very little action except for some street theater, where we would get together and act out scenarios in front of the student union. The student union closed at nine or nine thirty, and we would go there on Friday nights and stay longer, then the police would come and we would all leave. For a long time, that was all the activity we engaged in. It was pretty harmless.

The two incidents I was involved in that changed some perspectives and caused things to briefly heat up were the issue of the *Free Press* for which several of us were arrested and an attempted sit-in at the Student Activities Building. The issue of the *Free Press* in question published two pieces of information previously published in other alternative newspapers and over which there was a great deal of controversy. One item was a cartoon that took up the whole front of the newspaper showing police, as pigs I believe, raping the statues of Justice and Liberty. The other item was about a member of a street theater group in New York who had been tried and acquitted of some offense. The name of the group was the Motherfuckers and the headline read, "Motherfucker Acquitted."

My major activity was with the *Free Press.* In the fall of [1969], I had been back to my hometown for the weekend, and when I got back to campus I went directly to the meeting where they were putting together the paper. They were talking about doing this controversial stuff with the paper, where they were going to put in this cartoon and this headline that had gotten students at other campuses in some amount of trouble. I was putting together a movie review, and I was busy trying to paste that up, and didn't pay a whole lot of attention to what was going on. So the next day, Monday, I was working in the newsroom of the *Missourian* and I heard—we always had the police scanner on—I heard them talking about some kind of surveillance of people selling the *Free Press* up by the student union. And I thought, "That's really strange," so I just left the newsroom and went up there. They were recruiting people to sell the paper. I usually did that anyway, so I got a stack of papers—I think there were four of us standing in front of the student union selling newspapers. And Jack Matthews came out and said, "See this line in the sidewalk? This line is the difference between university property and city property. You can't sell these papers on university property anymore. You have to step across the line and sell them on city property." So we all did. We stepped across that line to the edge of the curb to sell the papers, and immediately a plainclothes policeperson walked up to each of us, bought a newspaper, and then put us under arrest. They put us in a police car, took us down to the police station and booked us [on obscenity charges] and put us in jail. We were in jail for a few hours. John Schuder bailed us all out as soon as he heard what was going on. The case went to trial and we were, amazingly, found guilty of distributing pornographic literature. The case, with Barbara Papish as the only remaining defendant, eventually was heard in the [U.S.] Supreme Court. The lower courts were overturned and she was cleared of obscenity charges. The argument that finally won in the Supreme Court was that the paper's main focus was not prurient literature. That became the standard for judging obscene literature: if a high proportion of content was obscene. . . .

When we got out of jail and went back up on campus, there were maybe a hundred people selling the paper. People just gathered in front of the student union selling the paper. Of course the police at that time were pretty overwhelmed so they didn't do anything with the people who sold it after that. Clearly we were the ones that they were after. I think the administration really was quite mild. Part of it was that they were a bit frightened by the difference between us and what they expected of students. And part of it was that the legislature was pretty conservative and was continually holding that over the university; if they didn't control that radical element, then funding would be cut. So I think the administration, even though they never seemed to be able to negotiate their problems with students, they were sort of caught in between. The activities on campus frightened them, and then there was the legislature.

The second incident involved the sit-in. There had been a rally earlier that day. And the police always attended those things. The person that got in the most difficulty was the main speaker at the rally. The rally was kind of a distraction for what was going to be the sit-in. So the people who were going to be part of the sit-in had already gone into the building. This was where the *Maneater* was published, and where the international student office was. Even though the building wasn't secured, there were people inside ready to stage a sit-in. And the police went into the building. Those of us who had been out at the rally, because we knew we were targets, stayed outside. But the police went in, and somebody said, "They're pushing people, they're hitting people, they're doing things to people inside the building." So we decided to go in and see what was

going on. And then we were the ones that were arrested. Mike Dea-
vers, the speaker at the rally, was thrown out of school and told he
could never go back to the University of Missouri again. I was
thrown out of school and told I had to stay out for a year. Another
student, who had never done anything before and just happened to
be at the rally with us, was kicked out for the rest of the semester, I
think. That was pretty much it. I got a job at the *Tribune,* and worked
there for about three and a half years.

The sit-in, I think, was about coed housing in the dorms, something really silly, really silly. I don't even know exactly how we all
got involved in that except that we saw it as some kind of personal
freedom issue, the university being dogmatic about controlling people's personal lives. It didn't generate the kind of response from the
student body that the *Free Press* incident did, maybe partly because
we weren't really arrested. It wasn't the same sort of rallying point
as the war. It was less spectacular in some ways than what had happened earlier. The *Maneater* managed to get some hidden micro-
phones into some of the hearings to hear exactly what was going on.
They published an exposé that suggested among other things that
the university had decided it was time to make an example of all of
us and that was the main reason that they dealt so harshly with us.

I think we staged a sit-in because everybody else was [doing it],
but we weren't very good at it. We didn't even do anything except
go in the building; I mean, the doors were all still open. It wasn't
like we had blocked up the place and the police couldn't get in. And
there were not very many people that did it. It became sort of a non-
event, I think. But the university just decided—and I guess to some
extent it did look like an escalation of activity—I think they decided
it was time to do something, to stop the escalation. This was not
long before Kent State . . . and it went downhill after that.

After Kent State, what happened was that everybody got pretty
scared, and the activity had a tendency to die down rather than
picking up after that. That's when the park on the edge of campus
became Peace Park and the memorial to Kent State was built in the
corner of the park. That was the community activity. So it did take a
shift away from doing anything more violent. There were a couple
of people who were kind of outliers, a guy who threw a Molotov
cocktail into the ROTC building and talked about doing some more
violent things. But he and one or two other people really were

outliers. There really never was that feeling of movement toward some more violent activity.

Kent State was really eye-opening. We never saw ourselves as revolutionaries in the sense that people in Mexico see themselves as revolutionaries. I don't think we ever really for the most part expected to put our bodies on the line. That kind of event, that students actually could get killed . . . that really was a wake-up call.

The SDS chapter was mostly rhetoric. There was a lot of street theater. There was the *Free Press,* but it was pretty benign. There were silent vigils against the war, and a few sit-ins—staying in the student union past closing hours until security showed up. People in the movement represented a small minority of the student body, and most of the university, except the administration, ignored us. The administration saw us as a threat and refused to engage in dialogue. The war was the main focus of activity for a while, but around that were specific problems with the administration and the fact that they weren't listening to us. People with authority didn't listen.

There were really three different groups in Columbia. The student radicals, that was quite a small group of people that were probably the most visible to the police and most visible to the Columbia community because we were in the paper so much. Then there was a drug counterculture that tended to be a different group from the activists. Activists knew that the best way the police could arrest you was for possession of marijuana or something. That group probably was a little bit bigger, but clearly not as visible. They were careful not to be visible. Then there were some other people that did things like go to the Chez Coffee House, where there were a lot of people singing protest songs who were really not activists. They were sort of fringe hippie types. They started the grocery co-op and did that kind of thing. They were hippies. There were people who had communes. . . . So there was that group that was quite different from the people who did drugs and that lived in town and from the activists. I guess if you counted up everybody that was different from the mainstream there was a decent-sized group, but there wasn't a lot of connecting up. The druggies were afraid of the activists and the activists were afraid of the druggies. . . . Eventually there was a fairly strong gay movement in Columbia, probably a surprising number of people involved in that. So there were a number of counterculture communities but they were not all connected. The activists tended to be students. The people who were doing drugs, the people who were starting communes, people who were doing some of these other things probably were not students.

The student movement at Missouri was not very aggressive compared to movements elsewhere, but I didn't think much about that at the time. I was pretty focused on the activities at hand, and though [I was] aware of what was going on elsewhere I didn't compare the activities much, until Kent State. I didn't know the term *prairie power.* I did go on a march on Washington in 1971 or 1972. There, I was more aware of other groups, and actually joined the Weathermen in their march on the Pentagon. Those in front of us were teargassed. I was too far back to get any of that. I don't think I was really aware of what the Weathermen stood for—it just seemed to be important to show my outrage at the war in a more active way.

I eventually completed an undergraduate general studies degree with an emphasis in peace studies. I did an internship with a peace education organization in New York City. As a result of that experience, I decided to work with children in some capacity and completed a master's in child development and a Ph.D. in experimental developmental psychology at MU. I was briefly a preschool teacher. I worked at the Medical Center and in [the Department of] Psychology in Columbia until 1992, then took my current position as an instructor and researcher at the University of St. Thomas. I teach courses about development, among other things. My research is about conflict resolution in children. I am working with some other professors at trying to establish a peace institute and a social justice curriculum here. I am a member of the Social Justice Committee, and in that capacity put together a seminar on social justice during spring semesters. I try and get across liberal ideas, particularly about tolerance, to my students at every opportunity.

It's important to point out that a lot of people involved in the movement had a different kind of social consciousness, different from their parents and the generation that came after us. This was reflected in people's later activities. Most of them still worked to change society, but they did it in more mainstream ways. There were some people who participated in demonstrations just because it seemed like an exciting thing to do, and those people might have gone to Wall Street later on. But those people with convictions, who were serious students and activists, continued to try to make changes.

LARRY BENNETT

Larry Bennett was born October 21, 1947, in Peoria, Illinois. He re-
ceived a BA in physics from Southern Illinois University, where he was
enrolled from 1965 to 1970. He went to Governors State University in
University Park, Illinois, for a year (1975–1976), where he received an
MA in human relations. He has MSW (master of social work) and Ph.D.
degrees from the University of Illinois at Chicago, where he is currently as-
sociate professor of social work. Bennett was interviewed on the telephone
on April 14, 1999.

I came from Danville, Illinois, from a family of Roosevelt Democrats. I came from a working-class family and my parents grew up
right around the time of the Depression. They were out of work,
and Roosevelt came along and saved people. So my family was typical working-class pro-Democratic. I wouldn't call them political. I
would call them racist and anti-Semitic, but pro-Democrat and pro-
union. I was the only one in my family to go to college.

I came to SIU in 1965. They had panty raids in 1965. I was a freshman leaving home for the first time. I was seventeen years old and I
was really glad to get the hell out of the house. So I was looking for
that kind of a fun scene.

I don't remember any kind of political awareness, with the exception of women's hours. I became aware of that as a freshman in the
dormitories. We were the first group in University Park [high-rise
dorms], and the issue was why there was this differential in hours
for women. I think they had to be in at ten or ten thirty at night.

The other issue was motorcycles. It was the days of the little 50cc
Honda and the place was just crawling with them. There was discussion about banning them, and any time that kind of discussion
takes place, there's a reaction. So there was that kind of political

consciousness. There was also an awareness on campus of the civil rights movement, and there was sort of a budding peace movement. I wasn't necessarily looking for it at the time.

There was a huge riot my freshman year that started with a panty raid and spilled over into the streets downtown. The police were called. There were lots of arrests. It was really amazing to me. I had never seen anything like it.

I participated in the Moo and Cackle riot the next year. How could you not? One of the places it started was at University Park. We were out talking, at least the males were. To call it a riot is putting it rather strongly. I'd call it a bunch of Iowa idiots out walking around. There were a bunch of people running up and down the street, because once you know the police are after you, it's fun time. But I wouldn't call it organized; it really wasn't a riot in the sense of violence occurring.

By my sophomore year, I was much more aware of Vietnam as an issue; this would have been spring of 1967. At that time I was conflicted about it. My family back home was supporting the government because the Democrats were in office at the time. I was torn. Some of the people I admired most—I lived off campus by then— were involved in the antiwar movement.

An important part of my politicization was *KA*. It was an insert in the *Daily Egyptian* once a week, and it had something called "Adventures of Linear Logic Man and Anti-Linear Logic Man." This whole underground newspaper was stuck in the *DE* and it was mind-boggling to me. I was just enthralled by it. It was a whole new way to think about things. I can't emphasize enough how straight and liberal my background was. So this was all very new to me, college and a whole way of thinking about things that was new to me. *KA* was very left-wing, student power oriented, antiadministration. I found it terribly, enthusiastically irreverent. So I became a *KA* aficionado. When the riots happened at Columbia University I looked at that and decided it wasn't right, what they were doing to students. So I became a student power person.

I took a job during the summer selling meat, and I went on the road with my car. That summer they began organizing for the Democratic National Convention in August. I decided that when I was done with work I'd travel to New York, because the Yippies were going to be there. So I hitchhiked to New York City and went to

Greenwich Village. I saw the Yippies and thought it was a really different way of thinking about things, and I was going to join the demonstrations in Chicago. But I didn't go to Chicago; I came back to school, and then the riots in Chicago happened. By then I was over the top. I had joined SDS that summer before going to New York, and by the time the Democratic National Convention happened I was a full-blown Communist.

SDS in Carbondale was peaceful; it had a typical Port Huron mentality at that time. Consciousness raising, antiwar, antiracist sorts of issues. There was a small cadre of people who would meet. . . . SDS was sort of the left wing of the Southern Illinois Peace Committee. It was a splinter of SIPC that was more interested in confrontational tactics. There was no violence, but a definite feeling that we liked what was going on at Columbia University and we thought we should deal with SIU that way.

There was a group of fifteen or twenty people and we would have regular meetings over in the Ag building, talk about stuff and have our local contingent at the larger antiwar demonstrations beginning to happen on campus. It wasn't until after the riots in Chicago that SDS tried to become a real force on campus. By then I was a resident fellow over in the Wright Hall dormitory. The way I joined SDS was I had organized an underground paper called the *University Park Free Press*, which emulated the *Big Muddy Gazette*. They had just published their first issue and I had gotten into a confrontation with the administration—looking back on it now, I can see that it was my fault—and I got fired. SDS took me under their wing. SDS and the *Big Muddy Gazette*, I might add, were pretty much indistinguishable. They took me under their wing on the grounds of university suppression: "Here's this guy trying to publish this little rag over there in the dorms, and he gets hassled." That's how I got sucked up into SDS. I had joined the national organization before then, but I hadn't had much to do with the local.

There was virtually no relationship between local SDS and the national. The national organization was dominated by Chicago and Michigan people, and Southern Illinois has a real complex about Chicago. The farther they get from Chicago, the better they like it. Our SDS actually called itself Coal City SDS because we wanted to make it clear that we thought differently than Chicago. While people in Carbondale SDS were engaged in confrontational action, they were not at the level of aggressive violence of the Weathermen. We saw that as Chicago stuff and distanced ourselves from it.

By 1969 we did view ourselves as revolutionaries. I think everyone agreed about that no matter what part of SDS you were identified with, but the issue was do you go out and start fighting in the street? Do you trash [property], blow up buildings, arm yourself, take to the streets with guns now, or do you continue to organize and use more traditional kinds of tactics? We were the latter and the Weathermen were the former.

One of the things SDS did at that time was supply money to support political activity [civil rights] in Cairo [Illinois]. Another focus for organizing on campus was the Vietnam[ese studies] center, which was a convenient target for our wrath. There were a lot of what we would call "OFF AID" [Agency for International Development] demonstrations that we were a part of. Part of our job was pushing the *Big Muddy Gazette*. We also met with other SDS types from all over Illinois and we drove around to different rallies within the state, antiwar and antiracism rallies, so we were active throughout the region. I was a graduate student by then, working my butt off trying to be a physicist. We did our share of demonstrating, but we weren't planning any revolutions in a serious sense, not like people thought.

There was a lot of activity around challenging the university in terms of student rights. Once they got rid of women's hours the energy was directed at the university administration for denying tenure to a pacifist professor, for giving aid and comfort to AID, the Vietnamese Studies Center, all those things became foci. Student rights became more reactive, in a sense. We wanted to have these demonstrations against AID and the police wouldn't let us do it, and the university was trying to put up these barricades to keep us from having these demonstrations. In a sense, the rights issue became more about personal freedom, our ability to organize and demonstrate on campus. It transformed itself into a more militant approach.

The *Big Muddy* went through a few different phases. It became a big hit when they published the issue with [President] Morris on the cover nude. Prior to that it had just been an interesting rag, but that became a student rights issue. When that first group of people dispersed, the *Big Muddy* was taken over by a second wave, of which I was a part. Then there was a third wave. . . . That paper lasted on into the seventies in one form or another. We viewed ourselves as a collective and used a collective decision-making model. By the late sixties and early seventies the women's liberation movement was under way. At the Big Muddy collective there were a lot of battles about gender issues and decision-making. It was a very intense group of people, political people.

In the spring of 1970 I was living at 508 N. Bridge, and that house was raided on May 9. We had a curfew and we had sixteen people over. That was the SDS house at the time—that's how it was thought of. We had about six people living in the house, and we were political people, and during that curfew [during the post–Kent State riots] we decided to bring a bunch of people over to the house and have a big party. We were observing the curfew, smoking dope, and drinking and partying. The police came. They shot tear gas canisters through the window and dragged all the people out into the street, beat the crap out of us in the street and took us all to jail. Sixteen people. And then they just went in and trashed the house looking for drugs. Oddly enough, they confiscated the tomato plants sitting on the kitchen table, one of the truly amazing things in my life. But they took us all to jail and dropped the charges the next day. I remember a guy who was stoned out of his head saying, "Hey, there's a cop car in your backyard." Next thing I know there's tear gas coming through the windows. That horrified me. I guess I thought nothing like that was going to happen to me. Even though I had been arrested before for demonstrating, I didn't think I was going to be a victim of a police raid. That really scared the crap out of me. So I actually spent the riot, when they shut down the university, that five or six days when there were thousands of people in the street . . . I was pretty much holed up in my girlfriend's dormitory, scared shitless that the cops were going to come and get me. So I pretty much missed it.

There were different leaders for different things. There were student leaders: Dwight Campbell, who was black, and Rich Wallace, who was his VP, who was white. There were the heads of the SIPC, and others who were peacenik types but who had a university affiliation of some sort. There were functional leaders, people who if a meeting needed to occur got it organized. There were leaders that were role models—Doug Allen [see p. 126] was that type of leader.

There were people who were just hell-raisers. If I had to say one thing about leadership, it would be that there were no charismatic leaders in that particular group who could stand up and rally the troops around them. This was pretty much a leaderless movement. In a sense it was a mob, a leaderless mob.

Faculty were not really involved. They had their heads up their asses, near as I could tell. There were a few—Fred White in English and Doug Allen, of course. The faculty were more liberal than they are now; there were a few in every department that would be supportive to the cause, but I don't recall any other faculty other than those two who were involved.

None of the Big Muddy collective or the SDS types wanted the university closed. I think . . . the riots became more of a party, and it sucked in a lot of people . . . who weren't politically on board and it just became like a happening, a way to be part of something that felt like a national movement. I think those people did want the university closed, but the serious movement people didn't think that was the thing to do because we understood that people were employed at the university. Close the university, you jeopardize people's jobs. We were also concerned about the way working-class people in the surrounding communities would regard the movement. We wanted to be popular; we didn't want to be elitist college students, especially those of us who were from working-class backgrounds. We didn't want to alienate the working class. I was kind of pissed off when they closed the university.

I was friends with Dwight Campbell and Rich Wallace and supported the Unity Party. I was a graduate student at the time so I wasn't involved in electing them, but I supported the cause and did what I could to help out. The idea that the movement had split along racial lines nationally . . . that didn't seem to be the case from the ground up. Looking from the inside out, it seemed to be too white of a movement, and we were never able to bring on board enough people from the [black] community, from the north end of town, to suit us, but in terms of splitting along racial lines, I just didn't see that. I saw the Unity Party as part of a long process of bringing people together as part of an antiracist movement. It was the latest attempt to do that, bringing it home to student government, but I don't see where we were split along racial lines.

This period cost me my career and I was kicked out of the university.

I lost my teaching assistantship in the physics department and was no longer training to be a physicist. When I say it cost me my career, I mean that's how I viewed it then. It definitely worked out for the better in the long run. I think I'm a much better social work professor than I would have been a physics professor. In a sense, it formed one of the foundations for my career now.

I don't miss the sixties at all. I get a kick out of people who are nostalgic for the sixties, but my politics haven't changed too much. I'm still left-wing, which makes me kind of cold and lonely. I'm a social work professor, and I'm pretty radical; in a sense, I sort of forged the steel of my profession back there in Carbondale. It basically formed what I am now. I can't look at the world in black and white anymore. I see too many variations, too much gray, to be quite as sure of things as I was back then.

I lived in Cobden [near Carbondale] until 1976 working for Synergy, becoming a human service–type person. I also wrote term papers for money for five years after that because I was pissed off at the university for taking away my teaching assistantship: "Fuck you, I'll just write term papers for money." It was actually through writing those term papers that I was first exposed to psychology and the whole area that I subsequently went into. So it was sort of a weird rebellious way of getting into another field. So I then left and got my graduate degrees and lived happily ever after.

PAT HARRIS

Pat Harris was born in Chicago in 1946. She attended SIU for four years, beginning in 1964, and received a BA in sociology. She returned to Chicago to work in social services (child abuse and neglect) for four years, but then came back to Southern Illinois, where she spent most of her career working as an affirmative action officer for the Illinois Department of Corrections. She is currently "refining the art of retirement," a subject about which she intends to write a book someday. Harris was interviewed in Carbondale, Illinois, on July 7, 1998.

I graduated from high school in 1964 and started down here [SIU] that fall. I had applied to SIU and the University of Wisconsin–Madison—that's where my father went. I did go see Madison's campus, but it had too many hills and it was too cold. So I decided to take the other option.

I came down here in August 1964 to start my freshman year, lived out at Thompson Point in Kellogg [Hall]. It was a real interesting experience, because I came from Chicago, the South Side, predominantly black schools. And here I was in Southern Illinois, the only black in the dorm, and that was my first real culture shock.

My mother and sister brought me down here on the train. They gave me my meal ticket and said, "Your room is paid for, your board is paid for, and if you need anything else get a job." They left on the next train. I thought it was a real sophisticated way of kicking me out of the house. So it was a little traumatic, the adjustment from urban to rural. I could not believe that was all there was to downtown—you'd blink and it was over. Other than catching a train to go back to Chicago for the weekend, I don't think I ever left campus that first year. I was afraid.

We had Freshman Orientation, a credit course that you did for a year, and they wanted us to wear these little gray beanies and stuff, which we didn't do, to distinguish us as freshmen. We had convocation over at Shryock [Auditorium] once a week; we had to go there and check in. We had hours [in the dorms] and it was wonderful. I think girls had to be in at 10 p.m., maybe on the weekends you could stay out until 12 a.m.—the only saving grace about that period, because once you're locked into the dorm, there wasn't a whole bunch left to do other than study. I think the retention rate now would be a lot better if they still had dorm hours.

I knew college was going to be different, but I had no real idea what to expect. Mom had, in her way, convinced me to apply to school and I did it more or less to keep her happy. When we looked at brochures about housing, I picked what appeared to be the best-looking and most expensive dorm, thinking that would stop Mom cold. But she surprised me and came up with the money for it. So I was kind of stunned. I had met one girl who had gone to school down here, so I knew it had a party reputation. That was appealing, but I hadn't thought that much about academics. It was overwhelming being the only black in the dorm, so it took three quarters for me to feel on an equal footing. By the third quarter we must have lost one-third of the dorm, and then I felt that I could do this.

There was pretty much one black person per dorm. That's how we were distributed around. It was tokenism. The good news was that the basketball team and the football team were at Baldwin [a nearby men's dorm], so our ratio of male to female was pretty good. The weekend was a party. That's how it was. Of course you couldn't party after 11 p.m. or so; you had to be back in the dorm. There were limits, but the fraternities and sororities always had something going on during the weekend. We played cards during the week and danced during the weekends. We didn't do a whole lot of [racial] mixing. There was one section in the cafeteria and generally the black students sat there, and then there was the rest of the college.

I graduated in 1968. It never occurred to me to take more than four years to go to college. I could explain to my mother an E, which was a failing grade, because an E was "excellent" in high school, and she never knew the difference. But being here longer than four years—that was not optional.

The war became an issue soon after I got here. It was no secret that blacks were being drafted and sent to the front line in greater proportion than whites. We all knew that. It touched me, because so many kids I went to school with were going off to war and not coming back. So we were politically interested in the war.

I guess it had started in 1963 with the civil rights movement, and there were so many folks on campus who were very much involved with that. There was a group of us that would meet at the student center every day and discuss the progress of the civil rights movement. There wasn't a lot about it in the media down here, so we had to have outside sources in order to get information. We were keeping up with Dr. King, Malcolm X, H. Rap Brown, Eldridge Cleaver. It was just day-to-day, come in and report. We were all black, but not all from Chicago. We had people from Cairo, East St. Louis, St. Louis, even a couple from California and Pennsylvania. So we came from different areas, but we had pretty much the same concerns. And we were just one small group. There were certainly others. A lot of the people in the group were older than me and came with different experiences. They came with military backgrounds, community activist backgrounds. I used to sit and listen, and of course throw my two cents in periodically, but I learned a lot. I started in nursing and switched over to sociology.

So for me the two big issues were the civil rights movement and the Vietnam War, although I felt more involved in protesting the war. That had more of a direct impact on me because I knew people who were dying. I still didn't understand why we were there; it's always been a mystery to me. They talked about the Communist threat, but that was so abstract it didn't make sense. We had reservations about going to another country. Why were we dying for democracy and still fighting to sit at the front of the bus? It didn't make an awful lot of sense at the time.

My family was politically dysfunctional. My stepfather was a staunch Democrat and my grandmother was a staunch Republican, so we had political warfare in the house at all times. As a kid wanting to get out and party, I often found if there was not a distraction going on and I raised the question about going to a party they could always find something else for me to do. But if I could get them engaged in a political war and then ask if I could go out, it was like "Go," because they were distracted. So consequently I had to spend a lot of time reading the [*Chicago*] *Tribune* and *Sun-Times* so I would know the issues, because then I could start a war and get out. So when I came down here I was probably a little more aware of what was going on politically than I would have been otherwise.

There were political organizations around, but I didn't join any. I did eventually end up working with a program called Intercul. It was a university program that provided support and assistance to students from different cultures. Intercul was the vehicle that was used to bring in the black studies program. I wasn't part of the group that was advocating to bring in a black studies program, but I was the student working at Intercul at that time. It was really interesting, because when black studies was introduced here it was not because of a huge protest. I remember people saying, "We were just getting geared up for [a protest] and then we got it. How dare they?" Which I always thought was pretty slick on the part of the university [administrators]. They could read the writing on the wall. It just seemed that [Chancellor Robert] McVicar was in tune to what was going on and willing to move before it became the kind of an issue that involved big protests.

There were big rallies against the war. There was one picture in the *DE*. I was right up in the front line, and they sent it off to war to my husband. "This is what your wife's doing while you're fighting the war."[1] There was a lot going on in Cairo, more than on campus. I was on the fringes of that whole thing. I wasn't as actively involved in the civil rights component other than our discussions, monitoring the progress of the movement as whole. The issues around the war were more personal for me, and a lot of it had to do with where I lived. A lot of the issues that were pressing issues for Montgomery [Alabama] weren't quite the same in Chicago, although there were areas you just never went to in Chicago. The issue of where you sat on the bus was not—unless you went to Skokie or something—it wasn't the same. It was always confusing. A lot of stuff that I took for granted was definitely different in other parts of the country, and it was kind of hard to make sense out of it all.

The closest I ever got to the South was going to Lexington, Ken-

1. Harris got married in 1966 following her sophomore year. Her husband volunteered for duty in Vietnam and served there in 1967–1968, the year the demonstrations picked up on the SIU campus. Harris does not remember who sent the *DE* article to her husband. The marriage did not last, but Harris was far from being the only antiwar protester who had a spouse in Vietnam.

tucky, in the summer, which is where my great-grandmother lived. I was too young to actually understand what was going on. I took so much for granted. I had all the potential in the world to be a female Emmett Till of Lexington, Kentucky. You'd go to Walgreen's in Chicago and sit down and order a pizza and lemonade. You go into a Walgreen's in Lexington, Kentucky, and you get snatched off a stool and thrown out of the store. My great-grandmother wouldn't ride the bus because she had to sit in the back. So we walked everywhere, and I didn't know that's why we were walking. Unless you get on the bus and have to sit in the back, you don't know. Coming from other parts of the nation, it's not an issue. So ignorance really was a dangerous thing, which is why they probably stopped sending me down there about that time. I do remember Emmett Till, and as much as it was hushed [by some of our elders], it just made us more curious.

What dragged me into the Vietnam issue was the disproportionate number of blacks in the war. Going to those rallies, I always felt more welcomed than I did at [the cafeteria] or in the classroom because there was that commonality in terms of where we were coming from about that issue.

When I was in the dorm it was really interesting. We all came from such different backgrounds and race was the unspoken issue. My question was, which one was going to leave this room first? But what happened was, one night we were sitting in the dorm and we pulled out our high school yearbooks. And each yearbook, despite where we came from, the front page of each yearbook was dedicated to John F. Kennedy. And that was the bridge that pulled us all together. We sat there and all cried together and reminisced. We felt that same pain, and that was the beginning of us being more than strangers.

It does not surprise me that the movement here was interracial. . . . You had to remember what King meant. His message was to all people, not the color of my skin but the content of my character. A lot of people had heard that message and were willing to risk—and I think that's what it is, willing to risk—open communication and work together to make the dream a reality. It seemed to me that Dwight Campbell [the African American student body president] was willing to put it on the line. He was, I think, ready to move a lot faster than a lot of other people. He was an organizer, and he tried very hard to get people away from the card table and the parties and everything. There were some real serious students that never came out of the library, and then there were some very serious white folks, and then there was the rest, who just jumped from issue to issue, season to season.

We had Hazel Scott [an African American] as homecoming queen, and that was a pretty big deal. For a lot of people, that's as political as they got, for that election. But it was a real learning experience to us, because we were so outnumbered. I think a lot of black students were stunned that actually happened, and felt empowered by it. They saw it as political strategy. It was a very idealistic time.

It was hard when you lived in the dorm and only had one TV. It wasn't like being at home, where you get a constant diet of civil rights movement and Vietnam War. Coming here did kind of re-move you from that; there just wasn't a whole lot of biting social commentary going on. In a way, we were kind of cut off from the rest of the world here. Not only did the newspaper screen out stuff and we didn't have access to TV, but there weren't an awful lot of outside sources of information coming in. I remember just before Freedom Summer: I had a friend from high school and she went to Ohio State, and when we finally came together again that summer she was asking me if I was going down South, and I asked, "Why?"[2] So there was a lot going on that we just weren't really aware of. When we'd come back from vacation it was always an exciting time because you had [had] a chance to go out into the real world and find out what was going on. You knew when you got back down here the discussions and information and perspectives were all going to be really exciting.

I would go back to Chicago and talk to students who had gone to other universities and were home for the summer. They always called Carbondale a pseudoreality or something; they never saw Carbondale as being quite on the same page as everyone else. They always said we were kind of in a dream world here, not really deal-ing with reality, because it seemed like there was a lot more antago-nism going on at other campuses, a lot more. Now, I wasn't here when they had the big riot [1970] and I never really understood what that was all about.

2. This incident could not have happened exactly as Harris remembers, since Freedom Summer took place in 1964, the summer before she started college.

I heard stories about black students who hated it down here, who swore they'd never come back here again because of their experiences, and I asked myself what they were experiencing that I missed. Part of it, I think, had to do with my living on this side of town [northeast Carbondale, where much of the black community lives]—I was also part of the community, so my experiences weren't solely based on my interaction with the university. Being female made a difference, too. My sense was that it was always harder on the fellas than it was on the girls. We all felt that we were under scrutiny at all times, but the consequences were much more severe for them. They were more likely to get into conflict with an instructor. Girls weren't taken seriously, anyway.

Today, what I do for the state is work with affirmative action issues, racism, sexism, and every other "ism" that's out there. This is what I went to college to do. These were the issues that I grappled with. I [still] come away [from problems at my work] sometimes, not so much as I did in the beginning, asking, "Is it because I'm black; is it because I'm female; is it . . . ?"

When you're in college, home is three hundred miles away. Overnight, you're in an entirely different environment. You go from urban to rural. In Carbondale, you could walk from one end of town to the other, and when you came from a place like Chicago it was all so different. We used to laugh about being in a hick town. We'd laugh about fertilizer commercials on TV: "Where are we? What planet have we arrived on?" That had just as strong an impact as everything else. It was all these different things competing. It was an emotional roller coaster. Coming to Carbondale in the sixties was rough. There were so many up-close issues that we had to deal with; just negotiating around all these was really a challenge. Partying was a way of keeping your sanity about all these different issues to be confronted and dealt with.

When you come here to a predominantly white campus, it's not only "What am I doing here?" but it's "Am I really inferior?" That's the question you have to grapple with. I don't think it matters what high school you came from—I went to a predominantly black school—the message within society was always about inferiority or superiority. Here you're really put on the line, put up or shut up. It was a scary experience coming down here. You had to negotiate all these things, and sink or swim.

I would tease my parents about sending me to college: "It's a real upscale way of doing it, but you were really just kicking me out of the house." But I'd thank my mom for it. I can't imagine what life would have been like or how I would have been different had I not come here, because SIU was pretty progressive. It was considered in a lot of ways to be pretty progressive at the time, and in a lot of ways kind of backward.

My father graduated from the University of Wisconsin–Madison, which is why he wanted me to go there. I did not want to follow in his footsteps, and I didn't like the hills and I hated winter. Mom did some college, then when Dad went into the service he was stationed in England. He went to Oxford and got a degree, but he was a victim of World War II, physically disabled, mentally wrecked, and nobody was going to employ a black man with a degree in economics and a law degree. It just wasn't going to happen. He was very frustrated and very bitter.

I didn't understand it as a kid, but as I became an adult . . . when I think of some of the frustrations that he had to have experienced every day of his life. He had run track with Jesse Owens, and to be crippled in the war by itself was just one trauma. But he was always pushing me to go to school. When I would get one of his letters here while I was in school, that would be one of the gathering points in the hall. By that time we had all become friends. They had me in charge of watching the time when they were sunbathing. I didn't understand the concept of sunbathing, and I didn't know that people actually burned. I was the wrong person for the job. When Dad's letters would come, we would all gather around and read. He used all those fifty-cent words, and you needed to have a dictionary just to understand the point he was making. It wasn't just me, it was all of us. We had to get out the thesaurus and encyclopedia and the dictionary. . . . He was pretty far out there, and he could have been a professor easily, but it wasn't to be.

CAROLJEAN BRUNE

Caroljean Brune was born in Clay Center, Kansas. She attended the University of Kansas on and off from 1964 to 1984, earning a BA in psychology in 1972 and an MBA in 1984. She is currently the business manager for the School of Education at KU. Brune was interviewed in Lawrence, Kansas, on April 17, 2002.

I was born in 1946, the first year of the baby boomers, in a small town, a very small town in middle northwestern Kansas, not too far from Manhattan, close to the Nebraska border. My brother and my sister and I were the first generation of our family to go to college. My dad was a postman. We also had a small family grocery store that everybody in the family worked in, my grandparents, my siblings, my parents. It was a small-town Kansas upbringing, not anything unusual.

My parents both worked in the grocery store, right across the street from where we lived. My father was a Roosevelt Democrat. In fact, back in the days when he worked in the postal department he did get an appointment as associate postmaster, or whatever, when Kennedy was elected. So I was acutely aware that there were political patronage things going on. My grandparents on the other side were strong Republicans. So it was a mix. My mother tended to be a Democrat, so I grew up I suppose in a more Democratic family. I remember the 1956 Democratic convention, the first one I clearly remember, with Adlai Stevenson. . . . I always thought politics was an exciting thing. I loved the old conventions, I loved to watch them on TV. I didn't [follow politics] too much locally because Kansas is a very strong Republican state, so there were never any Democrats running for anything locally. But I had very early Democratic roots.

My parents were Protestants. I joined the Catholic Church more out

247

of rebellion against what I considered my father's bigotry when I was a freshman in high school. I religiously attended Mass every Sunday for four years and then dropped it when I came to college. . . . I'm probably more agnostic than anything. My dad was superintendent of the Methodist Sunday school, and they were Methodists. My grandparents were Baptists. They never missed church.

I listened to a lot of Woody Guthrie when I was younger, as well as country, which was a favorite of my older brother. My first semester at KU, 1964, Bob Dylan hit the scene, followed by the Rolling Stones, and things were never the same again.

I was influenced, I think, very early by the Democratic tenets of fair play for the underdog, the working-class people. I didn't read any social activism sort of stuff in high school at all. It wasn't until I came down to college that I became acquainted with [that]. . . . Saul Alinsky[1] was one of the first people that I read that got me very excited about grassroots movements and what people banding together could do. There was none of that, of course, growing up in Clay Center. I think I always felt acutely that I was more for whoever I felt was being oppressed in a situation. It was kind of a vague, undefined feeling. Until I came down here [KU].

I came down here as soon as I graduated from high school; I came in the summer of 1964. Oh my gosh, it was pretty awful. I've got letters on the wall that the dean of women sent my parents, one letter right after another saying that your daughter probably is going to have a very short career here because she doesn't seem to respect the rules and follow them very well. Well, the rules were that women were second-, third-, fourth-class citizens. There were closing hours. You signed in and out of dorms, even if you were going to the library. Ten thirty, you had to be in your room—we had hall monitors. Women had to live in organized housing until their senior year. Women couldn't own cars down here. We had to go to lectures from the dean of women who told us that women, for instance, never sat this way [one leg crossed over another], you crossed your legs at the ankle. Somebody might be looking up your skirt. Let a gentleman light your cigarette. That was back in the days when cigarette-smoking was fine, but women were supposed to let gen-

---

1. An influential community organizer from Chicago whose writing laid out rules for organizers interested in bringing people together to work for social justice.

tlemen light their cigarettes for them. You couldn't wear jeans on campus. You could wear pantsuits if the temperature got below 35. Pantsuits, you know? It was unreal, just totally unreal. So of course, those rules, combined with the group of people I kind of got to know right away . . . it was a disaster. I got married in January of '65 simply to get away from university housing. I had two children from that marriage so I don't regret it a bit, but the marriage didn't last, of course. No marriage built on the premise that somebody is escaping from something is going to last.

There was this wonderful little neighborhood bar called the Bierstube, down on Tennessee about six blocks from here. It served German beer; it was run by graduate students in the German department here. And it was kind of a hangout for upper-class philosophy majors. These were the first people I ran into, people who were followers of Jean-Paul Sartre and Simone de Beauvoir,[2] people who introduced me to names I had never heard in my life. These were people who had been to places like Harvard or MIT and had come back for one reason or another. These were people who would stay up all night having philosophical arguments. Bertrand Russell[3] I heard about for the first time in my life. There was also a fringe group of people who were really into the Beat poetry and were writing their own poetry modeled on that. This was the time of Lawrence Ferlinghetti's[4] small-press poetry. There were a lot of small-press publications around. Lawrence Ferlinghetti, Jack Kerouac. These were people who just opened whole new worlds to me.

And then of course very quickly things started happening here. It's quite ironic—Walter Bgoya is speaking tonight in Kansas City. He was a student from a royal family in Tanganyika, and he was here at school, and he was black. He was very, very instrumental in getting the civil rights movement finally started here. He was well-spoken, very nice looking, and he wasn't an American. All of the horrible injustices that were being done to black people . . . There were fraternities here, the Sigma Nu house primarily, that still had in their bylaws that blacks need not apply. It was in the bylaws. There was a nightclub, the Thunderbird, on the corner of Iowa and

2. De Beauvoir was a French writer and philosopher whose work, especially *The Second Sex,* had a significant effect on the emerging feminist movement.
3. British philosopher noted for his many antiwar and antinuclear protests.
4. Influential Beat poet and part owner of the City Lights bookstore in San Francisco, a mecca for writers and artists.

23rd Street, where if a black showed up at the door or a white ac-
companied by a black, they were not allowed in. So [Bgoya] started
getting the movement rolling here as far as demonstrations. We had
a lot of picketing in front of the Sigma Nu house and the Thunderbird, which finally closed. The Sigma Nu house didn't close; they
changed their bylaws two or three years later. But the Thunderbird
closed. People just stopped going to it when they realized its racist
policies. Then that spring, Charlie Hook, who later committed suicide on the steps of the induction center in San Francisco by slash-
ing his wrists, was here at school. He was from an East Coast family.
And he started the antiwar movement. There were just an awful lot
of things starting up here. It got people involved in consciousness-
raising, at least those of us who [joined the movement]. I guess life
went on as normal in the major part of the university, but it seemed
like everything that was really exciting was happening in these
groups and these movements.

I got involved in civil rights. I got involved very much in the antiwar movement. One of the traditions at KU was a military ball held
every fall, in which the ROTC, which was very active here as it was
on most campuses, would have this big [event]. And women would
be invited by a group of guys in uniform who would come to their
sorority or residence hall. They would come to the dinner and read
your name out loud, and you'd come up and get the invitation. A
group of graduate students got the "unmilitary ball" started, which
was held at the Stables, a very, very popular pub here in Lawrence.
And the unmilitary ball became a tradition that lasted way beyond
[the event that inspired it]. The military ball finally stopped happening because there was so much controversy and so many demonstrations; it just wasn't a good thing to do.

We had peace vigils. Every Sunday from noon to one there would
be a silent vigil down in the park, Central Park, where you would
just stand, not necessarily holding signs or anything. A few people
had signs, but you would just go and stand for an hour for peace in
Southeast Asia. And the crowd grew and grew and grew. We started
out with maybe twenty people every Sunday. By the time we were
celebrating the second anniversary of this vigil, there were over five
hundred people in the park. It made a difference. I think it made a
difference.

Then I was having babies right along. I'm glad I had them young,
and I'm glad I had them at that time because I just took it right in

stride. I just took them with me most of the places I went. When the Kent State killings and the Cambodian invasion took place, and there were universities all over the United States that were closing down, we had a big demonstration during the spring ROTC review at the football stadium. And a whole bunch of us went. I took both my kids and went. We were all arrested. They had a mock court where they tried the first five, and dismissed the charges, so the rest of us didn't have a record, I guess. But they did [cancel the ROTC review], and it was a good thing. It did cause the Board of Regents and the state legislature to become so angry that they fired the chancellor because of that, but then this was happening all over the United States at that time.[5]

SNCC had a chapter here. Charlie Hook was president of that before he left. CORE had a chapter here. Some of the people who were initially involved in that, in fact the people whose house we met in, are still here, a retired faculty member and his wife. Those were the two major national movements that we had here. It wasn't until a little bit later, the late sixties and early seventies, that the black student movement really got going here. Of course, I wasn't involved in that other than being sympathetic to the cause. Then along came '72 and the feminist movement really got started. And I was involved in that. It's totally amazing that we just had the thirtieth anniversary of the February Sisters and I'm still very close friends of two of the women that were in that movement.

That started with Robin Morgan coming to campus, coming to talk to us as she did again this year. She's just the most amazing woman to listen to. She's just very empowering. You can't hear her without really being moved to do something. We had had a tradition here, a bunch of women . . . after having been in the civil rights movement and the antiwar movement, we knew how movements were supposed to happen. And we could see that women were getting the short end of most of what was going on. The guys loved to sit around and plan grandiose marches or demonstrations or sit-ins, but when it came down to working out the details of who was going to feed all these people, who was going to clean up after them, who was going to take care of the kids while we were all doing this, well, they couldn't be bothered. We were doing that. And who got interviewed by the press all the time? They did. And when you look

5. Brune is likely conflating the events of spring 1969 and spring 1970.

at pictures, the old pictures that were in the paper back then, the first six lines in any march were guys, white guys, okay? So we began to have issues.

We had been trying to get Watkins Hospital, the student hospital . . . it would dispense no birth control information or devices of any kind. And it didn't matter whether you were a married woman student or single or what. There would be no information, no birth control pills, no pelvic exams, no Pap smears—nothing was issued at the student hospital. A contingent of us went to talk to the director one day, who looked us in the eye and said he wasn't going to turn the student hospital into a whorehouse by providing these things, encouraging promiscuity. We said, "Look, we're married. We've got kids. It's very, very inconvenient"—most of us had campus jobs, were going to school, taking care of the kids—"to try and schedule a doctor's appointment at the public health clinic." It didn't make any difference.

Another thing is that there were absolutely no child care facilities on campus, and there were very few full-time places where we could take our kids while we worked and went to class. We wanted something available on campus. We were willing to pay what we could to get it going, but that was one of the things we wanted.

At that time, there was a glaring lack [of women]—in fact, there were zero women—in the administration. It was all white males, 100 percent: all of the deans of the schools, all of the top university administration in Strong Hall from the chancellor on down. We wanted a woman administrator.

We wanted a women's studies program, no matter how small. We knew we wouldn't have a full-fledged history department or philosophy department right off the bat. But, for heaven's sake, there was a lot of valuable material [that wasn't being taught]. Women's studies had started in other universities and we were willing to do the research and see how they started, what they were teaching, what kind of faculty were needed. But, no, totally out of the question. It wasn't "viable."

The other thing was that in the late sixties, or at least by the seventies, the federal government had mandated that every state-funded university or any university that received federal funding in any form had to have an affirmative action program. We had no affirmative action program. They kept saying, "We're working on it."

We said, "Good. We are now two years out of violation without an affirmative action program. We need it, now!" Nothing. There were groups of us with [all these] particular interests who were meeting on sort of a regular basis with the administrators who were in charge, and getting nowhere.

We met with Robin [Morgan] after her talk and told her all this. And she just kind of looked at us and said, "Well, what are you doing about it?" That was a Thursday night, and Friday we went about our business. And Friday night one of my friends called and said, "Hey, you know, Robin's got something. What are we doing about it? I think we ought to take over a building on our own." And that was kind of scary. I had two kids, I had a campus job, and I was getting close to finishing my degree. But we thought . . . we did have a building that was a likely possibility because one of the people in the group had a key to it. And it was off campus; it was the East Asian studies building that no longer exists. It was in an old house, right off campus. We agreed to get together in small groups at various locations and then maybe converge on the house all together at about eight. It sounds like a really paranoid way of going about it, but we were all paranoid. We had documented cases of the attorney general of Kansas, Vern Miller, who was notorious, coming to the demonstrations taking pictures—we've seen these pictures in the archives; we had them at the reunion—taking pictures of who was doing what around here. And we as women really had more at stake than our male counterparts because for the most part a lot of us had kids. But we did it anyway. We went in.

The stories we heard about the administration's reaction were kind of funny. Evidently Chancellor Chalmers, who was sort of an okay guy, probably one of the better chancellors we've had, was hosting a bridge game at the chancellor's house that night. Of course the campus cops called him, about eight thirty, and said, "Chancellor, there are a bunch of women and children that have taken over a building." And he said, "Look, I'm playing bridge. Get the police and get them out." One of the women who was playing bridge at the house was Emily Taylor, who was dean of women at the time, and she said, "Now, Chancellor, how is it going to look if you call the armed police in to a bunch of women and children who are sitting in a house having a picnic and not doing anybody any harm? That won't look good." So he says, "Well, you go over and try and talk to them." She and two other young women faculty members did come over to the house, outside the house. They didn't come in; we didn't invite them in, and they didn't come in. We designated one person as our spokesperson who did talk to them, did convey the frustration that we had been going through and had culminated in us taking over the building. Received assurances that "Oh, the affirmative action program is on the table," that was the next thing the administration was going do. And, oh, child care, yes, that was going to be coming. At any rate, assurances that at the very least we would be included in talks that would hopefully lead to these programs being enacted in the very, very near future. That was the most we could get; that was really all we could hope for.

And it happened. A lot of it did happen. We did get an affirmative action program right away. We did have Frances Horowitz, who was a very respected local scholar, appointed as vice chancellor for research and graduate studies. We did get Hilltop [Child Development Center]. It started out kind of small, but they just built a brand new building a year and a half ago. Health care came. We didn't get as far in health care services as we liked right away, because they really had to wait until this despicable director of the health center retired. They couldn't do much while he was still in the way, but he retired within five years. That came about.

We all went out [of the building] the next morning and went about our lives. I never in my mind thought that this would be anything that anybody would remember. With everything else that was happening here, I just didn't think that would be any more outstanding. But Robin Morgan called about a week later and she said, "This is the first time that women, on their own, for their own issues, have taken over a building." We didn't know it at the time, but it's nice to be the first. . . . We decided that night that we needed a name, and it was February, and Robin Morgan had just [published] *Sisterhood Is Powerful* and that's what she talked about, so we became the February Sisters, just amongst ourselves, and it stuck.

The civil rights movement started first and then kind of melded into the antiwar movement, and then the black [power] movement kind of was an offshoot, and feminism came last. . . . Of course, in the Midwest things always happen a little later than on the coasts, but they followed the same pattern as everything else around the United States. We didn't see ourselves as different from people on the coasts. We all admired them. They were role models, mentors in a way.... You read [about], or you saw in the news, Berkeley—Sproul Plaza—or Columbia [University]. And these people were so articulate and so well-read, such leaders. But then we had our own—we had Charlie Hook and Walter Bgoya, and we had great women, and we had local people who emerged as being every bit as good. I think the backlash against us was worse here than on either coast, because this is the Bible Belt. Good Kansas kids don't act like that, so it must be outside agitators. The only worse place would have been the South, I think. They shot people down there. We did have shootings here, too. It was pretty sobering. I was up on Jayhawk Boulevard the night that Rick Dowdell was killed. That was during one of Vern Miller's curfews. That was something you never want to see again.

That time was such a communal time. When I look back on it, the thing I treasure the most is the sense of being part of a group that you don't find now. Everybody is into their own little thing; for the most part people are much more solitary and much more individualistic. [But back then] people lived in communes; every third apartment building in Lawrence was a commune. We had wonderful bookstores. There was one, the Tansy Bookstore, that had local poetry readings every night, live music; it was kind of a combined coffeehouse and bookstore. Free University classes were held there on a regular basis. The Free University was something that started here in the late sixties, early seventies as an alternative to the courses that were offered for credit. And a lot of them were taught in the local bookstores. There were bars in town, like the Bierstube, that were known as places where you could sit around and have intellectual discussions. The Abington Bookstore, just down from the student union (it was torn down; now it's a parking lot) . . . the couple that owned it would open up the store at night for this sort of activity. If you needed a space to have a meeting about a demonstration the next day, they would come and open up their store for you. Word just got around that there's a meeting at the Gaslight tonight, somebody's doing something at the Tansy Bookstore. I guess students today have places like that, but sometimes I get discouraged that there's just not as much social activism. And then sometimes I get very encouraged because I see that students will declare a whole Volunteer Day where they'll open up Jayhawk

Boulevard and have table after table after table of things . . . sign up for Habitat for Humanity or come help us paint this black church in North Lawrence or something like that, and that's great.

For the most part they [political and cultural activists] were the same group of people. I think everybody was politicized back then. I really do. Even people whose lives were centered on their painting or their poetry or their music were politicized. The times were just like that. Within the group everybody helped everybody else and nobody felt threatened. You felt great. It was just such a good feeling.

When I got an undergraduate degree in psychology, finally, in '72, I wanted to go into social welfare graduate school, and that's what I started in. Saul Alinsky was just my hero. I started in social welfare, took the whole first year of classes, and was working part-time on campus. And then I got to the second year and they said, "Okay, it's time to do field experience for a year—and by the way, we don't pay you anything." It was eight to five for a whole two semesters and there was no way I could do that with kids. I had to have a job. So I dropped out of graduate school in social welfare at that point and got a full-time job on campus, one that enabled me to take classes. I started messing around with some math classes, which I'd always liked, and some accounting classes. I did that for about two years and I thought, "I am just wasting time here taking these classes. I should either go for a degree or not." So I decided to apply for the MBA program and I got accepted, and I completed my MBA in '84 here at KU. I always worked full-time. I really had good jobs on campus that allowed me to take two classes every semester in the business school. So I got an MBA. I'm almost embarrassed to say that's what I ended up with. But I don't think it changed me. I hated the program, but I had to do something to make a living.

I always worked on campus, but they were clerical jobs while I was getting my degree. When I got my MBA, I applied for and got a position in the budget office at the university, an accountant-type job, and I was there for seventeen years. Now I'm the business manager at the School of Education; I've been there for four years. I'm looking forward to retiring. . . .

You can imagine my parents' reaction when they started getting all of those letters [from the dean of women]. My dad's reaction was, "Well, obviously we shouldn't be sending you to school." They weren't really sending me to school anyway; I was getting government loans. You know the Lyndon Johnson [loans] . . . all of a sudden the baby boomers hit college age and there weren't enough jobs for them, so we had these huge government loan programs. The National Defense Loan, that was the first one. So I was really paying for all of my tuition and books and living expenses through loans, anyway. But the university's reaction coupled with my parents' reaction is why I got married. I thought, "Well, if I get married, then nobody is going to be able to tell me what I can do from now on." It was kind of an easy five years. I didn't see too much of my parents, despite the fact that I had two kids in that time period. My mother's not living anymore, but my dad and I . . . we've both mellowed. I guess I'm more of a Democrat now than a radical activist, so he's more comfortable with that.

Tomorrow night I'm going to a talk on the future of the peace movement. The Lawrence Coalition for Peace and Justice is still very active, and I attend most of the public meetings that they have. I try to get involved in leafleting on tax day about the huge amount of tax money that goes into the defense system as opposed to social programs. It's not in the streets anymore, but my beliefs haven't changed at all, not at all. Saul Alinsky's still my idol. My beliefs have not changed at all, and I'm glad of that. I don't think I'd like myself very well if [they had].

My kids have turned out great. They've turned out to be exactly what I would have hoped. I was afraid. . . . I remember seeing Dr. Spock when he spoke here. He was very involved in the anti–Vietnam War movement, and he told us—many of us families with small kids—"It doesn't matter how you bring your kids up. There's going to be a point in time when they're gonna rebel against you. They're going to join the Marines or join the DAR or hate feminism, or whatever. Just accept it." So I lived in fear that at some point my kids were going to join the army. I even went so far as to join the Quaker Church for about two years to protect them from the draft. After listening to Spock, I figured, what's the point? They're not going to turn out to be like me. But they did. It makes me have a renewed conviction that this is the right way to think. Ninety-nine percent of the people [who were student activists] have remained idealistic, with the same ideals, through their lives.

BIBLIOGRAPHY

Altbach, Philip G. *Student Politics in America: A Historical Analysis.* New Brunswick, NJ: Transaction Publishers, 1997.

Anderson, Terry H. *The Movement and the Sixties: Protest in America from Greensboro to Wounded Knee.* New York: Oxford University Press, 1995.

———. *The Sixties.* New York: Longman, 1999.

Angle, Paul M. *Bloody Williamson: A Chapter in American Lawlessness.* New York: Knopf, 1952.

Bailey, Beth. *Sex in the Heartland.* Cambridge: Harvard University Press, 1999.

Beahler, John. "Something's Happening Here." *Missouri Alumnus,* Summer 1990, pp. 20–21.

Billingsley, William J. *Communists on Campus: Race, Politics, and the Public University in Sixties North Carolina.* Athens: University of Georgia Press, 1999.

Bloom, Alexander, ed. *Long Time Gone; Sixties America Then and Now.* New York: Oxford University Press, 2001.

Bloom, Alexander, and Wini Breines, eds. *"Takin' It to the Streets": A Sixties Reader.* New York: Oxford University Press, 1995.

Braunstein, Peter, and Michael William Doyle, eds. *Imagine Nation: The American Counterculture of the 1960s and '70s.* New York: Routledge, 2002.

Breines, Wini. *Community and Organization in the New Left, 1962–1968: The Great Refusal.* New York: Praeger, 1982.

———. "Whose New Left?" *Journal of American History* 75 (September 1988): 528–45.

Brinkley, Alan. "Dreams of the Sixties." Review of *If I Had a Hammer: The Death of the Old Left and the Birth of the New Left,* by Maurice Isserman, and *"Democracy Is in the Streets": From Port*

Huron to the Siege of Chicago, by James Miller. *New York Review of Books,* October 22, 1987, pp. 10–16.

Brown, Clyde, and Gayle K. Pluta Brown. "Moo U and the Cambodian Invasion: Nonviolent Anti–Vietnam War Protest at Iowa State University." In *The Vietnam War on Campus: Other Voices, More Distant Drums,* ed. Marc Jason Gilbert, 119–41. Westport, CT: Praeger, 2001.

Calvert, Gregory Nevala. *Democracy from the Heart: Spiritualism, Decentralism, and Democratic Idealism in the Movement of the Sixties.* Eugene, OR: Communitas Press, 1991.

———. "In White America: Radical Consciousness and Social Change." In *"Takin' It to the Streets": A Sixties Reader,* ed. Alexander Bloom and Wini Breines, 126–31. New York: Oxford University Press, 1995.

Carson, Clayborne. *In Struggle: SNCC and the Black Awakening of the 1960s.* Cambridge: Harvard University Press, 1981.

Chepesiuk, Ron. *Sixties Radicals Then and Now: Candid Conversations with Those Who Shaped the Era.* Jefferson, NC: McFarland & Co., 1995.

Cohen, Mitchell, and Dennis Hale, eds. *The New Student Left: An Anthology.* Boston: Beacon Press, 1966.

Echols, Alice. *Daring to Be Bad: Radical Feminism in America, 1967–1975.* Minneapolis: University of Minnesota Press, 1989.

———. "Nothing Distant about It: Women's Liberation and Sixties Radicalism." in *The Sixties: From Memory to History,* ed. David Farber, 149–74. Chapel Hill: University of North Carolina Press, 1994.

———. "'We Gotta Get Out of This Place': Notes toward a Remapping of the Sixties." *Socialist Review* 22:2 (April–June 1992): 14–15.

Epstein, Barbara. *Political Protest and Cultural Revolution: Nonviolent Direct Action in the 1970s and 1980s.* Berkeley and Los Angeles: University of California Press, 1991.

Evans, Sara. *Personal Politics: The Roots of Women's Liberation in the Civil Rights Movement and the New Left.* New York: Random House, 1979.

Farber, David. *Chicago '68.* Chicago: University of Chicago Press, 1988.

———, ed. *The Sixties: From Memory to History.* Chapel Hill: University of North Carolina Press, 1994.

Farrell, James J. *The Spirit of the Sixties.* New York: Routledge, 1997.

FBI file on the Students for a Democratic Society and the Weatherman Underground Organization. Wilmington, DE: Scholarly Resources, 1991. Microform.

Fink, Carole, Philipp Gassert, and Detlef Junker, eds. *1968: The World Transformed*. Washington, DC: German Historical Institute, 1998.

Fisher, Michael P. "The Turbulent Years: The University of Kansas, 1960–1975." Ph.D. diss., University of Kansas, 1979.

Flacks, Richard. *Making History: The American Left and the American Mind*. New York: Columbia University Press, 1988.

Flacks, Richard, and Jack Whalen. *Beyond the Barricades: The Sixties Generation Grows Up*. Philadelphia: Temple University Press, 1989.

Garfinkle, Adam. *Telltale Hearts: The Origins and Impact of the Vietnam Antiwar Movement*. New York: St. Martin's Press, 1995.

Gitlin, Todd. *The Sixties: Years of Hope, Days of Rage*. New York: Bantam Books, 1987.

———. *The Whole World Is Watching; Mass Media in the Making and Unmaking of the New Left*. Berkeley and Los Angeles: University of California Press, 1980.

Green, Brent. *Noble Chaos*. Lincoln, NE: Writer's Showcase, 2000.

Harper, Robert A. *The University that Shouldn't Have Happened, But Did! Southern Illinois University during the Morris Years, 1948–1970*. Carbondale, IL: Devil's Kitchen Press, 1998.

Heineman, Kenneth J. *Campus Wars: The Peace Movement at American State Universities in the Vietnam Era*. New York: New York University Press, 1993.

Isserman, Maurice, and Michael Kazin. *America Divided: The Civil War of the 1960s*. New York: Oxford University Press, 2000.

Jacobs, Paul, and Saul Landau. *The New Radicals*. New York: Random House, 1966.

Jacobs, Ron. *The Way the Wind Blew: A History of the Weather Underground*. London: Verso, 1997.

Jones, Glenn W. "Gentle Thursday: An SDS Circus in Austin, Texas, 1966–1969." In *Sights on the Sixties*, ed. Barbara L. Tischler, 75–85. New Brunswick, NJ: Rutgers University Press, 1992.

Kelly, John F. *Center for Vietnamese Studies, Southern Illinois University*. N.p., 1971.

Keniston, Kenneth. *Radicals and Militants: An Annotated Bibliography of Empirical Research on Campus Unrest.* Lexington, MA: Lexington Books, 1973.

————. *Young Radicals: Notes on Committed Youth.* New York: Harcourt, Brace & World, 1968.

Kessler, Lauren. *After All These Years: Sixties Ideals in a Different World.* New York: Thunder's Mouth Press, 1990.

Klatch, Rebecca E. *A Generation Divided: The New Left, the New Right, and the 1960s.* Berkeley and Los Angeles: University of California Press, 1999.

Knoll, Robert E. *Prairie University: A History of the University of Nebraska.* Lincoln: University of Nebraska Press, 1995.

Koplowitz, H. B. *Carbondale after Dark and Other Stories.* Carbondale, IL: Dome, 1982.

Kunen, James Simon. *The Strawberry Statement: Notes of a College Revolutionary.* St. James, NY: Brandywine Press, 1968.

Lasch, Christopher. *The Agony of the American Left.* New York: Knopf, 1969.

Lyons, Paul. *New Left, New Right, and the Legacy of the Sixties.* Philadelphia: Temple University Press, 1996.

Mankoff, Milton, and Richard Flacks. "The Changing Social Base of the American Student Movement." In *The New Pilgrims: Youth Protest in Transition,* ed. Philip G. Altbach and Robert S. Laufer, 46–62. New York: David McKay, 1972.

Matusow, Allen J. *The Unraveling of America.* New York: Harper & Row, 1984.

McAdam, Doug. *Freedom Summer.* New York: Oxford University Press, 1988.

McMillian, John, and Paul Buhle, eds. *The New Left Revisited.* Philadelphia: Temple University Press, 2003.

Michener, James A. *Kent State: What Happened and Why.* New York: Fawcett Crest, 1971.

Miller, James. *"Democracy Is in the Streets": From Port Huron to the Siege of Chicago.* New York: Simon & Schuster, 1987.

Miller, Roy Eugene. "Student Ideology at Southern Illinois University: An Empirical Test of Theory." Ph.D. diss., University of Illinois at Urbana-Champaign, 1971.

Mitchell, Betty. *Delyte Morris of SIU.* Carbondale: Southern Illinois University Press, 1988.

Monhollon, Rusty L. "Taking the Plunge: Race, Rights, and the

Politics of Desegregation in Lawrence, Kansas, 1960." *Kansas History* 20:3 (Autumn 1997): 138–59.

———. *"This Is America?" The Sixties in Lawrence, Kansas.* New York: Palgrave, 2002.

Morgan, Edward P. *The Sixties Experience.* Philadelphia: Temple University Press, 1991.

Morrison, Joan, and Robert K. Morrison. *From Camelot to Kent State: The Sixties Experience in the Words of Those Who Lived It.* New York: Times Books, 1987.

Moyers, Bill. *Listening to America: A Traveler Rediscovers His Country.* New York: Harper & Row, 1971.

Myers, R. David, ed. *Toward a History of the New Left: Essays from within the Movement.* Brooklyn: Carlson, 1989.

Neumann, Osha. "Motherfuckers Then and Now: My Sixties Problem." In *Cultural Politics and Social Movements,* ed. Marcy Darnovsky, Barbara Epstein, and Richard Flacks, 71–73. Philadelphia: Temple University Press, 1995.

Ohle, David, Roger Martin, and Susan Brooseau, eds. *Cows Are Freaky When They Look at You: An Oral History of the Kaw Valley Hemp Pickers.* Wichita, KS: Watermark Press, 1991.

Olson, James C., and Vera Olson. *The University of Missouri: An Illustrated History.* Columbia: University of Missouri Press, 1988.

Pardun, Robert. *Prairie Radical: A Journey through the Sixties.* Los Gatos, CA: Shire Press, 2001.

Perlstein, Rick. *Before the Storm: Barry Goldwater and the Unmaking of the American Consensus.* New York: Hill & Wang, 2001.

———. "Who Owns the Sixties?" *Lingua Franca,* May–June 1996, pp. 30–37.

Pichaske, David. *A Generation in Motion: Popular Music and Culture in the Sixties.* New York: Schirmer Books, 1979.

President's Commission on Campus Unrest. *The Report of the President's Commission on Campus Unrest.* Washington, DC: U.S. Government Printing Office, 1970.

Rorabaugh, W. J. *Berkeley at War: The 1960s.* New York: Oxford University Press, 1989.

Rossinow, Doug. "The New Left in the Counterculture: Hypotheses and Evidence." *Radical History Review* 67 (Winter 1997): 79–120.

———. *The Politics of Authenticity: Liberalism, Christianity, and the*

New Left in America. New York: Columbia University Press, 1998.

Roszak, Theodore. *The Making of a Counterculture.* Garden City, NY: Doubleday, 1969.

Sale, Kirkpatrick. *SDS.* 1973. Reprint, New York: Vintage Books, 1974.

Small, Melvin. *Covering Dissent: The Media and the Anti–Vietnam War Movement.* New Brunswick, NJ: Rutgers University Press, 1994.

———, and William D. Hoover. *Give Peace a Chance: Exploring the Vietnam Antiwar Movement.* Syracuse, NY: Syracuse University Press, 1992.

Stock, Catherine McNicol. *Rural Radicals: Righteous Rage in the American Grain.* Ithaca, NY: Cornell University Press, 1996.

Students for a Democratic Society Papers, 1958–1970. Madison: State Historical Society of Wisconsin. Microfilm.

Teodori, Massimo, ed. *The New Left: A Documentary History.* Indianapolis: Bobbs-Merrill, 1969.

U.S. Congress. House. Special Subcommittee on Education of the Committee on Education and Labor. *Campus Unrest 1969.* 91st Cong., 1st Sess. February–May 1969.

Weisbrot, Robert. *Freedom Bound: A History of America's Civil Rights Movement.* New York: Plume, 1991.

Wells, Tom. *The War Within: America's Battle over Vietnam.* Berkeley and Los Angeles: University of California Press, 1994.

Wood, James L. *The Sources of American Student Activism.* Lexington, MA: Lexington Books, 1974.

Wynkoop, Mary Ann. *Dissent in the Heartland: The Sixties at Indiana University.* Bloomington: Indiana University Press, 2002.

———. "Dissent in the Heartland: The Student Protest Movement at Indiana University, Bloomington, Indiana, 1965–1970." Ph.D. diss., University of Indiana, 1992.

Young, Marilyn B. *The Vietnam Wars, 1945–1990.* New York: HarperCollins, 1991.

Young, Nigel. *An Infantile Disorder? The Crisis and Decline of the New Left.* London: Routledge & Kegan Paul, 1977.

Zaroulis, Nancy, and Gerald Sullivan. *Who Spoke Up? American Protest against the War in Vietnam, 1963–1975.* New York: Holt, Rinehart & Winston, 1985.